The Producer

Also by Christopher Davis

A Peep into the 20th Century
Ishmael
The Shamir of Dachau
Belmarch
A Kind of Darkness
First Family
Lost Summer

THE PRODUCER

by CHRISTOPHER DAVIS

HARPER & ROW, PUBLISHERS
NEW YORK — EVANSTON — SAN FRANCISCO — LONDON

A portion of this book appeared in *Esquire* magazine in slightly different form.

Grateful acknowledgment is made for permission to reprint excerpts from the following:

Lines on page 101 from "Ring Around a Rosy Rag" by Arlo Guthrie. Copyright © 1967, 1968 by Appleseed Music Inc. All Rights Reserved. Used by Permission.

Lines on page 155 from "Brother, Can You Spare a Dime?" by Gorney-Harburg. Copyright © 1932 by Harms, Inc. Used by permission of Warner Bros. Music. All Rights Reserved.

All lines taken from Sheldon Harnick's lyrics for *The Rothschilds* appear with permission of Sheldon Harnick and David Cogan.

All lines taken from Sherman Yellen's text for *The Rothschilds* appear with permission of Sherman Yellen.

FIRST EDITION

STANDARD BOOK NUMBER: 06–010994–7

LIBRARY OF CONGRESS CATALOG CARD NUMBER: 75–156518

For David I. Segal, whose idea it was

Contents

A section of photographs follows page 116.

"... the divine right of kings had been overthrown by the divine right of money. ..."

—The Rothschilds *by Frederic Morton*

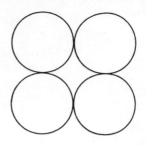

The Producer

Prologue   **July 6, 1970**

Ballet mirrors and barres line the room. John Bury's costume paintings, portrait prints of Rothschilds, engravings of eighteenth-century Frankfort and London cover the walls.

"*Is* everyone listening?" cries director Derek Goldby. "We're going to start at 11:30 this morning with a full reading and playing of the score, so there's nothing really to do till then. . . ."

The chosen cast (there will be changes even now), meeting for the first time, looks shy. Most of the production people are present, all of the creative people. Jerry Bock and Sheldon Harnick stand by a workmanlike upright piano. This, the first full-cast meeting and read-through, is in terms of theatrical production historic, and photographers are taking pictures. The small Rothschild boys, cast after many trials, having been awarded full scripts at last, are counting lines.

"Ladies . . . mothers? Can we say good-bye to you for the day?" asks stage manager Charles Gray.

Mayer Rothschild—Hal Linden—tall, Biblical-looking with long hair and grizzled beard and a prophet's yellow face—is

1

here. Joan Hackett, current choice for a female lead (she will pull out soon since the role does not yield much), is cool in a white pants suit, glasses shoved into her hair. Goldby is wearing an unaccustomed suit and tie and perhaps as a result is looking pinched. When it is time, he seats himself facing the cast, opens his script, and puts on heavy-rimmed glasses. Bock strikes a few bars of the opening for the photographers. Keene Curtis, who will play four roles, sits straight as a pole, legs neatly crossed, bald head gleaming in the mirrored light; at no point during the production will he appear to be anything but composed. The dancers have come in from rehearsing with Michael Kidd in a room down the hall (he has been at it for days, blocking his work in advance), tough as rubber bands, slim, the girls in deep-crotched dancers' work clothes.

"I am Derek Goldby, and I'm your director."

He introduces the co-producers and asks producer Hillard Elkins to take over. . . .

"This all began," the producer says, "when a fellow who is talking on the phone over there"—indicating Frederic Morton, author of *The Rothschilds*—"wrote a book. To compound his error, Sherman Yellen"—indicating—"wrote a book for a musical, for which Mr. Jerry Bock and Mr. Sheldon Harnick wrote words and music. Michael Kidd will be our choreographer. . . ." Hilly goes through the list and each rises or shows a hand. Then he makes a short speech beginning, "This has been rather a long road for some of us . . . ," after which Goldby again takes over.

". . . For the first time you're going to hear the whole show, which you may not do again for several weeks. Listen carefully. If there's a misunderstanding, someone doesn't come in with a line, I'm going to come in. . . .

"And finally, ladies and gentlemen: *The Rothschilds!*"

At first the actors walk through the lines, noses self-consciously lowered into their scripts, then relax, laugh at the wit in the unfolding tale, and start to act. They enjoy "Sons"; Harnick and Bock make "Everything" roar through the small upper Broadway rehearsal hall, so that we all sweat with inspiration. Elkins, in dark glasses, sits listening, arms folded, stylish musketeer sleeves turned back; he presents an odd physical expression of pride and lack of illusion.

The look belongs to a complex man.

He is volatile, open, others-oriented, secret, disingenuous, candid, ethically metamorphic, honest, and sweet-tempered. He is also violent, energetic, unfailingly courteous, and notably charming. He is articulate and witty, generous, dedicated to work; he is a number of other things, but in sum he is a brilliant, not to be denied show-business figure in a country where show business and activities contingent upon it are taken seriously. He is like a racing car (he has raced): though he must with the rest of us lose at last, he seems to have been designed only to win, and in this characteristic may be found the man's informing spirit. . . . To reach this point in the long road of the production of *The Rothschilds* Elkins has been traveling for more than six years; of these I will chronicle the year preceding the read-through described and the four months following.

"Only God Can Make a Three"

I

"It's not gonna hit me"

1

As a child in Brooklyn, the producer remembers, he was once walking across a street: ". . . Church Avenue it was—a boulevard—and I remember . . . I was crossing against the light of course, and out of the corner of my eye I caught this Department of Sanitation garbage truck bearing down—the colossal ego of the child—bearing down on me, and I kept walking into it. 'It's not gonna hit me . . . not gonna hit me . . . *not* gonna hit me.' Then it hit me. So I stopped believing in God. I threw down my tefillin and said, 'Fuck you!' . . . The fucking thing caught me by the coat, dragged me across the street, and I was in terrible pain, but I remember saying, 'Son of a bitch! The indignity . . . the fucking indignity!' "

2

Hillard Elkins lives and works in a brick-faced building on East Sixty-second Street in New York City. The neighborhood is a shifting border between the uptown takeover by new office buildings and an affluent turn-of-the-century home life with gargoyles and griffins looking down from lintels. Little galleries and flower shops are around the corner, as well as antique shops, well-known hairdressers, and up-to-the-minute boutiques, a few expensive restaurants, the inevitable delicatessen and Gristede chain grocer, paperback bookstore and dry cleaner. A block south are banks and business suits; and around the corner to the west are Central Park, dog-walkers, pretzel-chestnut men, the Pierre, the deep-browed Plaza, and, shrilly imperative in the morning and at dusk, the piping of doormen for cabs. The producer leases the top three floors of Number 19½, offices on the third floor, duplex apartment above that. Later the basement will be taken over and turned into offices and a receptionist added to the ground-floor foyer, a room will be added to the top floor, and so on.

At the time I came on the scene in the spring of 1969, Elkins' "entertainment with music," *Oh! Calcutta!,* was in previews and about to open; *The Rothschilds,* a musical for Broadway, was being written; and a film, *Alice's Restaurant,* was soon to be released. Other projects are listed on a brass plate in front of the building and on the directory by the elevator, among them the movie *A New Leaf; The $100 Misunderstanding,* for which the producer holds film rights; and *Golden Boy,* his successful production to date.

His corporation is Elkins Productions International Corporation—EPIC.

3

He has forgotten about the appointment for the first meeting, apparently because his secretary neglected to put it into the schedule. It is a piece of disorder that is not typical of the way the office is run. I wait while people phone around town. The predominant color in the office is brown: brown-gold carpet and brown louvered window shutters closed against the light, walls lined with brown cork, walnut shelves filled with bound copies of *Playbill, Hi-Fi/Stereo*, scripts, and so on. There are framed show cards—*Golden Boy, Bye Bye Birdie, Come On Strong*—heavy glass and metal-frame tables and leather sling chairs, a small projection booth, and a gold and black powder room. A good deal of activity goes on at walnut desks, on sandalwood phones with punch buttons; it seems appropriate. A man in a brown suit appears; he has a compassionate expression and brown eyes; a secretary, or maybe a girl who came in with him, lifts her skirt, and he, talking easily (it is not Elkins—he is looking for Elkins too but is doing this now), injects something into her buttock with a hypodermic syringe. I am told that the injected material is derived from the urine of a pregnant woman; at least I think I am told that. Whereupon my presence is noted more particularly, a phone call connects ("He's being very nice about it," Elkins is told), and a second appointment is made. Placidly, I take a cab to the producer's theater.

The photographs in the outer lobby of the Eden, which is in the East Village at Twelfth and Second Avenue, are staggering. There are naked people clasping each other. *Oh! Calcutta!* Some dance, and some appear to be singing; but they have no clothes on. A man with big muscles embraces a girl who, both knees raised, glancing haughtily floorward in a standard ballet pose, slides—appears to be sliding—down him. But where are their clothes? . . .

A short, strong-looking man has come into the lobby from the street holding a beautiful woman by the hand. He gives the writer a look, deciding (it is Hilly Elkins, and he is making up his mind at once whether or not to let me in on things). He introduces himself, then the woman. It is Claire Bloom, the actress. A truck has parked in front of the theater and pieces of furniture are being carried out of the Eden by a side door and fed into the back of the truck, which crunches them up and swallows them. A good desk goes in. The effect of Elkins' costume and to a lesser degree of Claire Bloom's—costumes are what they are—is one of brightness. In the clouded slum of lower Second Avenue, garbage everywhere, the producer is a blue and white racing car, the beautiful actress a canary-yellow one: or they are jockeys in their silks before the race, brilliant and small: also they are like neon signs in the rain. He nods.

I watch a moment of rehearsal, quickly blunted, Claire Bloom beside me. Hilly leans over the back of the seat to kiss her, with a glance my way: "My fiancée," he says. He goes off to phone. She came that day from England, where she is making a movie, and will return the next day. The nakedness, though expected, is new to her too. What's going on?

"I don't *know*," she cries.

While the office in the basement lounge of the theater is being redecorated, the producer conducts business in an Italian restaurant across the street. Soon, at four or so in the afternoon, rehearsal over, the place is crowded with *Calcutta* people, including the director, production staff, guests, and friends. They will remain until the preview curtain at 8:30. The compassionate-looking man shows up. Others get on the phone or run messages. Feeling fortunate to have been accepted (the nod), I make tentative notes under the checkered tablecloth. I had approached other producers asking to act as court biographer and been turned down out of hand, though one man would have said yes for money. Hilly darts in and out of the restaurant, constantly on the phone, or in conference at other tables. Some order food. There is no drinking of anything stronger than beer: it is a working day. How do you produce a show? Elkins does not smile. *The Rothschilds* files will be made available. I am not to hesitate to ask questions. There is still another office with forty employees, he says, in a house on Eighty-first Street, and here the business part of film production— *A New Leaf* with Walter Matthau and Elaine May (she writing and directing as well)—goes forward; it turns out that the house belongs to Elaine May. He is "setting up publicity" just now for *Alice's Restaurant*; there is to be a chain of franchise restaurants. The producer was thinking of opening *The Rothschilds* in London, perhaps Israel, but has decided on New York. The man with the syringe comes from California, is a good friend, and was once Elkins' analyst. Hilly's favorite color is brown, usually in combination with yellow. He is a compulsive eater of chocolate, and his analyst, when the producer was still in the agency business in Hollywood, tried to cure him of it by hypnosis. I write this down. A secretary at the same time is taking Hilly's notes on the rehearsal. He holds a long private conference with Jacques Levy, the director of *Oh! Calcutta!*, who is having a full meal. Fifty thousand dollars are being spent on the interior and exterior of the Eden; the amount will be recouped through profits and a deal with the theater's landlord. The truck is still across the street eating pieces of the old insides. The analyst tried to persuade Hilly under hypnosis to give up chocolate. The producer went home, ate a dozen chocolate cookies at once, and telephoned: "All right now, motherfucker . . ." I meet the sound man who "pioneered some good sound on Broadway" for *Golden Boy* and is doing the same for *Oh! Calcutta!* . . . Grove Press has given a $50,-000 advance on the trade text of the show. The producer spent $350,000 of his own money on *Golden Boy,* he says: "It was a great experience anyway, working with Sammy." He declares that he himself co-authored one of the librettos for the musical-in-the-making, *The Rothschilds*. Now and then, as he had earlier announcing the fact that Claire Bloom is his fiancée, the producer gives me a fast glance: all right. . . . The psychiatrist is saying to someone at the table, "I told him, 'Why do you feel guilty about it? You don't do it in the street, do you?' No! It turned out he felt guilty because he couldn't believe that he, in his dignity, of all people, could do such a thing." His patient's feeling of guilt had been based on an unrealistic appraisal of ethical priorities and of his value in the sight of the world. It's interesting. The compassionate man has come as Hilly's guest to see the evening preview, has seen two performances already, and does not want to see another. He wants to go back instead to the Plaza suite that Hilly provided, the grandeur of which embarrasses him, and take a nap; yet he does not. Later I learn that he went to school with Red Buttons in the Bronx.

Claire Bloom has been mostly silent.

The writer also is a guest at the preview, as he was in the restaurant. You do not pay for things with Hilly: "One of my hang-ups," he declares. As we go in, I overhear a couple; they are staring at a half-nude blowup in the lobby. "My God, it's Katie!" he says. "I just saw her in L.A.!"

"Well," she says, "you're going to see a lot more of her here." And he does.

Some notes on the producer's and his fiancée's appearance: ". . . Elkins about 45"—he was thirty-nine at the time—"collar-length hair, grayish, brushed forward, thin on top; scimitar white sideburns, trim gray-white mustache and goatee; thyroid heavy-lidded comedian's glance; no smiles . . . Athletic-looking —a tough tap-dancer or welterweight sailor: pink scrubbed glow, v/clean. White patent slip-ons with perforations, blue Edwardian suit, big collar, vent most of the way up the back, white silk shirt w/turtleneck (N.B.) collar w/loops through which is run a blue and white silk scarf; 'London $17' wristwatch threaded through cuff loops—a sliding melting Dali watch w/blue face. Blunt tough musician's hands, serpent rings on several fingers w/jeweled eyes. Claire Bloom: canary slacks, white patent shoes, serpent rings too, also earrings of rams' heads w/curling horns. The wonderful cheekbones, familiar steep widow's peak . . ." All the writer's kind of words, in this fresh and optimistic beginning, are underlined: ". . . scimitar, sliding melting Dali watch . . ."

II

"Don't open! Don't open!"

1

A long belted brown leather vest, tight-fitting brown shirt with yellow and brown silk scarf looped through the usual collar, glittering brown patent-leather moccasins with a ring and bit across each . . .

He cocks the small feet, ankles crossed, on his desk, where they reflect the Sixty-second Street office. This is an ad meeting. Hilly has proposed a budget in excess of $30,000 for TV time to cover *Calcutta*'s opening night—a week away—and the day following. Like the total cost of the off-Broadway show itself, a bit over the budgeted $100,000 (the first principle of off-Broadway is a modest budget), the proposal is unprecedented. Sam Friedman, a tall white-mustached Broadway veteran and EPIC's press agent, resists, as do the ad agency representatives. Hilly uses the word "overkill" to describe what he means by this kind of saturation coverage. He reasons, listens, and finally has his way.

"Opening night: 'We take you to the Eden Theater!'—the

announcer," says Hilly, acting it. "Interview one: 'I wasn't there. I wasn't there. You never saw me!' . . . Interview two: 'A doity show. Terrible. Disgusting. A very doity show.' . . . Three"—elegant, quizzical: " 'Obscene? No, I hardly think so. Amusing perhaps but not obscene.' We stand them up against the ass on the logo in front of the theater. The follow-up: announcer: 'We interrupt this program to bring you the Clive Barnes review of *Oh! Calcutta!'* "

"It's not a news show."

" 'We interrupt this *commercial* . . .' "

Sam likes the campaign but not the cost.

"Henry Morgan hates it. He can't stand the show. Get him to pan it on TV."

". . . It all hangs on our Sunday night preview."

"Ignore the critics," Sam says. "Don't invite 'em. Don't open. You can bust the theater wide open with this show. It's only Levy's and Tynan's egos . . ."

"*I* want to open," says Hilly.

"I didn't know you had more ego than Jacques and Tynan."

"That's specious. You don't know how my ego works."

"Suppose the reviews are bad?"

"Then we bury 'em! We fuck 'em and bury 'em!"

". . . protection. It doesn't matter what the critics say. I'm worried about the people who go to the parish priest, the rabbi; they'll complain and knock you in the head."

"Do you mind if you're wrong?" Hilly asks gently. "*You* think, I *know*. Listen and learn. I took the trouble to find out what the DA's response will be. I know. . . ."

He had invited an assistant district attorney with local authority in matters of pornography to a preview.

". . . *no* judicial confrontation. They don't want it. We don't want it. None."

"I tell Barnes what? 'You can't come to the Sunday preview'?"

"I'll call and tell him the truth, say the film clips aren't processed, and he won't be seeing the finished show," says Hilly reasonably. " 'I can't stop you coming, but I would prefer . . .' What's to make him mad?"

"*You* do it."

Hilly's valet, Robert, brings a pot of filtered coffee and cups on a tray that he places before the producer. Hilly pours fastidiously. He does not drink liquor. He smokes incessantly, and he drinks coffee.

"Coffee?"

Sam's ulcers: "Thanks to you, Hilly . . ."

"Maalox?"

He is back on Gelusil. He begins in his deep disenchanted voice, "Say by some chance we do get good reviews. . . ."

"Sam, Sam. If you ever again, ever, use pejorative language —ask a friend what it means, if you can find one: you will eat the *Times* page by page. . . . Wait!" Shouts: "George! Get Sam and me on the Carson show! In living color! My own press agent hates the show. We debate it. . . . Or get Brandman to book us on the Carson show!"

Hilly's associate, George Platt, gets Brandman on the phone, and the producer speaks to him.

"We'll do it naked! *Sam* and I! I'll use the Tynan stutter— 'Oh, f-f-fuck.' " Listens. "Okay, but you have to get Jacques Levy, the director, on anyway—a cute fella in a cowboy outfit and a big mustache . . . a big pot. . . . No, this whole thing came out of a fight we had right here in the office! Just now!"

His telephone voice is deep and reassuring. He is an artist of telephones. The calls are the constant: unless one is in progress or about to be, other activity suffers, as if in the way of doing the business of life the phone calls are the generative factor.

Yet the tone of his telephone talk is usually one of sweet seduction: if it is persistent or bullying, it is also modest and attentive; it is religious in the sense of being persuaded: urgent,
lighthearted, and interested in the humanity of the person
addressed. Hilly's personal interviews are a translation. He
will pantomime a left hook at the other: "Pow to the chin"—
to show the ultimate unimportance of the dispute to come, and
he will throw an arm across the other's shoulders. He is solemn,
keeps an eye on his own foot: the fight manager; alternatively,
the up-from-under scrapper. He steps back from the conference, closing it. He will look up at tall men as one would up a
hill from the bottom, eying with exaggerated intent. When
necessary with a secretary, or in a serious disagreement with
one whose vote equals his, he may shout.

HILLY (at the back of the Eden's lobby after a poor *Calcutta*
preview, suddenly loud): Ken, if I cannot make a suggestion,
the answer is no!

KENNETH TYNAN (who "devised" *Oh! Calcutta!*): Hilly . . .

HILLY: *If I cannot make a suggestion . . . !*

The producer will soon apologize, Tynan will say, "No, no
. . ." they will clasp each other in the chaste theaterman's
embrace, and Hilly will have succeeded in attracting attention
to the point he wanted to make. . . .

"Tell him Hilly Elkins—'Hilly,' like in small mountains.
E-L-K-I-N-S . . . *I'm* a lawyer! Also fourth-class matter! . . .
Judi, get me Claire in England: Winchelsea 36. . . ."

His barber, a girl named Sandra who is wearing mulberry-
colored jeans, trims his hair. George Platt says into another
phone: "The hottest ticket in town is *Oh! Calcutta!*" Celebrities
call for preview tickets, and George turns them down gleefully;
even Rock Hudson has to wait.

"Meet my lovely, petite English lady barber."

"I'm a hairdresser."

"Darling!"—on the phone to Claire Bloom—"Sorry if I woke you up!" He will meet her Thursday—Wednesday?—BOAC. Two crash helmets sit on their crowns on a shelf, gloves and dark glasses dropped into the well of one of them. The hairdresser asks, "When are you getting married, Hilly?" Soon. Has he been married before? "Three times."

He continues in the late afternoon to try to find someone who dislikes *Calcutta* and would be willing to debate with him on a talk show: Johnny Carson, or Barry Gray's late-night show. Sam Friedman, who is unwilling anyway, is not now being asked to do it. The producer canvasses Herman Shumlin, Henry Morgan, and others. No. Young associate Bill Liberman has developed a tension headache. Hilly works on Bill's neck, then, as the other cries out, gets a hammerlock on him, lifts him, and shakes him like a puppy. No help. It is twilight. Everyone's office pace slows. Not his. He prowls, demanding phone calls. Too many moments without one makes him jittery, but they are usually waiting, voices held in lights that blink silently under the punch buttons. He releases one from the hive. "You're holding up *my* fucking work, Jerry!"—the general contractor in charge of redecoration at the Eden: "Get more men, then! Push, push, push! Right?" But who will give Tynan and him a public argument about the possible corrupting influence of *Oh! Calcutta!*? Barry Gray on the phone, Hilly wades in: "I'm not charming. I surround myself with pricks, so I look charming. It's an old trick . . . Merrick won't do it. Shumlin won't do it. . . . Sam is grabbing at my leg like a dog— 'Don't open! Don't open!' " (The press agent wants to avoid a traditional, critics-invited opening, which it is possible to do; the producer feels they have had all the controversy possible from previews and is ready for the next stage—reviews and attendant publicity.) "Carson's out. . . ." He wonders aloud why he is especially manic this afternoon. His father, Max, appears; he is conservatively dressed, squarely barbered, gentle, laconic, and has a slight Russian-Jewish accent; he is put to work on a phone. Hilly is visited by a rare silent brooding mood. It lasts twenty seconds. Then he yawns crackingly, rubs his fists into his eyes, and is at once refreshed, "up." Chris Cerf of Random House phones (they are publishing the Alice *Cookbook*, a typical EPIC by-product intended both to promote and earn). "They're worried about five thousand dollars for shrink-wrapping the book," he says to the office, "and they'll get fifty thousand out of the deal!" He paces from desk to desk with his rolling, round-shouldered fighter's gait; a longish wait for incoming calls, the lights for the lines dying one by one; he snaps his fingers. "Calls!" Who will join in the debate? "Where's the Vitabath?"—looking into the black-marble, gold-trimmed bathroom for the office staff; a sign says "physiotherapy"; a phone with all the outside and inside lines on it is fixed to the wall within reach of the toilet: "Judi! Did you order it?" He is telephoning Judi from the powder room thirty-eight inches from her desk. More prowling. "Judi, I'm off the phone! Get me a call!"

There are multi-line phones everywhere in the triplex—next to bathtubs, in the sauna, in china closets and liquor cabinets, in the kitchen, an arrangement like a pilot's console beside the bed, and so on. He owns a portable wireless phone that he carries in an attaché case when he is afraid he will be out of reach of other lines, as on movie location. The office pace is not only kept fast but burdened and complicated by the number of lines, the intramural communication system, and master-slave system, a constantly used speaker-and-lock-release mechanism at the street door, bells, buzzers, lights, amplifiers. . . . One of the staff is always having to run to a booth in the street below to phone the phone company about breakdowns or to make the last-straw call that would break the office's back. Hilly has a favorite telephone call:

". . . driving in my car on Sunset Strip in Hollywood talking to Mike Stewart, at the time on an ocean liner sailing through the Straits of Gibraltar."

Derek Goldby, who is to direct *The Rothschilds,* arrives. We climb into the producer's convertible Impala and, everything else forgotten, top down, airconditioning up high, speed toward the Eden. A moment of fiery tidiness: a door flung open at a light, debris swept out. Hilly is late (he is almost always late) for a rehearsal of the sound cue for a *Calcutta* skit, which he has been giving his personal attention for days. We roar down Park Avenue, around the Grand Central ramp, tires screaming, at up to seventy miles an hour. Goldby and I are frightened and keep smiling. . . . "So this is New York!" ("I'll be glad to talk to you about *The Rothschilds,*" Goldby has said, and in fact thinks that talking problems over might help his work. "*What* will your book be about?" he keeps asking politely.) Cabbies, panicked and angry, shout at Hilly to slow down. I discover later that he used to race, so that the initially occurring image was appropriate. He has driven a Formula I Lotus at Riverside in California and MG's at Brand's Hatch in England, he says; he no longer races and no longer has a wish to keep expensive cars; he owns the Impala and Yamaha and Vespa motorbikes, on which he and Claire Bloom manage Manhattan traffic to shop or visit (the crash helmets). The producer, who has been alternately irascible and gloomily silent during the drive, parks in front of his theater at forty miles an hour and is off and running. "*Oh! Calcutta!*" on the marquee, yellow and chocolate; blazing naked girls and boys in house-front photos. The trip was belligerent, a threat, a descent into hell in heavy traffic, fifty bad blocks.

"Jesus!"

"Yes," says Goldby. "I'm glad it's over."

III

Second Act Trouble / ". . . a responsibility to go deeper"

1

"The main problem, as far as I'm concerned," says Derek Goldby, "is that at the moment we have not got an attitude toward the material that's sufficiently positive. We're not telling what we really feel about the Rothschilds. We're not telling the *why*. We're telling the story."

Goldby was signed to direct *The Rothschilds* in 1967, four years after Elkins optioned Morton's book. Progress from best seller to stage hit has been vexed. Old problems remain; new ones emerge weekly. A difficulty from the start has been to translate the chronicle of a family banking business that spans 150 years, includes in its range all the nations of Europe, and influenced most of the events of Western history since Napoleon came to power, into a frame for song, drama, and dance, and then to have all of that mean something.

Goldby, who directed the intellectual comedy *Rosencrantz and Guildenstern Are Dead*, is not satisfied on the last point. He has been in New York for two years, working and waiting.

He meets with Sherman Yellen, final choice for author and the man whom the trouble first of all burdens; and with Jerry Bock and Sheldon Harnick, the show's insurance (*Fiddler on the Roof* is about to enter its sixth Broadway year); and occasionally with Elkins to talk out problems. He is a young Englishman of energy and talent, a little frayed now because of the waiting.

"We're not telling the conflicts. The conclusions of course are foregone. They are in history. . . . I was originally attracted to the project as a sort of attack on the philosophy of capitalism, but I don't think now we can do that. I'm trying to find a way of at least investigating what makes people *have* to make a lot of money, and I don't think we've done *that* yet. . . ."

The basic structural problem was solved at once: start in the ghetto—late eighteenth century, early nineteenth—trace the rise of old Mayer's sons to eminence in five nations, and end with the acquisition of a coat of arms and the passing of an era.

"One admires the Rothschilds and one is disturbed by them as well," Goldby says, "since it shouldn't be necessary for people to have to be stimulated to the kind of ruthlessness that makes for success—if you have that kind of grit in the first place. As Brecht said—something of this sort: 'We shouldn't need heroes.' " And Goldby adds, "Wouldn't it be marvelous if people didn't need to be millionaires!"

The Frankfort ghetto in which Mayer founded his dynasty and where he and his brothers ran a shop for secondhand goods, with its money-changing sideline, was called Jew Street. A guard and chain cut it off at either end to enforce the curfew. Non-Jews entered in packs to tease the eternal foreigner —"Jew! Do your duty!" . . . the bared head, a bow—or to join a profitable pogrom.

"We must get away from the idea of this as the Jewish ghetto only," says Goldby. "The repression of the Jews must become universal. It must relate, for example, to today—to the blacks—not just be a story about poor Jews making it. Right now it is still a very Jewish show. Of course, I am not the writer or composer. Ultimately they're the ones who have to make it work. . . . It all must be crystallized in one central statement: someone realizes that you cannot buy self-respect; it comes from within. We cannot write this in 1969 and skirt the issues. You cannot write a romantic story about a family of millionaires today and let it go at that. One has a responsibility to go deeper."

2

David Merrick was the first Broadway producer to show an interest in Frederic Morton's "family portrait." It seemed to him that there was a musical in it, he offered $5,000 for an option, and Morton, considering it seriously, thought he might sign. Hillard Elkins, still relatively unknown in 1963 and engaged in the heroic travail of producing *Golden Boy* with Sammy Davis, saw the book's potential and wanted it too. All he asked was twenty minutes of Morton's time.

"I went to his place. He was in the apartment on Park Avenue then," Morton says. "Same Napoleonic style—the big portrait and so on—but smaller. There were seven or eight Weimaraners; anyhow, I remember pups all over. Hilly, looking like Napoleon, received me. He snapped his fingers. George Platt came in with a sheet of paper with a lot of titles on it. 'I never heard of these. What are they?' That was the point. I never heard of them because they were flops produced in the last several years by David Merrick! It was a carefully researched and rehearsed bit and very flattering, of course." Hilly raised Merrick's $5,000 by $2,500. "I more or less made up my mind to go with him on the spot, though I didn't tell him then. . . . The crucial factor involved here is the personality of Hilly." Morton, who will share in all aspects of the profits from the musical (in order to get Harnick and Bock his share had to be reduced, but he feels it is well worth it), despaired of seeing a good musical book, and even tried an outline himself. But when Yellen came in, everything seemed to fall into place: ". . . after a very low period here was a writer who used his imagination." He meets Merrick from time to time around New York, and the producer usually asks "facetiously, 'How many years has *The Rothschilds* been running by now?' "

3

Between Morton's first option and the hiring of Yellen, a number of attempts at a book were made: some complete, some partial with outlines; a number of full outlines, some detailed, some brief—all by different men. The Morton outline is six pages long. (The one Yellen used to sell Hilly is, with two scenes written, nearly fifty pages.) The English writer Wolf Mankowitz wrote a treatment (thirty-five pages; he was the first and for a long time the most serious contender). There were others. Most wrote scenes to go with the outlines; some wrote much more. None of it appeared to be what was needed.

Bock and Harnick were approached originally on the basis of the Mankowitz treatment and turned it down. Elmer Bernstein and Carolyn Leigh considered doing the music and lyrics. It was then that Hilly, optimistic, began to talk about an opening in Tel Aviv . . . in London.

"I go to Vienna," says Frederic Morton. "Hilly shows up from England with Wolf Mankowitz, who was going to do the book. Great. He had a great background for it. Hilly had a

girl he had simply kidnaped from Croydon—an actress working on a TV show in London who had come to see him off—
and a photographer to get publicity shots for *Rothschilds*. . . .
Vienna had never seen a real Broadway producer at his most
manic. He was on the phone to New York, London, Hollywood. We went to Drei Husaren—like '21' or Sardi's—a typical Hilly production in an old baroque restaurant: a table for
eating, one for special conferences, one for the photographer
. . . flashbulbs popping, Hilly running to the phone." The hat
check girl had charge of the telephone, and at the end of the
evening she was in tears. "She had a fast nervous breakdown.
. . . I made sure she got a good tip.

"Later Mankowitz and Hilly parted company. . . . He
flirted with Sidney Michaels; by now Hilly was concentrating
his energies on other things."

By the last day of 1964, $10,967.36 had been spent on the
project by EPIC and nothing to show for it except losses for
tax purposes. A period of confusion ensued. Creative people
were approached broadcast: John Osborne and Tony Richard-
son, Peter Ustinov and Lionel Bart (co-workers complain that
Hilly is "hung up" on English theater talent), even Leonard
Bernstein (Hilly had co-produced with Lester Osterman a
concert version of his *Candide*). Treatments continued to be
ground out. Then in 1966 Hilly wrote to an associate, "I
think we've found our writer at last"—meaning Yellen. Derek
Goldby, attracted by the quality of Yellen's work, was hired
to direct; and the bait of Goldby, with his current success, and
Yellen's first draft hooked Hilly's first choice, Bock and Harnick; in any case Leigh and Bernstein had gone on to another
project.

"It wasn't until April or May of '69 that there was a complete first act with music," says Morton. "I go over to Sheldon
and Margie's place on Central Park West to hear it. A queasy

moment: it had been so long; and of course I still had right of disapproval. I hear the tape. It's 1810's but *relevant*. Great! The Jewish ghetto becomes the black ghetto! A good Jewish mother says, 'Take it easy,' but the sons sing—I can't sing or even remember lyrics, but—'We have a dangerous, curious malady. We want everything!' . . . There's a parallel between the struggle for suffrage the Rothschilds led for the Jews and the changes now. It's in part a comment on what's going on today—the black movement. . . ."

The Rothschilds: "They're a phenomenon," says Morton. ". . . that a father could produce five sons with such talent and energy that each becomes the richest man in the country he goes to: they completed a giant step from a feudally oriented society, psychologically anyway, in reference to the upper classes, to a capitalistically oriented society. In that sense you could say I admire them. In another sense I don't. Some of them—by no means all—had to act tough."

4

"The problem is in the second act where I create the subsidiary romance between Nathan and Hannah," says Sherman Yellen. He is tall and thin, a pipe-smoker, has an M.A. in English literature from Columbia, and has been mostly, until now, a television writer. "We have to get out of the ghetto. I needed someone—Hannah Cohen—who could be an articulate spokesman for the idealism of the period, someone opposed to the plain pursuit of money; but this has been reduced, and we're back to the five brothers." Reluctantly, he has let himself be persuaded to move away from the love story and what he feels is its illuminating dialogues.

I mention Goldby's scruples.

"I have no feeling for *educating* people," Yellen says. "I

find Brecht cold. I love to entertain. I want real human people." He has been on the project for a long time now—nearly three years; at first he wanted to make his language the peer of the music in every sense; collaboration on a large scale has modified this wish. "I have to do material I feel will provide musical suggestions. The whole Hannah work, as it was, was looked upon as digression by Sheldon and Jerry. Hannah and the Rothschilds' mother would have been the play for me, but that's out. . . . I've got to finish. I've been with it too long." He sometimes likes Elkins, whose discovery he is in a sense, but usually is enraged by him. It seems to him in this idle period that the producer is slow in moving the project forward. On the other hand: "He sees me as an ivory tower scholar and patronizes me, and I don't mind. . . . Listen, it took Hilly Elkins to read my plays"—still unproduced—"about a murder in Jacobean England and a Bible play and have the vision to imagine I could do a big musical." He modifies it at once: "Of course, Derek had read my script and called it brilliant by then." (Yellen was commissioned by Hilly to do one of the sketches for his *Oh! Calcutta!*, which is one of the successes of the revue, and has just signed to do a movie script.) This particular week in the summer of 1969 he is not working at all on *The Rothschilds*; a current payment is past due, and he is, in a gentle but possibly not ineffectual way, holding out. Yellen cries wrathfully, "Always the agent. He throws curves *now* at this bad time!" But: "He's brilliant—the closest thing we have to Mike Todd today. He comes on like Sammy Glick, but he has genuine good taste in spite of that bedroom decor of his; and he's a good critic. Also, Hilly is the only man I know who speaks in whole sentences instead of fragments, the way I do or anyone else. . . ."

Yellen says of Bock and Harnick: "They are always vulnerable. Each time out, despite their great success, is like the first time for them." They are shy, particularly Bock. This book I am writing, and which you are reading, seems to them and to Yellen, I am told by him, to be no more at this point than "another of Hilly's self-gratifying promotion schemes," which makes them uneasy about it.

"Well, if the payments are made and we solve our second act problems, we may all feel more cheerful and be ready to talk. . . .

"I *don't* mind saying I'm upset that my use of Hannah as the spokesman has been voted out. . . ." Of course, it is a collaborative effort. He thinks: "It's not a folk opera. It's not based on a classic like *Fiddler*. It's not contained in one set. It's hard to find a line. It's a very big play."

IV

"You Have to See 'Oh! Calcutta!' to Believe It"

1

A rehearsal:

Ten more or less clothed figures make expressive swaying gestures on the stage. (In actual performance they will be naked.) They are like Stanislavski willows. This is solemn hard work. Jacques Levy, director, stands in the pit right against the stage watching intently and murmuring. Suddenly a girl slips out of her bell-bottoms—all she was wearing; then a heavily muscled boy is out of his. The company—five males, five females—pulls together, hands upraised, gesturing yearningly upward to the flies; they move against the beat of a stately rock rhythm and are drawn seemingly upward, as if levitated, closer to each other, clustering upon an invisible nucleus, drawn up, up; sparks must come of it, perhaps light itself. Levy speaks in low, encouraging rehearsal tones. The point is to feel it against the music and to improvise, each in terms of each, all, and self. One nude girl breaks from the group, hurries with small Martha Graham steps downstage

29

left, where she pulls up short of the edge, throws her arms over her head and downward as if they are a rope of hair (her own hair is short), bends with them, feet together, swaying right, then left, hands spread before her knees, then, apparently attracted past endurance, her bare behind as bright as the moon, helplessly rejoins the group; a couple breaks off in its turn, comes back. If unity is difficult to maintain, independence is almost impossible. There are consistent group people, but they don't count so much; the rebels and wanderers hold one rapt: naked prodigals. When at length ten are one, Levy is sweating. The "kids" are strung to an extraordinary pitch, greased with sweat, tremblingly still. The electronic music, having made its assault, is pulling out to sea: ten-in-one/one-in-ten, on a motor-operated sliding platform, drawn offstage, one feels to other halls for other eyes. Music ends. Silence. Then the actors amble back on. Levy, who holds a degree in psychiatry and was once on the staff at the Menninger Clinic, begins to talk it all out with them.

The rehearsal was of a new ending; it will be tried in one preview, taken out in the next, put back, taken out, shifted to just before intermission, etc. When he is not on the phone below, Hilly sits still at the rear of the theater, Judi beside him to take his notes; he watches the stage with a rueful, humorous gambler's glance.

2

A preview:

Redecoration cannot be finished by opening. Under Jerry Simek's direction workmen hammer and saw during intermission, even between scenes, though some of the customers upstairs have paid the $35 official scalper's rate for a preview ticket. Jerry is a tall plump harassed young man who came to do a household job for Hilly several years ago and never got away.

The producer is on the phone in the unfinished office off the basement lounge of the Eden (it had once been a serious house, the Phoenix, but for years before Hilly acquired his long-term lease was a strip-tease palace with, it is said, beds set up in the dressing rooms; the whole of the theater was in disrepair). One of *Playboy* magazine's editors, a near-bald Chinese with a shoulder-length fringe and mirror-bright loafers, is tonight's special guest. He is in conference with press agent Sam Friedman and, whenever Hilly is off the phone, with Hilly.

"Sam, Sam, I *want* to give them an exclusive!" cries Hilly during a phone break. (He cannot, since *Time* is doing a cover with inside pictures, and *Newsweek* will do a feature, and *Esquire* is talking too.) "Sam? . . . Sam," he says, "stop the shit. . . ."

"We'll really cover the show," the editor says. *"Esquire?"* (Onstage the sketch "Will Answer All Sincere Replies" is in progress, and a burst of laughter and applause is heard.) "We sell six million copies a week!" Sam wears a tired look and, on his lapel, a campaign button: "I WOULD SLEEP BETTER IF NORMAN MAILER WERE MAYOR." *Oh! Calcutta!*'s opening and the New York mayoral primary are to be on the same day.

Kenneth Tynan is upstairs, standing and taking notes. "I've been on the verge of tearing up my contract with Hilly several times since last we met, but he's always talked me 'round. He has great charm. . . ." Tynan devised *Oh! Calcutta!* and wrote one of its sketches. Hilly and the *Playboy* man join him. A police sergeant in short-sleeved summer uniform walks in, as the producer later observes, like a cop taking an apple off a cart, looks at the stageful of handsome, entirely naked men and women, and his jaw sags. Hilly describes the look as one of "traumatized disbelief." One of the audience again tonight is the assistant district attorney in charge of the city's morals, keeping up to date on changes at the producer's invitation. Hilly, protecting his investment, wants only to be assured that the show, which might be described as tastefully pornographic, won't be closed or restricted. It will turn out that the morals man is troubled by something: one of the paintings shown as background to music (it is by Clovis Trouille, a patriarch of French Surrealism) gives us a cardinal of the Roman Church lifting aside his red robe to display women's stockings, garters, and underpants. "It bugged the shit out of him," Hilly would report later.

With its audience gone, the house lights up, the rear doors propped open to the summer night, the Eden is stark and shabby. Cars, cabs, and scooters shoot by on Twelfth Street under the tenements, head-lamps pale in the blue street light. Actors come up the aisles with that transcendent air performers have after a performance—the theater's own mixture of night work, art, and exhaustion—dressed in their street clothes— stripes, vests, beads, see-through stuff; they seem relieved of the burden of other men's dialogue, yet in need of lines to speak. There is a great deal of smoking, a hardening of class lines. Director, producers, manager, press man, "deviser," certain actors, technical men (film and sound are major parts of this mixed-media revue), and other staff hold councils at the velvet-cushioned half wall in the theater's rear. Some actors step gingerly out into the hot night. Levy takes a moment to say good-bye to guests—a man and his wife: "Now, go home and make it. That's the effect the show's *supposed* to have"— smiling the smile of psychiatry and William Blake. Notes are produced, pen flashlights brought out, clipboards full of cues. The show is taken apart, its numbers rearranged for the twentieth time. The actor Bill Macy is interviewed by a reporter from *New York* magazine: "You don't know it?" asks the reporter, astonished, as they sit side by side in theater seats. "It's on all the newsstands." Hilly's notes: "Tell that cunt to change her hair ribbon." Someone shouts, "Oh, *fuck!*" Tynan and Hilly argue briefly. Later Jacques Levy, Hilly, Tynan, and the actress concerned hold a long parley of a technical nature: how, efficiently, are they to get the girl's bra off in the medical laboratory burlesque called "Was It Good for You Too?" It did not break away fast enough and hurt her slightly. The *Playboy* editor has gone. Sam drifts out onto Second Avenue. Hilly will stay up until five, sleep for a couple of hours, and be on location on Long Island for the morning's shooting of his movie *A New Leaf* by 8:30. . . . What was it he wanted to say? Yes. He has invited the Mormon Sheriff of Las Vegas to opening night. The title rings in the deserted theater. The Mormon Sheriff's seal means something since Hilly plans to have a *Calcutta* company there as well as in half a dozen other cities. If the reviews work for him? Reviews don't matter. I write it down.

3

Opening night in the afternoon:

Hilly is in conference in the Napoleon dining room in his apartment at 19½ East Sixty-second. A seated Bonaparte, pale as wax, gloomy with greatness, has his thinking cap on in a spotlit portrait five by three feet—a baroque frame above a Spanish baroque mantel. Wine-red velvet walls match the drapes in the portrait. The dining table, very long, also Spanish perhaps, is surrounded by carved, crown-surmounted thrones which are covered in red plush. A phone console is in the cabinet behind the end chair, light buttons pulsing. There are small brass cannon and French Revolutionists in plaster, chess sets, snuffboxes and Empire knickknacks. The floor is in blocks of white and black. There is a pier glass, gold-flecked. Lesser Bonapartes, steel-engraved, whisper in the red corners.

"The idea is to deal with you so that I'm not required to deal with So-and-so. You know him?"

"No."

"To know him is not to love him. Anyhow. I asked for an advance of fifty thousand, and they came back with twenty-five. Now they're up to thirty. Okay. This is not an issue, so let's go over the points. The advance is standard."

"No, it's not."

"For a hit?"

"It's not a hit yet."

"Did you see *Newsweek?* We're a hit before we open. We're a *Time* cover. You want to wait and negotiate after that?"

They discuss the proposed campaign. Hilly talks of Times Square and Jersey meadows billboards, three-sheets all over the city, cards in cabs, in buses, in airline terminals and train stations, and so on, plus Hilly's planned opening night TV blitz, and *Playboy*'s eight pages. . . . "When I tell you I'm going to spend thirty-four thousand dollars in twenty-four hours on a show that can gross at this point maybe twenty-six thousand, when I could put fifteen grand in my pocket . . . I need the maximum help I can get on this. . . . Okay: what can I hit you for?"

"Whatever the advance is: it depends."

"I'll keep the advance at twenty-five if you'll come up with a heavy ad budget."

"Ten thousand . . . ?"

"Oh, come on!"

"Twenty-five percent isn't heavy?"

". . . I said to Vanguard, 'Don't talk unless you're prepared to give me a top deal. I'll tell you what a top deal is: 15 percent, but not a Rodgers and Hammerstein 17½ percent.' They called back: '12 percent.' I said, 'I won't talk! Say no more!' "

Mitty, Hilly's Weimaraner, old and blind, wanders into the dining room. He knows the duplex apartment and rarely hesitates, but when furniture is out of line—a chair pulled out—he bumps into it gently. He is a good-looking affectionate old pet; the deep cloudy blindness of his eyes reflects colors near him, so that sometimes his eyes are gold and sometimes green or scarlet. When Hilly is not busy, he will rub his dog's ears and love him.

An hour later BBC is setting up lights and a TV tape camera in the dining room. The man from the recording company has gone. Hilly, saunaed, changed into one of his all-brown ensembles, reappears. The interviewer has an Englishman's thick gray hair and wears a red-checked shirt. To warm up they talk in tones that grow softer, more upper-class and refined by the moment until both are nearly silent. The camera runs. *"Calcutta,"* says Hilly with an air of gentility, "is a satire of a sexual nature." Are children prohibited? "No one under eighteen." "Now, as far as the cast is concerned," asks BBC: aren't they risking imprisonment and fines? "Does the management provide . . . ?" When Hilly makes his joke—"We hire rich actors" —BBC hesitates, then puts up his chin and laughs, "Ahhh," silently. . . . "Which is more difficult for the actors—the nudity or the language?"

"Everyone says 'fuck,' " declares Hilly, loosening up a little. "We're involved in problems that pertain to exposure of the psyche, not exposure of the body."

In the downstairs office he gets on the phone with Mark Cross, where he has an account. The monograms on some wallets and cigarette cases are badly done or wrongly placed, it's hard to tell which. "Fuck it," he says, but sweetly. "I can't live with this." They are sent back with the office boy who had picked them up. A talk with general manager Norm Kean: "Window cards, back page of the *Times,* three-sheets. Not *various* locations! Get the locations! I want a true sample . . . complete lineup: subway three-sheets . . ."

Norm advises: "Stay out of subways in the summer."

Should there be kliegs at the opening night? It is given consideration: yellow? bastard amber? The city will send twenty cops. Kenneth Tynan walks into the busy office with an advance copy of the Sunday *Times* theater section. There on the front page at the top is his *Calcutta* piece, "Pornography? And Is That Bad?" (*Intelligent Puritan: But is this a job for first-rate writers to be doing? Kenneth Tynan: Perhaps it isn't the most majestic or awe-inspiring thing they could do. But nobody ever said it [voyeurism] was. . . . The pursuit of happiness through sex is our principal theme.*)

He has not been paid for the piece and is advised to call the *Times.* The money will be coming through, so that's all right.

4

Opening night in the evening:

"I have a clothes fetish. I really do."

Walls from floor to ceiling behind the pictures in the bedroom are all closets and cabinets, racks of drawers, numbered plastic boxes, glass-fronted bins. Even the elevator in Hilly's fifth-floor private hallway has been sealed off and converted into closet space. Shoes and boots rise everywhere in tiers. A train of bins contains shirts, socks, and handkerchiefs, each sort identified by an embossed tag; others hold ascots and scarves, which have by now replaced ties in the producer's wardrobe, to overflowing. One closet holds sixty pairs of slacks and twenty or thirty jackets, as well as several dozen pairs of boots and shoes and sandals, also vests, heavy shirts, sweaters, etc.—a fraction of the total.

The bedroom is burnt-orange velvet draped from the ceiling like an Arab's tent, the bed very large with a carved frame, a canopy, and a coat of arms on a shield that hangs above the pillows: a cross with hawks and roses. ("A put-on," says Hilly.) Books, magazines, playscripts, filmscripts are piled everywhere. No windows are apparent (it is hard to find the out-of-doors from anywhere in Hilly's triplex, though there is a garden terrace with fountain off the living room; all windows are shuttered or draped or, as in the bedroom and dining room, both). An airconditioner keeps the room at 55 or 60 degrees. The sauna is located at the bed end of the bedroom, the bath at the hallway end; the latter is of black marble, has a whirlpool tub and mirrors on the ceiling as well as the walls. Pictures, except for a Modigliani drawing, tend to be Victorian whimsical, as are the *objets* (a rosary, a bronze lady, framed grants and warrants). Mitty has his own chair, in which no one else may sit. The place is comfortable, Edison-Roman in feeling, the modern of 1931, like the lobbies of the skyscrapers of that year or a plutocrat's waiting room. . . . Photographs: Claire Bloom with Hilly, Claire in jeans and sweatshirt alone running along a surf. There is an album: baby Hilly naked on a sheepskin; then he is on a pony, his boy's face suspicious; then in the Air Force, usually on the telephone or with a girl: "Always you, darling." Then there are grown-up naked girls, and an essay of Weimaraners, Mitty's family; Hilly's wives. There is also, in the album, his old Lexington Exchange card (actors' employment): "Age, 17; Voice Range, 13-28; Experience: second lead in *What a Life,* Ernest in *The Admirable Crichton,* MC'd variety shows; Remarks: comedy impersonations." . . . Books: Sydney Omarr's *Astrological Guide for You in 1969*; art books; current magazines and journals (U.S.,

English, French, Italian, German); McLuhan; *The Joys of Yiddish*; *The Pearl: A Journal of Voluptuous Reading*; *Psychoanalysis of Dreams*; *The Hobbit*; *1001 Ways to Make Love;* as well as dozens of novels.

Judi is here with her notebook. Hilly, in a yellow terry-cloth robe, lies across a bed scattered with notes, cigarettes, coffee cups. . . . In attendance are three men in business suits. They are like European emissaries to an emir. June 17, 1969: two hours to opening-night curtain at the Eden.

Clive Barnes, the theater reviewer for the daily *Times* and, financially speaking, the single most potent voice in the New York theatrical world, has already seen *Oh! Calcutta!* (he could not be prevented after all) and written his review. He did not like it. "Negative" is the word Hilly uses. (He has been told about the review, not seen it.) But Hilly is riding high on this particular night, and he is not worried. "I'm hot," he says in the way a gambler talks of his luck, referring to the evening, to his life, and to the future. The men with him, all of whose fortunes are in one way or another tied to his and one of whom is a relatively heavy investor in the show, are worried. The producer's brand of invincibility, which combines yoga indifference and inspired optimism, scares them.

"I'm hot today," he says.

An hour to go. One of the businessmen has remained. He did not bring a dinner jacket with him, and Hilly produces a black Nehru jacket, black satin-striped trousers, and gleaming patent pumps: everything fits perfectly. "Would you believe this?" The man is astonished. Judi, desperate to change into her own new evening gown, reads a letter back to Hilly, who is engaged in combing the businessman's hair forward. ("I don't know myself!") Hilly's valet, Robert, appears with a fresh pot of coffee. Disaster for him: he must replace the buttons on the producer's own new evening jacket, just bought, and there is no time; he carries it off to cope. Hilly goes back to Judi: "File this." News clips; a piece from a London paper about him and Claire Bloom. She is still in England filming Iris Murdoch's *A Severed Head*. Less than an hour, and Hilly has not yet bathed. A hired limousine waits in front of the house. The Kenneth Tynans, who are the producer's house guests and have been for some time, are in their little suite at the rear of the house, and Mrs. Tynan is preparing to go with Hilly to the opening. Tynan will appear at intermission looking pale.

"My *sons* have been trying to get me to dress this way!" cries the businessman, looking over his shoulder at himself in the eight-foot swivel mirror. Judi groans with impatience. Hilly dismisses her at last, flings his notes away, leaps from the bed, drops to the rug embracing his knees, rocks with energy, then does ten sit-ups and ten push-ups. He finds a Wonder Wheel in the bottom of a closet, rolls forward on it, extending his body, and then back five times, while the businessman watches approvingly ("Great! Best thing in the world for you!"), hurls the wheel aside, disappears into the bathroom. The other takes a call from his office. Half an hour to curtain . . . He describes his costume to the secretary, asks her to put the other secretary on another line and describes it again (neither he nor I know that Nehru jackets have been out of style for more than a year). "I don't *know* myself! I intend to really have a ball with this outfit." . . . Hilly reappears. Twenty minutes; it takes that long to get to the theater. "Where's my socks?" He searches high and low. "I laid them out with fucking care. That's the trouble with servants. They don't ask, they just"—searching— "do things." He finds them. Robert returns. A new set of buttons was found and sewed on. Hilly's jacket, which is of a royal-looking black velvet, is double-breasted, has a large collar, high waist, and a flaring skirt. Hilly also wears black trousers with a gold-braid stripe down each leg like a raj officer in dress uniform, and pumps that appear to be made of black glass: magnificent. "I paid twenty-nine dollars for the jacket this afternoon at Alexander's"—his joker's look as solemn as the sea: "Don't put it down."

Some celebrities are present. There is the football player Joe Namath. Ed Sullivan, Dick Cavett, Carol Channing, Anita Loos, Julie Newmar, Hedy Lamarr are there. The actor Lloyd Bridges stands in the twilight before the theater. At intermission there is free champagne in the basement lounge (the bill will be in the office next day: $460) and high-piled platters of hors d'oeuvres. The smoke is thick—"God! My bronchitis!" —and customers chase it here and there with their tasseled golden-bound souvenir programs. Uniformed servants move in the crowd with trays of coffee. A number of people carry opera glasses; one man wears two pairs of binoculars—apparently high-powered ones—crossing his chest like bandoliers. Everyone is smartly dressed or, failing that, wittily dressed. There are a number of well-trimmed beards, brass and beads, lace, velvet, bells, patent leather, fishnet: "I love this generation because they can spoof everything," a woman says. Members of the EPIC staff deploy themselves, listen hungrily for comments, but there are few. No one really knows how to talk about the cheerful pornography upstairs. Sheepskin vests with wool turned in, embroidered vests the purple of Jesus, swinging old men in side whiskers, stripes and checks, and ominous box-heeled square-toed shoes. Celebrities stand separated from each other, famous actors and actresses (the latter favoring pants suits), tall, tanned, upright, silent: inexpressible pilings. A young man, celebrity-watching, narrow as sugar cane, pecks at his plastic champagne glass, tense: leather vest to his knees, fringed to his moccasins, beads, silk slacks, and a leather band —a garrote—tight around his neck. Someone else: ". . . flew

in from Chicago for this: the plane, my wife, the shopping
. . . ten-buck seats, to see what you see in Cicero for a
buck . . ." But he likes it. Usherettes wear yellow and chocolate
smocks with "Oh! Calcutta!" embroidered on the backs.

(At first curtain no one wanted to sit down. Hilly inspected
the progress of Jerry's work in the lounge—"Fair, only fair"
—and disappeared backstage. Mrs. Tynan stood at the rear
barricade. The initial shock that was a true one for the audience—nakedness in this situation is no more than mildly sur-
prising and then only to some people—was to hear a pretty
girl in evening dress who is seated on a stool on the stage with
other young men and women in evening dress—it is the "Suite
for Five Letters"—describe masturbating fantasies in vivid
detail, and then to see her, writhing, eyes closed in ecstasy
[all five are doing this separately in a fugue to their own
thoughts], reach a hand up the front of her skirt to her crotch
and seem to manipulate herself. There was a notable gasp.)

"Spread it thin," Norm Kean warns the bartender who is
dispensing champagne. "We're short."

A buzzer sounds. The lounge is suddenly emptied, cigarettes
doused in the plastic glasses, the glasses in nests in boxes of
plastic plants.

Act II.

Ten people dance in half light. "We are over . . ." Five
sentimental couples. They drift here and there, at length, absently, remove all of their clothing. "Life is over much too
soon. . . . The world keeps floating all alone in space. . . ." A
girl comes smiling upstairs late from the ladies' room in a
transparent blouse; she glances at the naked stage, her smile
dissolves, and she becomes sad; her own nakedness is eclipsed.

Jack and Jill leave a party. He wants to play a game; Jill
will try anything, because she is in love with Jack. With a
ruler Jill is to measure Jack's "thing," which is "up in the air."

Then he measures Jill. The winner will choose whether or not they are to make love then and there. To her delight and his chagrin, Jill wins: she is eight inches deep, he is seven inches long. She chooses not to make love at all, but Jack is getting ugly; he wants his way; in fact he rapes Jill to get it. The rape is as real to her as the game was and all but destroys her. At Jack's exit ("Hey, baby! Hey, baby! What's your name anyway? . . . My name is Joe," which it is not any more than it was Jack), the raped girl is left alone, half-conscious.

A men's club meets once a week, sits in swivel chairs facing upstage, and its individual members, by an effort of imagination, project erotic images onto screens; whereupon, to the increasing excitement of rock music and rapidly shifting images that finally become an ensemble image—it is a club, after all —they masturbate to climax. Tonight the new man is introduced, and they get to work at once, but the new man, true to his own notion of beauty, excites himself by visualizing the Lone Ranger and his horse Silver in action against their theme from the *William Tell* Overture. The others protest—that each can see all of the screens is essential to the ultimate togetherness; their standard images of *Playboy* girls fight his unique ones. But after all the new man wins and all screens, at the organization's ensemble climax, are filled with a single Lone Ranger mural. (I am told that John Lennon, one of the Beatles, wrote this and used General Custer instead of the Lone Ranger. Hilly made the substitution and threw in the theme from the *William Tell* Overture. Lennon's autobiography in the program: "Born 1940. Lived. Met Yoko 1966!")

The audience has warmed up noticeably. There are cheers, even a few bravos. There is loud laughter at the right places. Opening-night first act was badly timed and wearying; this is better. Hilly looks pleased and alert; Tynan remains reserved; Jacques Levy's glance has brightened. Only Hilly knows about the Barnes review, and even that may turn out to have some saving gifts when its full text is known. There are the other reviews still to come. . . .

(The show is at its best in a burlesque mood, and sometimes it is appropriately moving. Its worst, when it is being philosophical, is not worse than it ought to be and is sentimental merely. It suffers from the theaterman's itch to tinker, rewrite, rearrange: make perfect what has no business being so. Elkins, who had his *Golden Boy* on the road for twenty-two weeks, which is longer than most Broadway shows run, is known for endless dissatisfaction with his productions and endless problems. The result of the tinkering with *Calcutta* is that its structure is self-conscious and tight.

The best of the sketches was thrown out early in the previews, a victim of tinkering. Cartoon slides are cast on a screen, the voices of the characters—a man and wife approaching middle age; he is a gas station attendant—are heard through loudspeakers. It is bedtime Saturday night. The couple tosses a gargantuan fight; they transfix each other with obscenities and insults, throw things—"CRASH!" says the cartoon; it crescendos to the point of his being about to bring a chair down on her head—it looks like murder—when he discovers, and we too, that he is sexually excited. Argument ceases. The voices now caress each other roughly; we miss dialogue, things grow so intimate. We see the man descend upon his wife. We see the house from outside; their cartoon bedroom window goes dark. "In a printed box, as in comic strips, camera holds on lettering: 'A scene of this kind is necessary, now, to their rare evenings of love-making.' " Hilly felt that, with some other sketches, it was too real and made a transition to the next scene difficult.

In another sketch that was dropped a mixed group of senior citizens meets in a house where one old couple is baby-sitting its grandchildren, who are asleep; they throw their Social Security cards onto a coffee table and pick one each to find a partner; then they hold a wheezing, tottering orgy. They use canes; someone sucks on someone else's feet. There are accidents and incontinence, and there is even some success. Then the evening is over: "Who's got my surgical bra . . . ?" "Ralph was a little soggy tonight," and so on.)

5

"There's no personal connection between art and psychology in my life," says Levy, *Calcutta*'s director. "When I majored in psychology, it was because I didn't have the guts to go into writing." The hoped-for liberating effect of the show has, for Levy, a political rather than a psychological purpose. "Nothing in psychology prepares you for getting people undressed and easy with nudity and sex in public. At the beginning I had some Freudian notions about voyeurism and exhibitionism to put them at their ease; it had very little other effect. One thing: I asked the *Calcutta* cast not to be involved with each other socially, not to ball each other, in order to maintain a high degree of tension in the group. I guess that's Freudian. As they got more and more used to it, the excitement of their naked bodies diminished." Therefore another tension-maintaining rule was that they not be naked with each other except while working. "But that broke down after a while. . . . I never worked so hard in my life—the continued work of unifying this group. To be in the middle of ten naked, writhing bodies on the stage: you don't run into that every day in life. . . . Also, technically the show is a bitch."

6

Hilly and the chauffeur remove packages—gifts for the cast and staff—from the trunk of the big car and load them into the arms of Tony, the Sardi's doorman. A pack of autograph hunters, all boys apparently under fourteen, look us over in a sharp professional way. No stars, let alone superstars. (When Claire Bloom will emerge from Sardi's with Hilly a few days later, they will be upon her at once, armed with her portrait in eight-by-ten prints, pens for writing on the glossy surface, and information about her latest movie release and her private life.) Hilly is everywhere, drawing everything to him, the combined optimism and mystic indifference in full control. More sharp stares from the ordinary people inside Sardi's waiting for tables (in this theaterman's restaurant on West Forty-fourth Street the distinction between being ordinary and being important is accepted by all hands; equal rights would spoil the fun: in is in, out is out).

Because of the 7:30 opening-night curtain we are ahead of the Broadway theater crowd. Our party is upstairs, and here the stares stop. . . . Whiskey, gin, and their mixers at the bar —no cocktails. The buffet is jammed with cast, staff, agents, backers, lawyers, accountants, friends, friends of friends. Almost before the curtain was down at the Eden forty blocks away nearly two hundred people had arrived at the cast party. There is Hilly's father, gentle, owlish behind his glasses, implacably conservative; he has a date with him, an old friend. Hilly's mother has been dead for some years. (I will be told by several people that Hilly was late for his own mother's funeral; the word "own" is invariably used. He was in fact late, but it was because he had had to fly to the funeral from California.) Kenneth Tynan sits against a wall, head exhaustedly back so that he must look down over his chin at the man he addresses; he wears a pale suit, pleated shirt, and an orange seersucker tie; he listens, tortured, polite. Later a few take the Sardi Building elevator upstairs to Blaine Thompson, theatrical ad agency and "war room," where an inner circle will wait for reviews. There are telephones, two small TV receivers; the windows overlook the Majestic, where Bock and Harnick's *Fiddler* is playing ("The best theater in New York," says Hilly, who promised it to Sammy Davis and got it for him for *Golden Boy*), the Broadhurst and the Shubert; to the right of Shubert Alley with its hoardings of theatrical posters is a half-block square hole in the ground that was the Astor Hotel, in the lobby of which generations of young men met their dates. To the west stands the St. James, where *Hello, Dolly!* still runs. There are a half dozen more theaters in the immediate area, but many fewer than there were a few years ago and more probably than there will be a few years from now, as Broadway is going.

Hilly sends a tired wink from his post behind an executive's desk. Sam Friedman, Bill Liberman, Norman Kean with his wife, Mrs. Tynan, apparently cool, are here. Judi in her new gown, very nude, is present without her notebook. Tynan's appearance is silent and ghostly. Both TV sets are running and primary mayoral election results are coming in on all channels. It is a significant primary, and already it begins to look like a candidate named Procaccino. ("White backlash," murmurs someone in the room.) Then at 10:55 Stuart Klein's broadcast theater review: ". . . no wit . . . all the sophistication of a men's room wall . . ."

(Procaccino's campaign headquarters were in the Commodore Hotel. The *Post* next day: " 'Boss, we got it,' said campaign volunteer Murray Isaacs, who had been downstairs tallying the first votes in from the Bronx. . . .")

No liquor. Coffee is brought for Hilly and the rest. He smokes a cigar briefly, but it has a party appearance, and the occasion calls for chain-smoking cigarettes. . . . What did Klein say? "He thought the sketches were like dirty jokes except for the *sex*?" Hilly is baffled. It is a bad review. "Okay," he says absently to Tynan, "you're going to make nothing but money." The producer's coat is off; all eyes are on him (except veteran Friedman's), as if bad news filtered through Hilly may be better. Someone suggests the review line be used. "I never have and never will use a false quote in an ad. . . . If my theory is right and that's the worst review we get and still pick up nine or ten thousand at the box office tomorrow, we're all right." A waiter has brought cigarettes and Hilly fills his case, spilling some. He is not trying to be calm. Tynan dematerializes. At 11:20 first the Shubert, then the Broadhurst, breaks, and the crowd spills blinking from the icy lobbies into the hot street. . . . Edwin Newman "is not projecting for Procaccino," which is a mistake. We wait for his taped theater review. "The actors were in the pink," he says at last. "The reviews are immaterial. If it's legal, the box office will be busy for a long time." We applaud. "Sam, it was worth it whatever you paid him," cries Hilly. (In the event it is not clear, he is joking.) We wait for Marya Mannes; then there will be James Davis in the *Daily News,* and the following day Jerry Tallmer in the *Post.* Tynan reappears. Hilly tells him what Newman said. ". . . don't worry."

(Candidate Wagner, at the Biltmore, said, "This is a strange night, isn't it?"

"This is only the first round," said Lindsay, who lost.

"If I'm right about this city being on the edge of doom," said candidate Mailer, "then heaven help this city, because there's not much to look forward to with the men elected today."

"For two of the sweetest hours of his life, John Marchi closeted himself in his hotel room. . . .")

There is hardly a way anyone can find of making clear the misery and anxiety of a New York opening night for those connected with the production.

Hilly is now on the phone taking something down in rapid, crazed script. He is sweating heavily, hungrily taking smoke deep into his lungs. Yet he is also calm; neat fingers are lightly on his hip like a fighter at ease. Tynan cries out as the producer, off the phone, begins to read from his notes: "Don't bother about the good things! Let's have the lot!" There are no good things. It is the Barnes review for the *Times*: ". . . To be honest, I think I can recommend the show with any vigor only to people who are extraordinarily underprivileged either sexually, socially, or emotionally. Now is your chance to stand up and be counted. . . ." (*"I'll* stand up and be counted," cries Tynan, pale.) ". . . I have enormous respect for Ken Tynan. . . . But what a nice dirty-minded boy like him is doing in a place like this I fail to understand."

"Well, I'll have to call him on that. I don't mind so much if he says the show's lousy. . . ."

The *Daily News*: "STAG STAGE SHOW OPENS TO THE GENERAL PUBLIC. . . . Hard-core pornography . . ." Hilly's sardonic chuckle. Everyone crowds around the desk where he sits transmitting from the phone. ". . . the bodies of the men and girls were naked and active, and the sketches, made up of small writings, just lay there. . . ." "I think we should take a full page in the *Times* and quote the stag-stage-show line."

"No, no."

"I'm kidding."

Tynan uses his fingers to stretch his lips. "Smile when you say that," he says sadly.

". . . some very raw and disgustingly clinical doings . . ."

No one in the room understands at all what James Davis means by disgusting. They are grinning, tired, defeated, and angry, and everyone suddenly looks too smartly dressed. "It's the worst review I ever read," says Hilly. "It's a vendetta," says Bill Liberman; and quickly: "I mean, against this kind of show." Hilly paces, notes in hand. Marya Mannes on the little screen: "If you're out for an erotic evening, this is not your dish. Nudity is not news any more . . . callow laughter, sophomoric . . . wit and lusty joy totally absent." Hilly says at last to Tynan urgently, "The show *is in no trouble*. Do not electioneer. Do not discuss. You and I will discuss *only*."

Everyone has grown silent. The *Post:* ". . . the good things down first: . . . trim, taut, well-developed torsos . . . truly beautiful dancings in the buff. But the words, the skits, that come between . . ."

There is belated, gloomy interest in the primary results. Hilly takes the elevator down to the party. The eating and drinking are over; the wrong word has spread. Most of those who are not directly connected with the show have left in a mood peculiar to show-business ritual, compounded of cynical optimism, happy pessimism, and a desire to escape the scene. Hilly seats himself against the red Sardi's wall that has seen many such moments, cast and staff gather around; he shoves empty platters aside, opens the *Times.*

"This is," he says in a pulpit voice—formal, fraternal— "perhaps the worst review in the history of reviews." Then straight up through his eyebrows: "First! I have just bet one hundred dollars that we will wrap ten thousand tomorrow." It sinks in. "This is one of several bad reviews." A pause. "Of course, CBS was good. . . ."

He reads. " '. . . destined to make the shrewd entrepreneurs the crock of gold that lies somewhere over the rainbow.' This is the one point at which I agree with him." Nervous laughter. They prop hips on table edges or stand on chairs to see him, not drinking the drinks in their hands, smiling with rage, feeling the producer's affection and loyalty. He reads from the *Daily News,* makes jokes that are less humorous than loving. "My point is that in the next four weeks we'll be spending forty thousand dollars on ads to promote the show. There's a deal just closed for Las Vegas that runs into six figures, London and Stockholm are set up, we have the UA cast-album deal. . . ."

Director Jacques Levy says, "In a few days we'll know if we're going to go on. . . ."

"Wait a minute!" cries Hilly. "Wait! We are going on. I will buy out any backer! I guarantee we will go on. Right now we're sold out for two weeks. . . ."

Levy agrees at once: "We'll go on as we have." He makes his own jokes. "I know there are some people in the cast whose parents haven't liked the show; well, I can only say to them . . ." And: "What time is the call tomorrow?"

Later Norman Kean, Sam Friedman, and Hilly hold a council. Kean is ruthlessly optimistic; Sam is solid and plain: anything is possible, even success; it can be done. "We have Michael White in London," says Kean, giving the producer the same list Hilly gave the cast, ". . . the UA record deal, the Rome deal, the Las Vegas deal. These are hard facts. . . . Save the ad budget . . . not even with Minsky's . . . Every night is opening night down there. Now I'm just throwing out something. . . ."

If Kean is working on Hilly, Hilly is working on himself and the others, but his speech is slightly slurred now. "It hasn't entered my mind that we'll run less than three years. . . ."

"If you wrap seven thousand tomorrow . . ."

"We'll wrap eleven thousand!"

An observer senses that the producer is only beginning to ride his considerable stamina and courage. ". . . Ads on the buses. Good, *because buses are moving slower every day*," says Kean.

Hilly begins, "All I want is that transparency—*Oh! Calcutta! . . .*"

"Eden Theater . . ." Sam begins.

Norm: " '*See Oh! Calcutta!*' . . . If we wrap four thousand consistent, don't be unhappy. Of course, if we wrap that on Saturday and Sunday, I'll scream. Keep the ad schedule as it was set last week; sit and wait. You can afford to wait and see."

It is two in the morning. The producer takes a sheet from the writer's notebook and sketches a layout for an ad, which he passes around:

> **HA\$ HA\$**
> **THAT WAS THE LAST**
> **LAUGH**
> **—Oh! Calcutta!**

"You're kidding."

It is decided to call off the overkill TV ad campaign with its $34,000 budget.

The cast gift is a paperweight of clear heavy plastic in which a reproduction of the handsome Clovis Trouille painting—the show's logo for all posters and ads—is buried: a reclining girl, her back to the artist, her lovingly rendered behind exposed, a trefoil on each buttock. It is signed "Clovis," and the artist has lettered underneath: "Oh! Calcutta! Calcutta!"—the punning English translation of several French phrases, most of which were unprintable until recently. The producer has inscribed the reproduction: "Thanks! Hilly" and the date: "6/17/69." He drops one into my hand.

7

Billy Graham, the evangelist, was in the city that week, his New York crusade pronounced a success; he spoke out against smut. A man in Brooklyn whose son had been killed in action told a reporter, "I wouldn't mind if he had been fighting for

America, for a cause, like I did." He doesn't mean it in exactly that way. "But whoever heard of this country, Vietnam? It's a politician's war. Our sons are killed while they argue about the shape of the conference table." The boy's vision had been poor. He wrote home that he could not see the rifle targets during basic training. "We wanted him to be assigned as a dental technician," said his mother. "What I should do is invite Nixon and Johnson to the funeral and tell them to bring their sons-in-law. Maybe if they saw how all the parents hate this war it would be ended." More than twenty thousand New Yorkers and out-of-towners, as New Yorkers refer to the rest of the world, had a look at Judy Garland's body in its coffin in a chapel at Madison Avenue and Eighty-first Street. The weather was hot. A file of sandaled men and women sweltering in monk-like robes carried signs up Fifth Avenue to the fountain in front of the Plaza and there paused to distribute leaflets—love and peace—and sell a magazine. The Long Island trains were late morning and evening; the 7:55 from Babylon to Brooklyn was almost invariably canceled or late. By fall the monks will be a sort of popular success, and the Governor of the state himself will try to deal with the 7:55. The city was not yet off-stride, though it would be soon; it buildings were falling as if in a war (relevant to this book, Loew's Sheridan Theatre in the Village, a landmark, was about to come down), and the moon was on the eve of being penetrated. In Penn Station men's rooms, on walls inside trains, on sidewalks and subway pillars: "Stop American and English World Rule." Boys wearing white cotton socks and heavily welted shoes, hair trimmed, girls with a strawberry-festival look were in town jamming the buses, converging on Madison Square Garden to hear the evangelist; a wallet-size leaflet: "What Is Hell?"

"If you can't laugh, you can't live," a woman, unsmiling, said addressing me, a stranger, on a New York street corner. "I saw Judy in her coffin." She had been standing outside the funeral home waiting, and suddenly, unexpectedly and frighteningly, though it was why she had come, she was inside. "I'm next to the coffin. I look down and I see this tortured face. . . ." She touched my arm because I had been about to break away. "You have a minute? Wait . . ."

"Was the coffin open?"—stupidly.

It had a glass cover. The woman made a bell gesture to show the shape of the cover. "The next day I had a bad arthritic attack. I looked in the mirror this morning, and I looked just like Garland in the coffin, so I decided what the hell: if possible I was going to enjoy my life, because that was terrible what happened to hers; her mother gave her sleeping pills at the age of twelve. . . ."

Oh! Calcutta! is a hit.

The disaster of opening-night reviews is simply ignored. Tickets are hard to get (at first Hilly claims they are scarce to turn the slowly developing demand into a panic; then they really are); it is sold out for two weeks, then four, then a couple of months. Everyone gives it the calculated play; whatever else it is, it is copy: in a summer of war and riot and little other theater, the pleasure of nonideological controversy. The Sunday *Times* theater section runs article after article about pornography and nudity ("Not Funny, Just Naked," "To Be or Not to Be Nude—That Is the Question," "Truth, Not Titillation"); there is a boom of letters with leads like "More on Nudity—Can You Bare It?," "Disaster for Actors?," "Something Lacking," " 'No, No,' Says Ned to Nudity," etc. And, of course, jokes (the wardrobe mistress at *Oh! Calcutta!* as a victim of progress), and serious questions from Actors Equity and other organizations about the seemliness of nude auditions and proposals for control of them. When the Sub-Dean of Westminster Abbey attacks the play in a sermon—"If our sexual appetites are free to roam, then no man is safe from seduction, no woman safe from rape"—EPIC is delighted, and the success of the promised English company seems assured. It is not as if there hasn't been plenty of nudity on and off-Broadway and in movies, but *Oh! Calcutta!* has moved to the center overnight; somehow it is easy to grasp and use.

Hilly exploits it in his way. Having doubled his bets in defeat, in victory he goes for broke (more in spirit than tangible ways; the producer is cautious with his money: free publicity is best). An idea of Hilly's after opening was to cast slide transparencies on a screen above the marquee outside of the Eden in order to seduce men: the bare breasts and writhing backsides in color stopped Second Avenue traffic and threatened to cause an accident, so, while Hilly was in London for a day to see Claire, Bill Liberman had it stopped; when he returned, the producer ordered the slide show resumed and saw that its focus was sharpened. . . . He is interviewed in front of the theater during an intermission by Gene Rayburn, host for the WNEW-TV show *Helluva Town.* Rayburn also interviews patrons now and after the show, hoping for shocked responses. Not to waste time, Metromedia has brought along a Sister Marlene McLaine, who is running for Mayor of New York City on a sex-for-everyone platform and has set her up outside *Oh! Calcutta!* with a volunteer who shakes a tambourine. She wears a black cloak, has a fleshless, handsome phantom face; her voice is thin: "We're going to have a world steering committee to set up a universal erotic zone. I will run on a sodomy ticket if I have to. . . . We will make peace —that's P-I-E-C-E—all over the world, and to me that's religion!" The neighborhood is fascinated by the excitement Hilly has brought into its midst. Hippies drift through, floating here and there in the lingering summer light of the East Village, idle, hoping like children for thrills and gawking like any American at celebrities. Hard-bitten Villagers in undershirts—older residents full of beer and philosophy—consider the mobile TV unit, its staff, Hilly in his costume, Rayburn in his Cardin outfit and makeup, whispering into a hand mike, smiling below eyes that succumbed long ago. One of them takes Sister Marlene's platform to respond. "This is good—to have an open forum here," he says. "It's the way it used to be on this street." Lights are on, cameras running, and a shill, worried about the budget, interrupts: "Let's see what she has to *say!*" On she goes, terrible with her torn voice and jokes, kliegs lighting her for a moment: "Now, when I'm Mayor . . . " The tambourine man, a drifter picked out of the crowd, admires her and can't bring himself to leave her side. Another man, drugged or drunk, black, negotiates the press in front of the Eden and blinks at the candidate; it makes him angry; whatever it is, he is venomously angry. " . . . mothafucka, you ain't sayin' nothin'. Go on, get offa theah, bitch, you ain't none of you sayin' nothin'! . . . " When the lights are snapped off, the street is restored to reality. The candidate steps down; her portable dais is folded up and, with the flag on its collapsible staff, put into the back of the truck unit, to be brought out again when the show breaks. It seems to the angry man that he achieved this, and he blinks with surprise.

(Inside, in the basement office of the theater, Hilly is saying to Judi, "Yes! Posters in Moscow! Yes. Write it down!" An usher lounges at the bar whistling while Tynan's "Who: Whom" is performed upstairs. You do not whistle in a theater during performance, and the boy gets a bad moment from Hilly.)

8

Because redecorating never stops, Hilly's office shifts constantly from bedroom to dining room, to a desk in the third-floor complex, to his car, to the Eden. Generally speaking, where there is a phone there his office is. He reclines across the big bed; employees and co-workers sit on it; papers, books, box-office statements, correspondence and files, charts, filled ashtrays, coffee pot and cups, cigarettes and Zippo are scattered over it. The room is freezing, because summer or winter Hilly is warm, and he runs his airconditioners until they frost over and are disabled; now and then a secretary or lawyer goes shivering into the hallway outside where it is warmer to thaw out a little.

"I need one minute of your time, Hilly," says Bill Liberman. The bed distracts him: "Why is the *blanket* on?"

"It always is," Judi says.

And Hilly: "Bill, you never know when I'll have a cold ass." He is dictating: "Ken, Don Pedro Hotel, Porto Ercole" —Grisolia, it sounds like—"Italy: Belated thanks for your very thoughtful gift. I hope this finds you and delicious Kathleen enjoying your well-earned rest. While we still have our police hassles, the prognosis is very healthy. . . . It is with reluctance that I have to advise you . . . " Bill has ad layouts for *Calcutta*. ". . . one minute of your time." A secretary wants to know what happened to a check for $12,000. "Since when are you my wife?" Hilly asks. "This putz is taking down every word, so it's okay if he hears we're bankrupt. I gave it to the Governor to stay out of jail." (Hilly joking, if it is not clear.) He takes a call, studies the layouts ("You Have to See *Oh! Calcutta!* to Believe It"). He likes the layouts (the copy is his). He finishes the note: ". . . I have to advise you that we have to pull 'Who: Whom' "—a Victorian servant kneels, facing away from the audience, presents her bare behind to be spanked, and remains so throughout the sketch —"while I personally like the piece and feel it would be most effective in the proper context. It seems too rough." He is now in good humor. Blind Mitty feels his way past, and the producer gives his muzzle an affectionate squeeze. "Good old man, good old faggy dog." He muses briefly. "There will be such a scream from the middle of Italy. . . . I want daily wrap and daily mail figures up to date and daily from now on." The phone: "Ah . . . "—elegant: "I have made no commitment on the Japanese rights to *Calcutta.* You may pursue it. Ah call me from Tokyo. . . . I am *delighted* with that response, and I am extremely interested. . . ." Another line: "Wally, will you call Paramount and get my next payment on *Leaf?*—twelve thousand dollars . . . "

It is another afternoon. The producer Roger Vadim is on the phone from Paris. He wants to do *Calcutta* there. Hilly, in the dining room, is in a regally high swivel chair. Phone lights blink in the Empire cabinet at his back.

"I have several contacts, but I'll wait. . . . No, it will not be too late, Mr. Vadim. I look forward to your arrival. I give you my word that I will do nothing until you arrive. . . . It is nineteen and a half" ("hahlf" for this call) "East Sixty-second Street. Thank you. . . . Yes. Very hot here."

A *Taxi News* representative arrives; Hilly wants to know if the card—"You Have to See *Oh! Calcutta!* to Believe It," with the nude Trouille girl—may go into New York City cabs. The man brings an impenetrable air of neutrality into the room, like a priest in a low place. "There has been a debate," Hilly begins, "between my point of view and the public morality, and the times seem to be running in my favor." A plump exclamation point—Hilly's own idea—has been pasted across the girl's buttocks in a layout by way of compromise: "An attempt to obviate any anal problem . . ."

"We've had far less *décolleté* than that and been turned down," says the man carefully. The card must be submitted to the Hack Bureau and the police. "The trouble with taxis is that they are private places, locations for possible perverted acts. You place a poster of this kind, and the result may be . . . well, bathroom art. I'll *submit* it, but my honest feeling is that they will have you cover the whole behind. All you have to do is let some warp-minded person get in and start scribbling on it—hundreds of people ride in the cabs each day—or say someone complains, and the police become the police all of a sudden instead of intelligent people. . . ."

The San Francisco production of *Calcutta* is set. Which theater? Norman Kean suggests the Kabuki, but it has only four hundred seats. He or production supervisor Mike Thoma must go and look at theaters in San Francisco and Los Angeles. Exactly where is the one in Los Angeles? "Look, you're on Wilshire, right? Your simplest bet is to take a left on Santa Monica . . . "—the pleasure of knowing cities. The producer sits in the big chair, neat and glowing, bare-ankled in white moccasins. . . .

Hilly needs operating capital.

His West Coast lawyer, who deals largely with the film-making aspect of EPIC, arrives to talk it over. . . . "I want a nice clean money deal to get off the nickels-and-dimes thing, which is damned uncomfortable. What will it cost me to get a hundred thousand for six months?"

The other is quiet, competent, and young. Instead of borrowing money and "collateralizing" it with *Oh! Calcutta!*, why doesn't Hilly sell his interest—say it's worth two million ultimately—structuring the sale so that it is a percentage of what the show finally makes? If he sells now, even at a discount, it takes the pressure off. He has been running his organization on little profit for several years, etc. . . .

A TDI representative (subway, train, and plane terminal posters and billboards) comes to look over the *Calcutta* lady. He puts on his glasses, spreads his knees, puts a hand on each, and studies her with her exclamation point.

"This is—um—a great improvement. Still . . . The point is there are a lot of people . . . a lot of people . . . It only takes five letters to Mr. Perlman . . . It is always the active minority . . ." He winds up firmly: "Much too potent."

"I understand your problem," says Hilly.

"You're a client and a valued one. I can recall only one case—it was a railroad—when we were told to take something down that we had put up."

Hilly will work on it some more.

"I understand you're going to take the show to Tokyo. We can hold the same location open for you that we had for *Golden Boy.* . . ."

Later, during a rare private late-afternoon quarter of an hour, Hilly settles down with some scraps of paper torn into different shapes to see how the bareness may be all or partly covered and remain the advertising he feels he needs. Judi drinks Pepsis and watches. Mitty walks in bumping into chairs. . . . Then the operating-capital problem again: maybe a stock swap, but that would mean moving properties out of EPIC. . . . It is too quiet. A letter on a recording deal should have gone out by hand, but it went instead by ordinary mail. People get bad moments as a result. Judi goes off somewhere while Hilly constructs a temper to fight the stillness. At last a fight on the phone.

"Moishe, we didn't agree on anything. I'll see you at 12:30 here. Okay. No . . . Moishe. Moishe, don't tell me *your* decision and say we agreed! . . . No more. We'll discuss it across a table . . . Moishe, if you want a deal . . . No, not tomorrow night, *not* at the theater: *when during the business day* can you come to my office? . . ."

It appears to be settled, but the same man calls back ten minutes later.

"Don't insult me, Moishe. There's a . . . Moishe. Moishe? Stop saying you're getting screwed and stop behaving as if

we're in the middle of Orchard Street selling apples. . . .
Don't be insulting, and I won't be. . . . Moishe, I believe you.
. . . Let's sit down like gentlemen, not a couple of peddlers.
. . ." A long pause. The fight is cheering him. "Moishe! . . .
Judi! . . . Moishe, I'll see you tomorrow. At what time?"—
formally, crisply: "I mean, how much time do you think I
can spend listening to you give me this nonsense? . . . No.
Hold it! No, I can't *do* that, Moishe. What time? . . ." Mitty
sits in the corridor outside the dining room staring blindly
into the kitchen, which adjoins, his nose up for food odors.
"If you come here with that attitude, forget the money, forget
the deal. . . . *I am not looking to screw you!* . . . Moishe,
I'm not *telling.* . . . Jesus! Moishe, I can't . . . I just can't
live with this. . . . What?"—listens; in a softer tone: "No.
That seven-hundred-dollar rise . . . Moishe, *stop* it, Moishe,
I'm telling you. I'm not giving you conditions. Don't you! I'm
asking you! Don't! I haven't *got* a minute! . . . Moishe,
don't, Moishe. Then *don't come*! Keep your money. I don't
want any favors. . . . Moishe, you keep *doing* it to me. . . .
Fine, don't waste your time or money. Keep your extra money.
I'm trying to make a picture, and I don't need this kind of
aggravation. . . ."

A late afternoon meeting—Hilly's New York lawyer, Norman Kean, Bill, Judi, etc.—concerning setting up the San
Francisco production and other matters.
   ". . . a deal in France, I made a deal in London, I'm
negotiating in Germany, Spain, Japan. . . .
   "Okay: can we get on to the heavy stuff, gentlemen?"
   The phone. The others confer among themselves and drink
coffee, which Robert has brought. Hilly's courtesy: "Sir? I
thank you. . . ." About the theater for *Calcutta* in Paris:
"Grand Opera? Near the Boulevard . . . eight hundred seats;

I love it, sir. It's beautiful!" Dale Burg, Kean's assistant, has hired a new secretary who will try out the next day. Hilly off the phone: "What's she like?"

"She's from Alabama and very pretty."

"I'm not looking to get laid"—with his happy snort. "What's her typing?"

Recoupment of investment in *Calcutta* will take longer than expected since the *Calcutta* budget went over the estimated $100,000, and it will take longer for backers to benefit (a theatrical limited-partnership agreement provides for investors to be repaid first: after they recoup, net profits are, normally, split fifty-fifty between them and the producer or general partner). Kean says, "We'll come out in eighteen weeks from August 10—around January 1."

". . . I want to make a deal everyone in this room thinks is fair, but I don't want to make gestures." Hilly is thinking hard. At length he proposes his own scheme for spreading percentages over the five-week middle period in San Francisco; it seems reasonable; the others agree. . . .

Hilly's meeting style is relatively complicated. It is supported by affection, more or less modified by respect for the people with whom he is meeting. His voice, a good deep radio-trained one, capable of modulation and variety in its quiet range, is his best weapon. (A writer in the *Village Voice* described the tone as one that "makes Chet Huntley reporting the progress of the Eisenhower funeral cortege sound hysterical.") The occasional raised-voice battle, such as the telephone one reported, is rare and usually deliberate. There are other apparently deliberate techniques employed: to get something he may have to demand everything; conversely, he may yield nothing grudgingly in order to wind up with much; part-facts will be iterated hypnotically; there is apt to be the sudden timely switch from business to personal ("You keep *doing* it

to me!"); he is disarmingly open about himself. He learns
with speed, is flexible, and can change his mind in mid-argu-
ment; he makes decisions about deals and people in split
seconds and then stands by the decisions. He can make the
payment of a debt feel like a gift. He listens with flattering attention. Ultimately he has his way. With his office staff the
manner is bullying on the right side of friendliness, with business associates it's friendliness on the edge of bullying.

The percentage scheme he proposed made him appear to
have been talked around, but what he gets also appears to
be close to what he wanted. Then suddenly, rather magnificently, he reveals that any money gained by his initially
proposed way of doing things was not to have gone to him
but was, all the time, intended to be split among his associate
producer, general manager, and assistant. This had been his
plan from the outset, he says. They are bowled over. Is it, after
all, a beau geste? He is very high now. "You didn't know that:
putz." His color is hot, green eyes shooting sparks. "I'm fucking proud to make this deal. . . ."

And later: a deal is afoot with Paramount to make a movie
of *The $100 Misunderstanding*, the rights to which Hilly owns,
treatment by Elaine May; the idea is that it is to be in a package with the filmed version of *Oh! Calcutta!*, Hilly to produce
both, and—this is the news—Hilly to direct the former. (How
did he learn to direct? By watching Arthur Penn direct *Alice's
Restaurant*. It is a joke.) "They give us two million or a mil-
lion-eight"—on the phone, excited: "for two pictures. I believe *Calcutta* can come in for under a million. We'll be using
young people for it, Jacques to direct: my cast cost is bubkes;
but it's going to be like the stage show—imagination! . . .
There's no rushing into this. I think I can put *$100* on the
screen. I believe I can deliver *$100* done my way for $750,-
000. I can *make* this fucking picture, and I'm going to make

a good picture if I have to go out with a tin cup to do it or if an orangutan directs! . . . When you talk to Bernie, 'Gee, Bernie,' you say, 'I understand you're going into home movies. . . .' "

It is getting late. He and Claire Bloom, in America again, have a dinner date with Gore Vidal. Vidal is to come to the apartment, and then they will go to "21." Hilly's Dali watch has stopped, the blue one; it is removed and exiled. What time is it?

On runs the meeting. Hilly nods solemnly "No," and keeps nodding, unsmiling, delighted, gleaming head lowered, eyes rolled up so that he peers through his own brows: No. Napoleon gazes from his place over the mantel. No. He and Hilly are serious jokers. They share the ability to make reality of their fantasies and to do it with such consistency and self-knowing verisimilitude that reality at last becomes Reality. The portrait of the Emperor, which is in the same order of put-on as the crest over the bed, is itself an example of Hilly's Reality, one of his productions.

Someone comes up in the elevator and is greeted by Robert in the hall.

"Is that Gore?" Hilly goes and looks. "Oh, hi. How are you? I'll be with you in a second!" It is not Gore.

He is due at "21" in eighteen minutes and is not dressed. Robert hovers.

"You won't be with him in a second," says Norm.

"Be quiet. Everyone knows I lie."

"Who is he?"

"My tailor."

Operating capital, next day: "All you want is the three hundred thousand so people won't bug you," says still another lawyer. "*License* your share to get the cash"—a new idea.

"The buyer's bringing in income and sheltering it against his real estate. You keep a long-range interest, and eventually you're back in. You don't know where this thing is going to go."

Hilly taps an unlit cigarette, listening closely, considering; he revolves the cigarette: tap, tap; revolves it again, lights it at last, points it: the decision. Alternatively, he extends the hand, cigarette casual in it, and makes gentle open chopping gestures of persuasion with it: the decision.

Men wait in the living room; they have been waiting since two. At 2:45 Hilly hangs up a phone in the dining room, stalks down the corridor banging the hard heels of his boots, shoulders rolling; he faces the living-room men, hands at his sides, palms out, turning from one to the other to appeal for time: a busy appeal; there is no time to appeal for time.

Andy Warhol's *Blue Movie*, its ads congested with innuendo ("Come anytime"), has been closed by the police. Now he is advertising a new picture, *Oh! Bombay!*, and is not only using type-face for the title similar to that *Oh! Calcutta!* uses but mentions Hilly's show by name as come-on: "The REAL THING —up close."

"Great," says Hilly. "I'll sue his fucking ass from here to China."

"You have sold yourself to the Devil and he is ruining the Youth of this country! The Devil is a powerful creature for Evil! Beware of the judgment of God!" . . . Judi keeps a file of *Calcutta* hate and libidinous mail. It grows every day. General scrapbooks for clippings are filled one after another.

"Claire Bloom, radiant these days and pleased at the success of Hilly Elkins' 'Oh! Calcutta!' says their marriage 'late this month' is still that indefinite!" writes Earl Wilson in his *Post* column. " 'It'll be when Hilly gets time to get the ring.' "

Claire has come in from shopping, having been, among other places, to a flower shop where the salesman treated her to some old-fashioned New York customer relations. She quotes herself: "Well, why the bloody hell"—in a sweetly reasonable tone—"do you have to be so *rude* about it?"

Robert drifts into the living room, with its hunting-lodge decor, to complain (Claire is gone). He is a frail-looking anxious man of considerable temperament who used to be a Pearl Primus dancer; he is now professionally a gentleman's gentleman. It is difficult for him with the non-stop redecorating and building (a room is being added for Claire's daughter, who will come to live at 19½): "I'm not young any longer. They're trackin' up the man's house with plaster, sawin' wood on the man's chair." He pauses, thimble on finger, needle and thread in hand. "I was here till two yesterday morning, and the girl's only part-time—she can't come in to the dinner dishes. She has the office downstairs to do, and she has to walk the dog. The man is never done fixin' up. I'm immaculate, immaculate! . . . For one year he ought to live in his house and be satisfied with it the way it is. . . ."

Hilly is hopelessly late for two meetings. "I gotta duck out," he says. "We're going to get a wedding ring. I'll be back in . . ." He looks at his watch, a twin to the disgraced one except that its face is brown. The joke: ". . . twelve minutes."

6:10 P.M.: a staff meeting (the other two have been disposed of) in the Napoleon room. Spirits are sunk in weariness. It is quiet. Hilly's father sits aside, inscrutable, later paces jingling the coins in his pocket. Claire reads *The Immortalist*. A hot and humid gray-yellow summer twilight presses against the windows on Sixty-second Street; inside it is chilly, growing more silent and menacing. Hilly is nearly inaudible. A new man, Leo Morgan, who used to be a producer of *The Sid Caesar Show* on TV, sits with pad and pencil ready, looking a

bit conscientious and square among the swinging modes. Judi
wants to get away for a date. Hilly is "at the end of his tether."
Silence . . . "I cannot survive this environment. I am going to
chuck the whole fucking thing. . . ."

Judi stays.

6:45: better. "All right, my love," he says to someone on
the phone in his Liverpool manner with a little sigh, but up-
beat now; he is coming to the surface. Another call. His voice
comes up higher, audible again. He flicks the hand receiver of
the phone as if there were dew on it and glances at the writer
with delight: "I'm waking up!" he says, feeling his metabolism
work.

Bill presents a dummy of the *Calcutta* souvenir book—
naked photos; Hilly is delighted. "We'll get busted for sure
with this!"

Claire makes hamburgers and salad for everyone, the former with a machine that bakes sandwiches into pics and will
be used in the chain of Alice restaurants; both are good. . . .
"Now, what I'm about to say is not meant to be in any way
kind," begins the producer. The purpose of the meeting is
emerging.

"Norm, this whole situation is due to your and my negli-
gence—not in that order. . . ." Off-Broadway minimum scale
is $100 a week, and Hilly, Hilly explains, started the *Calcutta*
people at $175, then raised them to $200, and now for the
cast album demands are being made. . . . "They sing—some
of them—one-fifth of a song, but they read that we're selling
out. They know the *Dames at Sea* kids got a thousand each
for the cast album. I am offering them, after all, two weeks'
salary, one now, one when we recoup. All right," he says
cheerfully, "now I'm going to get new people and replace the
cast. I don't have to take this shit. I've taken it from stars who
were worth it, but I don't have to take this. Norm, what we
should have had was a firm recording rider in the contract.

. . ." Kean catches something in his windpipe and chokes; Hilly waits. "Are you all through with the sympathy cop-out, Norm?" Everyone is cheered, despite the subject: at least wide-awake. "We knew we had a potential album. It would have been a piece of cake to put it in the contract. I should have caught it. Norm should have. The cast is impossible. If you give, they're entitled, and if you don't, they're deprived. . . . We must tighten up these contracts . . . fucking outlaw contract takes a month to do. . . ."

Norm says, "Obviously, we're going to give in over the deal with the actors. I sense that coming."

"Dad, are you going to jingle those coins all night?" Hilly is thinking. "If they accept the week's salary now and a week on recoupment, I'd be inclined to go forward on it, with total seriousness, subject only to finding bodies to replace the ones now in the company." All that works is his anger. Jacques Levy is reached at the ranch in Wyoming where he is vacationing. "Jacques, I've had it," says Hilly into the phone. "It's give-a-finger-take-a-hand time. . . . They're all being martyrs, and it's a totally unhealthy atmosphere. The first person I want to lose out of the show because she's the second biggest mouth and the least biggest talent is What's-her-name. Yes. And *he's* a paranoid. . . . Judi, put him down for a call tomorrow, and that other one—that cunt." To me: "Your book will never be published. . . ." Now, at 9:30 in the evening, he is nearly at the top of his climb, as high on work as if it were a drug. "Listen, Jacques, if I get a coupla bucks, do you want to do this as a movie? . . . I'll tell you one thing, I think the dance stuff would be absolutely remarkable as an exterior. . . . Um-hm . . . um-hm . . . I agree. I agree. . . . I *agree.*"

Norm says later, hot-eyed, as if needing to say it: "That's a very angry and intelligent group of people down there. They don't hate *us.* They hate."

"We cannot win this battle. Or this round. Or this *war*." To Judi: "I want this noted loud and clear for the principal players in *Rothschilds*. Norm, incidentally, set up a meeting with Goldby on budgeting *Rothschilds*."

Bill raises a point about the souvenir book. The *Calcutta* cast signed releases but was promised approval. "When they see these, they're going to say no to anything below the nose."

"They won't be here! I would like to replace the entire company. I will fall back on replacing the troublemakers—one rotten apple. . . . Do you have *one single indication* that the situation will get better? . . . Okay, I'll sit down with them. They'll get the shit out of their blood. I'll get the shit out of my blood. I'll play that. But if they say no, I'll have no choice but to behave like David Merrick! . . ."

"It's a shame."

"It's *life*, Norm. At least we haven't got anyone stabbed in the dressing rooms the way we did in *Golden Boy*. . . ."

(The matter will be more or less smoothly straightened out; no one is to be dropped.)

". . . the laundry bills. We got a bill for three hundred dollars for one week. . . . The rugs at the Eden, for example: the work's supposed to be done by contract; I find dirt accumulating in the crevices of the steps. Security guards: we've got one at two hundred dollars a week, and I have seen three fights where security guards couldn't be found. Norman, I want to cut this budget"—*Calcutta* is Kean's job now—"pare it down to the bone. I want this tight. We're spending too much for a hundred reasons . . ." etcetera.

10:15: "Okay, I think everyone's officially exhausted. Any comments or questions?"

A few side conferences. The meeting is over. People yawn and stretch. Judi has missed her date. "I'm not emotionally stable in any kind of relationship," someone says at large.

"Too bad"—yawning.

"Oh, no, it's groovy" is the bitter response.

In a *Time* magazine symposium that included Kenneth Tynan, Sally Kirkland, an actress who helped break the theater nudity barrier, and a psychoanalyst named Vandenhaag, Miss Kirkland said, "With nudity, we'll get some honesty, which we haven't had in the arts in a long time." And Vandenhaag replied, "Why do you insist that a naked man cannot lie?" *Oh! Calcutta!*'s virtue lies in its relative lack of solemnity; its naked men seem able to lie just as if they were dressed.

By early August, a few weeks after its opening, the show was an assured commercial success, and EPIC was filling mail orders promptly through January of 1970. . . . " '69's Most Controversial Musical Hit! . . . Suggested for Mature Audiences Only . . . a few seats in the first two rows at $25.00 for those who insist on being up front. NEW YEAR'S EVE: $35.00, $25.00, $20.00, $10.00, $7.50."

V

Second Act Trouble / Summer

1

Work on *The Rothschilds* goes slowly forward. Bock and Harnick are in their summer houses, communicating about the job now and then by phone. One or the other drifts into New York briefly, and they are briefly bachelors. Harnick particularly is part of what is being called the New York liberal establishment, so that the results of the mayoral primaries was a blow. Money must be raised, Lindsay elected; it is a matter of the first importance. Yellen has bought a house on Long Island and is redecorating it. He comes into the city to get writing done or to see his agent. (Work on the contract continues. Size of names on posters, in ads and programs needs specifying in this profession; proscriptions and privileges are the contractual medium of exchange, and each item has weight.) Key scenes are developing in the heat of the summer to make clear what *The Rothschilds* is about. . . . Nathan must abandon his father's style of servility; he rallies his brothers: "If they want to make Europe bleed when they are cut, they must beat Metternich on the loan. . . ." The point is to have that parallel available to

70

an audience—the ghettos at the turn of the nineteenth century, America's black ghettos today: *"and* the founding of the State of Israel." These people are no longer to be good servants: the parallel tracks of Jewishness and social significance, today and yesterday, must lead to an understanding, persuasively set forth, which can justify not merely the telling of the tale but the collaboration itself. In a way, it almost seems, you have to be Jewish (or black) to do the work, and it becomes a peripherally vexed matter: Derek Goldby loves the word "chutzpa," for example. How can he explain now, having written it into the book himself, that it's a tired old word, ought not to be considered an important discovery, and ought to be cut? Simply say so? In addition to which, Yellen has taken on that film script. He looks tired.

Goldby waits it out, spends occasional weekends on Fire Island. Things must begin to move soon. If rehearsals are delayed past January, 1970, he will think of taking other work; it has been two years since the success of *Rosencrantz and Guildenstern Are Dead*, memories are short, and new names come along all the time.

Hilly, occupied with other things anyway, keeps clear of creative difficulties, feeling apparently that the producer's job at this point is to be available but not readily so. He wants the Englishman John Bury for costumes and sets for *The Rothschilds,* but it might be difficult to get him (Boris Aronson was initially approached; he was not free.) The choreographer may be a young American named Grover Dale. If Bock, Harnick, and Bury are insurance, then comparative newcomers Yellen, Dale, and a no-star cast can be signed for relatively less; it appears to be Hilly's producing pattern now to engage in this kind of self-regulating extravagance. In any event, he moves deliberately this summer, and it is Yellen to whom the collaborators turn now as they would in ordinary times to a producer with fewer irons in his fire.

VI

"Oh, God, the movies really did screw us up!"/one

1

A United Artists picture.

Arlo Guthrie is starring, Arthur Penn co-writing and directing, Hilly co-producing; it is his first movie. He sits tanned and jeweled in the advertising director's office at United Artists in New York, reserved, being shown.

"Who!" The UA adman fixes Hilly. "Who bought it: the *Alice* album? What: *how many*?" Rough layouts are being displayed on an easel, and this is the pitch for them. Young men in variously modified British-American hover. Sideburns are long. A young artist, brute from a world of crafts, sits silent on the edge of the couch, mechanic's hands folded; his work is done, the ball in the other court. An older man, painfully engaged by trade in the metamorphoses of generation gaps, as it were himself all ages from nine to ninety, hangs back, and one senses caches of power. His spokesman says, "The half million who bought the *Alice* album compared to the number who'll see the picture? A piss in the snow, Hilly!" Then the producer is assured that these are only rough explorations for

72

display ads. The producer looks on silently as each is replaced by the next after a glance at him that is both humble and proud. Arlo is featured: his young face has replaced Washington's on the dollar bill, on a stamp, Lincoln's on a penny: "IN ARLO WE TRUST."

"Right? Look . . .

"It'll jump out of the fucking movie page and smack you in the kisser!"

A trailer for the film, designed to be modified for a TV campaign, has been written. Its author acts it skillfully, using Arlo's own intonations. Hilly is mostly quiet but appears to be appreciative and says that he likes the face on the bill and stamp and coin—the teaser ads. Later, when he feels it is his turn, he asks each one what he thinks the album, *The Alice's Restaurant Massacree*, is really about; and each, after an agonized pause (it is like Statues: each where he is—facing a wall, a window, another man—paralyzes himself with concentration), tells him. There is ritual in being put on the carpet in this way, and they are good at it. They become the new generation as they speak, accuse the "uptight" generation, in fact accusing what they are themselves—a gift that separates the adman from the moneyman and puts him in the artist's camp. Things are more relaxed, though Hilly has objected to the use of Arlo's album photo in the ad layouts for the film. He is not selling the album.

"Show him the rejects."

"No!" others protest.

All glance with hard shyness at Hilly, who is up to any glance; the rejects are displayed (church and stained-glass variations, for example) and rejected once more. A portfolio is found and Hilly takes the ad campaign with him.

"I don't know, man."

Arlo Guthrie wears his flowered shirt, bell-bottoms, and

soft moccasins; he has pushed dark glasses into his thick boll of long curls, so that they look at the ceiling while he screws his own eyes small to peer at the layouts in Hilly's office. He is slim, with a narrow, near-beardless face and a small mouth; it is an original, two-dimensional face like a flounder's or a Modigliani. Another layout.

"Groovy," he says politely.

Yet he does not like the substitution of "Arlo" for "God" in the teasers. "If you put like 'in food we trust' or something I think that would be a lot groovier," he says. Another design shows Arlo's head and bare shoulders on a paper dinner plate, seated at a restaurant table and about to dine on his own small derbied head on a plate before him. "I dig that. It's a gas. Let's use it."

"IN ARLO WE TRUST . . ."

"I don't think anybody who's really groovy would dig that. I wouldn't wear like . . . a Beatles T-shirt." The objection is hard to pin down, but even if he is inarticulate and soft-seeming, Arlo is apt to have his way. Hilly has known him for some time as a result of their work on the film. He is merely surprised: "That never occurred to me." Another man in the office says heavily, "It knocks the establishment, Arlo," as if to push him over. No, no. How can he express it? They'd take a look at the ads, his friends—"Ah, come on!" they'd say.

Silence. That's that.

"Did you have fun making the movie?"

"Yeah, it was a gas."

Hilly shows him the script for the trailer. "You should've heard the guy at UA doing your voice."

"It's good," Arlo says having read it. "I don't know if I like it, but it's good for what it is."

Hilly pantomimes the left in Arlo's direction: pow to the chin.

2

Judi has brought Hilly's car from the garage, and we are sitting in it in front of 19½ East Sixty-second at 7:30 in the morning drinking coffee and eating Danish from the delicatessen around the corner. Hilly is supposed to be on location for the filming of *A New Leaf* at 8:30. She has phoned and rung the bell of the apartment in vain. Is he asleep—in his bath still? "This is impossible. He's impossible!" He had insisted upon being awakened at seven. "He's a dinosaur in the morning," Judi says, despairing. "If he has a ten o'clock meeting he goes to bed at 7 A.M., sleeps till eleven, and it takes him like four million hours to get dressed."

The maid, Elizabeth, comes by with a key, and there is an anxious consultation. Liz has a bad back and would like to have Hilly try his chiropractics on it but is shy about asking. (He is experienced after years of agonizing "back." During *Golden Boy* he used to be carried into meetings on a stretcher.) Judi will ask him for her, and Liz will see what's keeping him. When Hilly appears at last, he is incensed: "Wake me up! That's your job. I don't care how! If you have to claw the door down or call the Holmes people. . . ." He drives, and I sit beside him. Judi is in the back with her notebook and the RCA radio-telephone in its attaché case. He wakes himself up by chewing at the edges of Judi's patience. All she wants in her defense is one word. A word? One word, then. He listens elaborately, nodding, maneuvering the car (top down, air-conditioning on high) fast through Manhattan's summer rush-hour traffic toward the Midtown Bridge, now and then glancing back at her. "That's not one word in anybody's lexicon. Call Claire's mother."

"On *this* phone?"

It rarely works, which he knows. He decides to wait until they are outside of the interference of skyscrapers, and by that time the call is forgotten. "*Who?*"—outraged. Judi, having given the matter some thought, has suggested an actor, Beau Bridges, for the important part of Nathan in *The Rothschilds*. "He is Charlie Goy, Judi. Judi? Judi, remember what you say reflects on this office: remember. Memo to Robert: 'What did you put on the brown patent-leather shoes? And if you didn't put anything on the brown patent-leather shoes, take it off!' " His humor improves, and the tone of the kidding belligerence becomes increasingly loving. Once in a while he interrupts the attack on Judi to flip a friendly insult at the writer. An expressway toll booth man nods at him: "Looks good." "My beard," the producer explains with lowered lids and his Oriental smile as we roar out of the gate. Then he begins to reminisce about his years in the management business (Steve McQueen and Robert Culp were Hilly discoveries; other clients were Mel Brooks, Gypsy Rose Lee, Billie Burke, Martyn Green, also Elaine May); that's not it; he is reminded of a story about a financial involvement, impossible for me to unravel, which he tells at length: ". . . guy's overweight; he marries the girl he was going with; then bit by bit he builds this paper fortune of eighteen million and suddenly discovers his cock, drops his wife, finds this girl, and showers her with cars—Spiders and what not—and the whole thing folds up. Over three years I lent him $25,000." Max, Hilly's father, showed Hilly the palm of his hand: "When hair grows, you'll get your money back." (The producer was paid, as a matter of fact, he says later.) He talks about *A New Leaf*. Elaine May had not directed a film any more than Hilly has; and his West Coast lawyer persuaded Paramount, he says, to let her do it as well as write the script and co-star. Costs have been alarming, and he tells how he has worked to cut them down and keep things going (many of the economies as well as some of the best promotion ideas for EPIC productions come from associate Platt); there has been a recent shaking up, a reworking of the film production's dollar structure, but costs go on rising. "It'll be two and a half million," says Hilly. "Face it or drop it."

The producer's driving is violent, but, as in a dog's attack or in illness, the idea is not to seem frightened or it will get worse. His multitrack consciousness permits him to tell anecdotes and jokes, figure "approaches" to production problems, invent nonsense, do impersonations, chew out Judi, and make his way through rustic unmarked sections of Long Island to find the filming location at Glen Cove where he is awaited— all at once.

The scene is to be shot on the lawn of the Alan Lerner (*My Fair Lady*) estate, which has been loaned for the purpose. The writer is absent. His lawn slopes to a pool and cabanas, beyond which, separated by a fence, is Glen Cove filled with power boats and water-skiers; one of the latter, who passes intermittently, is part of the scene. The property is crammed with equipment trucks and gear, dressing-room trailers, mobile kitchens for the outdoor hot-food lunch buffet required by union regulations; wires and cables are everywhere like tidal weed, lights on dollies, etc. Here and there on the bright grass, near the camera and sound gear, are those chairs of wood and canvas with the owner's name on the inside of the back rest and his title on the outside: "Elaine May/Director-Writer; Gayne Rescher/Director of Photography; Walter Matthau; J. Manduke/Producer"; etc. Joe Manduke is the line producer. Hilly and Howard Koch are executive producers. Paramount will present. The camera is the ruffian on the scene: battered on its scarred tripod, it is as black as night; scrim has been wired across its lens, and it glances across the lawn to the pool, waiting as if with confidence. Extras sit in bathing suits under beach umbrellas drinking from empty glasses. Others are at poolside (this is a country club). A few child extras keep going off the diving board. People play word games, work puzzles. Hilly stands with one group or another, his small presence like the generating figure in a Japanese landscape.

"Stay in position down there, please!" an assistant director with shoulder-length hair shouts across fifty yards to the poolside people. Elaine May, slim and baggily dressed (she is not in shot #40, which this is), chain-smokes in endless conference with Hilly, or with Hilly and Manduke, or with the cameraman, or in other combinations. She cups her left elbow in her right palm, cigarette aloft, looking like a skinnier young Bette Davis. Matthau appears with his son Charlie, who, since he is to be a diving extra, wears a pair of trunks. His father, tall, shambling, and long-armed, grins at everyone from under a saffron-colored cap, wrinkling affably. He shows a scrap of paper: "Charlie's autograph." The boy wears a black cap with "A New Leaf" embroidered across its front. "Come on!" cries the long-haired assistant. "Here comes the sun! We'll blow the shot!" Kliegs on fifteen-foot derricks are shifted, turned briefly on to blaze through the damp light, then off again. Matthau has disappeared to reappear in paisley robe and slippers, carrying an attaché case in one hand and a spring exerciser that he works with his other, and followed by a woman in a white maid's uniform for whom he fetches a seat that says "Howard Koch" on it. Elaine May is now squinting uneasily through the camera's lens, physically remote from it (palm, elbow, cigarette aloft), and conferring aside with Rescher. "Here we are on the Alan Jay Lerner estate," Matthau announces, "six hundred people sitting around at ten thousand dollars an hour, and it's all worth it because *this picture will never be released!*" Someone appears with water-skis and waist-floats—props. The star produces three tiny pairs of bathing trunks from the attaché case and offers them for May's inspection. She chooses, Matthau nods solemnly (they are for #41; #40 is only his voice). It is hotter by the moment. The long-haired assistant has tied back his hair in a ponytail. A couple of little girls, children of Lerner's caretaker, want Matthau's autograph but will not come to his terms: a kiss in exchange. Charlie is now in the pool.

"Walk away, everybody, will you? Let's have a set!"

They do the scene, which is voice-over for Matthau and the actor who plays his friend; the blonde "Sally Hart" is on camera under a beach umbrella; she rises, acknowledges the invisible pair, extends her hand into the camera. All of this is done repeatedly for dialogue. Then the recorded voices are played back for the shooting and for Sally's appearance (she does the acting, even when she is not on film, just as Matthau and the other actor actually walk downhill toward her to do sound, though they will not be seen in the shot at all). They do the voice recording three times. They shoot the scene three times. Matthau picks up a bull horn: "That's lunch, everybody! Two hours!" and everyone laughs. Later he is irritated because towels were not provided for the children in the pool. Who is to blame?

3

Hilly and Claire Bloom go to a sneak preview of *Alice's Restaurant* at the Baronet on Third Avenue. The staff is there, lawyers, accountants, agents, family, and friends. There are no seats except a few in the first row. From there, the screen rises like a cliff, and Arlo looms on the screen in color. Then he comes himself shambling down the aisle, big hat on, grinning shyly, having had trouble being admitted to the theater without a ticket. ("Hey, man, this movie is all about me!" he is reported to have said to the man on the door.) Someone gives Claire a seat at the rear of the theater. An elderly woman keeps offering Hilly her seat, and at last, rapt by his movie, he takes it. Pat Quinn, who in the film plays Alice, has a sexy thyroid look. Arlo moves easily and remotely from frame to frame. Arthur Penn's directing hand is everywhere apparent, so that there is distance and coolness between us and the actors; it is his movie. A sense of loss is induced in the audience and is undefined, which, like loss sensed in poetry, is gratifying. Technically, Penn has good brief visions and cold tricky ones; when, as in the last shot, he doesn't trust our brains (or hearts as a movie-man might put it) and makes his camera do our responding for us, his infatuation with his subject shows. At its best his characterization is documentary; characters are reported with a minimum of interpretation and without being understood in the least. It is what cameras, which have no use for stories as men have, are for. In story terms everyone loves Alice; Arlo is the scholar preparing for a secret exam; Ray is growing old; Shelly (who dies) is the anti-saint. The camera, on the other hand, plainly says that Alice is an unappeasable egoist, that Ray is mentally ill (or an actor), that Arlo does not exist at all, and that Shelly is a developing realistic movie performer. The dynamics lies in dramatizing and underlining such disparate factors rather than trying to gloss over, or ignore, or synthesize them as in old-fashioned movies: resolution is up to the audience.

Leonard Lyons sits with Hilly and Claire Bloom and Hilly's father afterward at Sardi's. Lyons is courtly: what is Claire doing? She has just finished filming *A Severed Head*? He makes a tiny note. She and Hilly share steak and eggs. There had been applause at the end of the preview and good comments in the lobby, and Hilly is feeling fine. Things are breaking. Claire signs autographs outside of Sardi's. Tony gets the cab. Hilly, holding his fiancée's hand, says, "When do things stop going right?" Claire at once crosses her fingers.

A check of rushes of *A New Leaf,* which is an old-fashioned movie, in a West Side studio. Hilly drives the open car, Claire with him. He races a delivery truck south on Seventh Avenue, full of zest; sun flashes on Hilly's jewels. The truck driver cuts in front of Hilly, who bides his time, takes advantage of cross-traffic, noses out his challenger at a light, and then sits beating his palms on the wheel, ready. "Oh, I'm sick!" cries the truck driver from the cab of his vehicle. "I'm sick!" And Hilly grins.

Matthau is at the studio with his mother, a long arm across her shoulders; he slouches and crinkles. "Don't try to ingrar-shiate yourself with my mother." Shot #88, over and over, at least six takes, the actors looking awkward, blowing lines, bursting into laughter when the scene is over. It is an interior. Actors fall down, fight, faint, sing: it is shot long, then medium, then close, then a mixture, then some odd floor and hip angles; we see the whole of #88 each time. Later it will be edited into one scene combining a variety of shots and angles, clipping speeches, using the best bits of acting: the director and editor working with their jigsawed raw material, trying to make a scene. Sound will be cleaned up or rerecorded and dubbed where needed, and then perhaps the whole thing taken back to the studio to be shot a few times more.

Promotion for *Alice's Restaurant*:

Alice (the real one) has written and illustrated a cookbook (Random House), which is to include a recording by Arlo; fifty thousand copies will be placed prepublication. There is to be a chain of Alice restaurants and franchises with stand-ardized decor and menu. Both promotion ideas, originally

George Platt's, are being developed by the producer. There is a meeting in the Napoleon room, and the long polished table is littered with samples: orange cup holders, disposable plastic eating utensils, pressed-cardboard disposable trays, disposable casseroles, partitioned dinner plates of gleaming "ceramicized" paper. . . .

"I want to make this completely idiotproof. If we are right and ever get this motherfucker off the ground . . ." The restaurants may turn out to be tremendously profitable.

"It all comes in the tray. Put the tray in the oven: no dishwashing, and that's what we're aiming for—zoom! Done and out. Furthermore . . ." The men around the table have an air of transcendent solemnity: this is money without nonsense about art. Neither Alice, with her give-it-away style, nor Arlo, with his sweetness and optimistic children's crusade, is present.

"Comments?" asks the producer-franchiser after a short speech.

"Well, I have some off-the-top-of-my-head-type things: philosophical. *Is* this the image we want to create?" asks a businessman.

"Let me say this about that"—doing Kennedy or Nixon. "If we use a real collar on the tray, our image will be good. Let's call it the twenty-first-century concept. Let's call it the astronaut aspect." It is hard to tell if Hilly is being funny and, if he is, what kind of humor it is. He watches the other.

"The kids are not your sole clientele," says the other. "During lunch hour it sure as hell better be the community surrounding also."

"What are you saying?"

"I'm not saying, I'm questioning."

The man is unsure: time after all is the big factor, he appears to feel.

Hilly grows ominously laconic. "Well?"

Someone else: "We have all the prices specked out, and we're talking in the neighborhood of an eighteen-thousand-dollar package. . . . We'll know the bottom line on specs and know what kind of dollars we have to get. . . ."

"Go!"

"Hilly, we need a firm menu to determine the shape of the utensils. . . ." And: "Hilly . . ."

He has been on the phone, hangs up. "Yep!"

"Time is a critical factor."

"Yep!"

Later he and the businessman confer alone in the living room that is like a set for *Mayerling*. The other, due in Washington, must leave for his plane and says good-bye. Hilly returns and sits.

"I just got rid of a guy on *A New Leaf* because he went around telling everybody when it was five o'clock. I want to get this restaurant operation on the track. We have problems. You have. We all have. We have negatives. We're going to make them positives. We have too many tiny nit-picking details that can only be solved with all of us around a table, and we're working from two coasts. . . . On costs: do you go with Walter Matthau or Jack Smith?" He develops his theme. "Okay," he says quietly when he is finished. "I'm through yelling."

Later: "He has not moved. I don't know why. So-and-so could go out and sell a million dollars in franchises right now. *He* says he has no problem. I think he has a problem."

Downstairs in the offices an associate is saying into a phone: "David Merrick may have the right idea—treat actors like little babies. Shit on them and they behave themselves. You wouldn't believe the problems we're getting with this company." A secretary is on another phone: "No, I don't want to get married. I don't want a child. If I really loved somebody..."

Now it appears to be certain that Hilly will direct as well as produce *The $100 Misunderstanding* for Paramount, which is also doing *A New Leaf*. He has had dinners with Charles Bludhorn, head of Gulf & Western and Paramount's owner. Phone calls flash back and forth concerning the present two-picture deal—*$100* and *Calcutta*—and people around Hilly are sworn to secrecy on the directing chance. "A million-two for the package." He watched Penn work. He has watched Elaine May apparently learning the craft as she goes. "You *learn*," he says deadpan. "This was your first day on the set? Tomorrow you'll be setting up shots too. Everyone sets up shots." Other things fade for the moment. *The Rothschilds* remains bogged in second act difficulties. *Alice* is about to be released. *Leaf* is for the moment in charge of Stanley Jaffe and Joe Manduke, Hilly's associate on *Alice*, and though he is still an executive producer, Hilly will stay away from the set. *Oh! Calcutta!* is a secure hit. *Lenny,* another possible project of the producer's, which is to be an off-Broadway mixed-media revue dealing with Lenny Bruce's life, is in a stew of legal difficulties; as George Platt says, Bruce made dozens of conflicting deals during his last years. Hilly, using Elaine May's outline (apparently she did not want to do the screenplay) for *The $100 Misunderstanding*, has hired a young screenwriter, Julian Barry (like Yellen, he did a *Calcutta* skit), to write it, and works with him, reading the new script in hotly typed sections, and making changes. In the midst of this, one of his lawyers advises him to turn the Alice restaurant franchise business over to someone else.

"You are capable of making money in a hundred different ways. Which ways are best for you? If you stay with it, okay.

Maybe. But I say give it to So-and-so and let him run with it. . . ."

That's the trouble. "Of course, he's adorable. . . ." And at length, seriously, because the producer is not only a business-man: "I want to disinvolve myself."

"This cuts two ways. You don't want some company to do a crappy job and give the picture a bad name: 'That lousy restaurant downtown.' Big companies, though, don't move fast. You're almost forced to go with what you've got now." The lawyer offers the name of a man who is in the restaurant and coffee fixtures business "for the whole of the Western United States. . . . What is So-and-so's posture now?"—con-sidering. "Well, Hilly," the lawyer, who is young, says finally, "you're a perfectionist who, once you're involved in something, are not satisfied until you see it done in an absolutely perfect way."

Hilly gives this piece of flora a look. "That's true," he admits. And at last: "Hell, even if it fails, we'll make a fuck-ing fortune!"—referring to the film.

Hilly is riding the swell of a wave that has been traveling for fifteen years. "Things are really breaking now," George Platt, his assistant, says; or: "Now that things are finally starting to break we can do so-and-so." The Broadway professionals who, six months before, were skeptical of Hilly's high-flying enterprises, are becoming, as they will before success, respect-ful. Yet George, who wants to produce too, begins to wonder where he will be and what he will be doing in a year. If this isn't his chance, when will it come? He is bogged in details. The office force generally—assistants, associates, managers, secretaries—is irritable in that special way that accompanies the promise of success. It has been hard work, but the work is only getting harder. The office is cramped, and autonomy and authority become problems. Apparently all are still open and affectionate in the high-energy, gossipy, profane theatrical style; yet the experience of the breaking wave is exacerbating. Hilly turns his old office over to Bill Liberman to make space in the cramped main office where desks are back to back and there is no privacy for anyone and where the noise volume is terrific. George stays in his familiar place on the other side of what is now Bill's desk, and Bill, youthful, curly-headed, dressed up to the minute, looks splendid and kidding in Hilly's board chairman's throne. To answer in part a variety of complaints, Hilly appears with Bob, who is to redesign the office space.

"They're complainers. I have to do something." He bristles with ideas, does the redesigning himself, making sketches, leaping from side to side of the room, pausing with his fingertips on his hips to give a ferocious stare into his thoughts.

"I'm not complaining," says secretary Merissa in English English. "I'm temporary."

"You're a temporary complainer."

He wants an intercom put in, independent of the phone system, for the staff.

"In this small area? They can talk to each other."

He wants it, he says, to keep phone lines free.

For the moment only minor changes are effected; Hilly moves his office to the bedroom on the fifth floor, then again to the Napoleon room on the fourth—wherever he happens to be —and acquires a new portable phone that really works. George takes a week in August; then Judi, who has a new boy friend, gets time off; nerves are quieted. For a time there is talk of buying a new house and moving into it—Claire and her daughter, office staff, Mitty, maid Elizabeth, valet Robert, and all. . . . "We just found a house I really like," he says getting off the phone on another late afternoon with a self-conscious grin of pleasure. "Sixty-ninth and Fifth. Thirty rooms. Inner court.

Ten years ago they were asking two million, but the most recent deal fell through and it can be gotten cheap, a steal: six hundred thousand. It adjoins the Westbury Hotel. Floors: lapis lazuli. But it needs a lot of work. Jerry!"

Jerry Simek, contractor and builder in residence—he is currently adding the bedroom to the house for Claire's daughter, to Robert's dismay ("I'm immaculate")—appears. He is usually hard at work at the theater or here, or is at the producer's elbow trying to get a little money out of him. He is a good craftsman. Now his plump youthful face assumes a shrewd expression.

"How much is it? I'll tell you if it's worthwhile." And when he learns: "You definitely can't lose on New York real estate." Both are awed; the grins fade; Hilly is more than half-serious, and Jerry matches the mood. It is the starriness of grownups' make-believe: why not? Hilly, a gambler rolling one seven after another, never minds superstition, while Claire, shocked, crosses her fingers in the cab when he demands, challenging his luck with belligerent indifference, "When will things stop going right?"

The producer is an occasional occasional poet:

> *Fate*
> *If we could choose*
> *We'd never lose.*

He composes them in cabs or on the rare two-block walk when there is no cab or car, then hurries into the office—"Bring your book! Judi!"—and dictates the poem; Judi types and files it. . . .

> *Hers & His*
> *Time wuz*
> *Time iz*
> *That's Show Biz.*

Untitled
Why, when it is so plain that any child can see
Is it totally invisible to me?
A plant, an ant, a shrub, a tree
Just plain reality.

Untitled
It is better to give than to receive
If you really dig poverty.

Untitled
When losing and winning become the same
We can play for keeps and forget the game.

Craps
Sevens are made by fools like me
But only God can make a three.

The city was still hot. Sardi's had closed for three weeks, which was unprecedented, while Vincent Sardi pursued negotiations to buy a London theatrical restaurant and his staff had vacations. Hilly and Claire flew to Juarez for her divorce from actor Rod Steiger.

The young men and women in jonquil-colored robes chanting peace and love were out. They sat on the cracked lip of the fountain before the Plaza, Fifty-ninth and Fifth: "We are Krishna-conscious—spreading love of the Supreme One." The Plaza stood as if helpless before them, Central Park was quelled. They had shaved heads, the boys, with a queue left in back, the queues sometimes red or blond since these were Americans, and rectangles painted on their foreheads. "These are the signs of our calling. No, not Buddhist. We are Krishna-conscious only, and we speak of the love of God." It is a functional exploitation of the youthful cult that has taken up traditional Eastern doctrines. . . . It was Hiroshima/Nagasaki Week in New York: a mass march from Forty-first and Broadway to the park. There would be a floating-lantern ceremony on Hiroshima Day, August 6; a garment district rally on the seventh; draft board actions on the eighth; and the big antiwar march on Nagasaki Day, August 9. In the tremendous hole in the ground left by the destruction of the Astor Hotel (Shubert Alley and its theaters blink in the unaccustomed light) a few girders were growing like a mold. At night after the theater at Forty-fifth and Seventh tough old men who had been saved discussed the Gospel ("The whole thing is *still* twelve men and their teaching"). Every black man, or so it seemed, carried what appeared to be a sap on his hip but turned out to be one of the new fast-selling bush-combs. A desperate couple, banana-pale, Southern-sounding, put out of a Broadway flea-box hotel: she sat on the suitcase; he looked hopelessly one way and another in the street, angrily blinking, panicked; in a moment he would do something violent. Three warrior-hippies—big hats, bare feet: real unmoneyed ones—were charcoal smudges on the steps at the side door of a theater. . . . Peace descending, love rising. That special black soul-hipster's broken-kneed turkey-shuffle, hands flipped back at the wrist at each step: you make way. Men stared through taproom doors as if they were in banks—through the litter of club seals and the brass hand-bars—gazed sexually at the poor; if one is dying, another is balding or putting on weight: transcendental sound vibrations. We were quelled too at last. At dawn in the Port Authority Bus Terminal an old lady rooting in a trash can wearing a battered felt and shawl, big Christmas ball beads, and skin-tight jeans cut off mid-thigh was a teenager picking up yesterday's *Post*. That day men landed on the moon, which had never been done.

"Hilly and Claire got married yesterday," Judi says on the phone a couple of weeks later. She sounds thrilled in her sour way.

I talk to Hilly. "Thank you, darling," he says. "I am going up to the Cape for a few days to honeymoon and see Kurt Vonnegut about *Cat's Cradle*, then to Boston for the *Alice* world premiere. We do promotion Monday and Tuesday. The premiere is Tuesday. Arlo will be there and Alice. If you think it's worthwhile, come up. It might interest you." They will go back to New York Wednesday, to Los Angeles Wednesday night to set up the *Alice* premiere there, then to San Francisco about the *Calcutta* company there. He has been working on *The $100 Misunderstanding* rewrite. He is formal throughout the conversation, as if these were news releases: "I'm batting out *$100*, which I'm directing, and it's brilliant . . . dynamite."

VII

"Oh, God, the movies really did screw us up!"/two

1

Claire and Hilly are at the Ritz in Boston in a suite of yellow
and gold. Arlo Guthrie will appear later in the morning on
Monday. Alice Brock is staying at the Sheraton-Plaza on Cop-
ley Square. The lady in charge of reservations at the Ritz,
which is an elegant and expensive hotel, says that if she had
known Mr. Guthrie was going to appear at the front desk
dressed as he was she would not have made the reservation.
Arlo has his bells and frilled shirt, his big hat and sack of belongings, his hair that is worn the way Hedy Lamarr wore hers
in movies. He has come from Bethel, New York, near Woodstock, where he performed with others before a jam of nearly
half a million people and had to be flown in and out by helicop-
ter. "Groovy." He comes hunched, grinning shyly into the Ritz
lobby: everything is mute, glowing; Arlo's Indian moccasins
sink into the Ritz carpet. Alice Brock, who has a financial interest in the chain of restaurants, is here for the fun and promotion. Boston is hotter than New York. The writer is at the
Parker House and dines next door on scrod at Dini's.

91

"One more," says the old pair in the next booth. "Whiskey shtimulates the heart." A couple of old loves, declares the waitress of the ladies, aside; they have been there having their night out for four hours, trying to make it to dinner, as it were to a harbor, stimulating their hearts: "We deserve a night out," they keep saying to each other.

Claire and Hilly are in 901-902, which he finds cramped. Also, Claire, perhaps because she is English, came into the living room and secretly threw a window open, so that Boston's late August heat wave came in like catastrophe. "Who did this? My God!" It is early morning Monday, and Hilly is uncannily real. He is rosy, gleaming, smelling of Arden for Men, entirely three-dimensional in Boston. He has pages of the new *$100* script and waves them, exhilarated. They read well. He has decided to put the Tynan sketch back into *Calcutta*, having read a Tynan essay in praise of Claire's 1952 Juliet. Claire, beautiful, charming, and simple, is also entirely three-dimensional. They look happy.

"My God, who did this?"—dressing: difficulty with the trousers because he has put on a few married pounds (we will go shopping later in the day); he grins under the Lancelot mustache and calls Claire vile names affectionately. The local press agent coordinating Hilly's week arrives; a car and driver wait. The agent once worked for Belasco (who died in 1931), the producer who wore a priest's collar, and he nods at Hilly's bizarre costume: old times. Is the airconditioning running while the car waits? "If it is, I'll kiss your ear." The press veteran, in a maroon jacket and chocolate straw hat, approves of flair. "Love of my life?" Claire will meet us. The car is cold.

"She comes in wearing a spade wig"—talking of Judi. "Right? She looked like a bad, racially oriented *Sambo* illustration. 'Take it off! If I were a spade, I'd run you right through with a shiv! Take it off!' " We are waiting in a television studio for his guest turn on *The Dave Garroway Show*, and Hilly is chafing because the schedule the agent set up for him is loose, half hours left hanging. He describes the adventure of simultaneously trying to get a marriage license (complicated by their total of four divorces; papers for all are required) and a liquor license for his bar at the Eden: " 'You have to be a felon to get fingerprinted.' 'Suppose I hit you?' " And the wedding: "Sam Friedman had ABC-TV there to shoot; he'd have had all the networks if we didn't stop him." His father, Max, was best man; two chocolate cakes from Blum's, one with nuts and one with cherries and whipped cream—innuendo. Caviar; Dom Perignon; guests were staff, a few friends; they were married by Amos Basil, the New York judge who closed the nude play *Che!* and who went directly from Claire and Hilly to a Plaza wedding, which was walking distance. . . . At last a young lady escorts him to the makeup table and, before ranks of lights, Hilly's forehead is powdered; he recombs his hair. Claire appears, and he goes before the cameras while she, nervous for him in the snake's cage of cables behind the three-folds, watches. On the air Garroway goes at once to *Oh! Calcutta!*

"I understand the writers don't identify their parts."

"I beg your pardon?"

"Isn't he awful?" Claire's look says.

She coughs rackingly and silently. "My graveyard cough from the hotel airconditioning."

"Do you think he's nervous?" she asks. "I am on these shows. He looks nice." I had described his eyes as green in earlier writing (". . . green eyes shooting sparks . . .") when in fact they are brown. She says, gazing across the cables and through the sun-white floods, "He has lovely eyes." "Did the cast have to audition in the nude?" asks Garroway.

"They read, sang a little, danced a little. Then if they

qualified," Hilly finishes the drill, "did an improvisation that involved nudity."

Garroway gets to *Alice*.

"At the risk of sounding McLuhanesque," says Hilly about the movie's plot, "it is not linear."

The chauffeur mentions the fact that he drove recently for the director of *Midnight Cowboy*, the current hit film. Hilly appears to be unaffected. . . . Plowing through Bonwits, Claire leaves the wake ("I swear it is! Look!") usually, but the morning is also marked by a saleslady: "Are you a celebrity, sir?"

"No, I am merely a sneppy dresser," he replies.

Nothing in Bonwits.

The chauffeur locates boutiques, and the producer and his wife move quickly from the cool car, across the hot pavement, down into the airconditioned basements, and back. Occasionally, they go from shop to shop while the Cadillac drifts behind them like a dog at heel. They hold hands and pause to kiss.

The Boston shops, like their Greenwich Village twins, are named P.J.'s and Paraphernalia; they play rock music. The salesgirls stand on ladders arranging display material, showing their behinds to the producer of *Oh! Calcutta!*

Summer lines have been picked over, and the fall lines aren't ready yet. Vest suits are coming in, and Hilly wants one. No. He buys a belt: "Size 34, if you'll keep it to yourself."

Into the car and out.

Claire Bloom tries Capezio's, where Simon and Garfunkel fill the shop. Nothing.

The Young New Yorker Shop at Lord & Taylor's (the sound system plays Bob Dylan): nothing here. Hilly moves with his high-energy dance from case to counter, where the merest glance is enough. Claire wanders into lingerie, Hilly into shoes. There are no patent-leather boots. There is no patent at all. Nothing. By now he has managed to irritate himself: "If I had a deal with me, I'd punch myself in the mouth and forget it."

Claire watches him disappear and reappear among shutters of hanging garments. "I find these jaunts very . . . interesting," she says with objectivity in English instead of American.

It is astonishing: here on Commonwealth Avenue in Boston are the Krishna-conscious ones. Did they walk? Claire Bloom, who saw them in New York, is certain they are the same ones. Chanting, they sway in white and yellow robes and carry signs with the words of their prayer on them.

Pleased to get Claire in the bargain, a reporter interviews Hilly at lunch at the Ritz. Did he ever act? Hilly rolls his eyes: "Does a fish swim?"—elegant tones. Most of the talk turns around *Oh! Calcutta!*, which does not please the producer as much as it might, since he is in Boston to promote his movie. "I've been a hit," he says at last, "and I've been a flop. A hit is better." (In New York Judi, sorting the Boston news clips, will read this and say, "I don't believe he said that. It doesn't sound like him.") About Guthrie he says to the reporter: "Arlo is really a beautiful fella, a bright young man. . . ." And about the movie: "The picture is not linear. . . ."

"How much credence do you think you'll give the reviews?"

Later, without Claire, Hilly goes to a men's shop and buys slacks, which are altered on the spot. It is an up-to-the-moment place, and he is fondly remembered from *Golden Boy* days with Sammy Davis, both of them having spent hours among their fashions. "I could cross the country in men's shops," says Hilly. While he waits, we cover odds and ends. Hillard, as a name, was as close as his mother could come in English to Hillel. A closed-circuit in-theater TV deal to enable cities cross country that would otherwise miss *Calcutta* to see it is afoot: with a package foreign deal for a million and a half. How does a man of his energy unwind to sleep? He does not sleep much. He plans "approaches" instead. He talks about his father and Max Elkins' attitude toward his son. "He's gotten over the initial shock of a sick mutation. As long as I'm out of jail he's content. He criticizes my entire physical situation, of course, the less than totally organized way in which I live and work—my lack of respect for money."

At the Ritz again Hilly inspects other suites more ample than his, an elderly desk man at his heels, but decides that the move is not worthwhile. . . . WEZE radio tapes an interview in his own rooms. "We got *Alice* in L.A., *Calcutta* in San Francisco. I'm on my honeymoon. What the hell are we doing?" The tape starts: Welcome to Boston. "I'm glad to be here. Lie. . . . At the risk of sounding McLuhanesque, it's not linear . . . my first film and a very interesting and valuable experience. Message? I think messages are overrated. You take out of something what you take out of it. . . . It's funny and sad and, I think, basically honest. Things happened on the screen as they happened . . . a film about disinvolvement. I think we'll make a bundle on it. . . ." NBC *Monitor* arrives to make its tape.

Dinner is at the Charles with Arlo Guthrie, Alice Brock, Hilly, Claire, and the Jerry Williamses. Williams runs a local late-night phone-in radio show on which Hilly and Arlo are to appear later. The producer is grateful to Williams; when he was in Boston with *Golden Boy* and the musical was in trouble ("I got clobbered"), Williams put him on the air for some fifteen hours of broadcast talk and helped save it. Arlo sips a Bloody Mary; Alice drinks a tiny glass of wine and says a few words about her cookbook ("They said I shouldn't have four dots, or I misspelled a word or something. I don't care. I like four or five dots, and I like the way a word's spelled").

There is Stockbridge talk (the town in Massachusetts where the picture was filmed). Officer Obie is still directing traffic in the center of town. I ask if she was at Woodstock with Arlo. No, there were too many of her own sort there, she says; she would rather be among people unlike her, like us. There is astrology talk, naming birth dates and signs; I am on the cusp, which I had not known. "That's cool," says Arlo shyly. He was "on Tarot" for two years. . . . We eat a specialty of the place, which is lobster covered with spiced bread like turkey stuffing (the bill for it will come into Hilly's office a month later: over $130). The producer and Jerry Williams tease each other, jabbing, working up to the mood they feel they will need for the show.

"All of the things that were in the record," Arlo replies later on the air to Williams' question, "were based on my life in Stockbridge for two years. When I was sitting in jail for littering, my friend said, 'This should be a movie.' We never said, 'This should be a record. . . .' At Newport everybody freaked and dug it. I'm glad especially that Arthur dug it, because I loved *Bonnie and Clyde*." Guthrie is doing his job for promotion. Williams reads a commercial with force and flips the copy into a wastebasket. Another guest is a lawyer Williams calls Irv, who represents Grove Press in its suit to be allowed to show the film *I Am Curious (Yellow)* in Boston theaters. That film and *Calcutta* are discussed: what is obscenity? Another commercial.

"What's happening, Arlo?" asks Williams suddenly in a strong grave radio voice.

" . . . I'm, you know, I'm a part of that whole trip. The kids, man, know that the only reliable source of information is each other. I mean plastic is not real. . . . The music world is in front of this whole trip right now."

Hilly gets "tired" on mike. He is low at first. "I'm trying,

Jerry." Then mysteriously: "You've got *Putney Swope*, which was made for $1.57 on a negative pickup.

"We're living in the dregs of a crumbling society," says Hilly.

Arlo: "The world is bigger, or smaller, than when you were kids. We're today talking about Chinese cats, about Russian cats, about Vietnamese cats: we're at the dawn of a new trip. . . ."

Claire sits in silence. Coffee and doughnuts are brought. The telephone-talk part of the show begins. Williams is brief, firm, and rather tough with the callers; their voices are piped through speakers into the studio:

"Hi, Jerry. Long time no see. I used to go to bed with you when I was a kid. Well . . . About *Oh! Calcutta!* Will the original cast come to Boston? Will it be cut?"

Hilly is warming up. "If we cut out the nude scenes, it will be a ten-minute show." He argues happily with other callers: "Sir! Sir! That is not the case!"—instant affection, instant loving conflict with the talk-show phoners. Arlo is cooler, more public in a sense: the group leader conscious of his standing. Hilly cries, "Jerry, let him talk! Sir, wait a minute! Arlo said . . ." A boy calls and declares that he is visiting Boston and comes from a town "where nothing at all is happening."

Jerry insists on the name; he bullies the young man, and at last the boy says, "Syracuse, New York"—throwing away his secret.

"Well, you can drop out, man," says Arlo to the boy from Syracuse, "and make it with us."

It is an attractive invitation. In this situation, in his inaudible way, Arlo shows the signs; it is possible to imagine that he might call and that some might come running. A girl phones, wants to speak to Arlo. Her bodyless voice fills the studio.

"I'm eating my pickle."

"Great. Far out, man. Do your thing."

"I'm from New Hampshire."

"Good! What's happening up there?"

"Nothin'. We're all eatin' pickles."

Later Arlo explains, "It's a whole big pickle rap. You know: 'I don't want a pickle. I just want my motor-sickle'?"

Claire is invited by Williams to answer questions too, and she accepts. A caller attacks Hilly and pornography.

"We're going to the moon with *Calcutta*, and we're going to *skip Boston!*" cries Hilly.

"I am a normal human being!" the caller wails.

And another: "Why does Miss Bloom sound so giggly lately? I've seen her a lot recently on TV." The voice seems to detect Claire where she sits frozen in the studio. "Can't you tone it down a bit, not be so hysterical?" Hilly at once is furious. "I don't care what you say about Arlo or Jerry, but don't talk this way about my wife!" And Jerry, after hanging up: "Boy, they're out there tonight."

Arlo objects. "No, they're groovy, man. That's what life is like."

A sympathy call: "Some of these *comments* from people out there. Awful!" Jerry is angered too and talks about "the Yahoos with the white socks, the brogues, and the cuffs."

"Beautiful"—Arlo. "*In*-credible." He is talking again of Woodstock. "Even the fuzz. People are afraid to live and go out and see where these people live. . . .

"There are thirty-two ways to God. . . . *I* don't know them. I know I'm not . . . *I'm* in no position to be oppressive. . . ." On the way out of the studio when the show is over Claire says reasonably, "You know that lady was perfectly right. I have been giggly lately."

Businessmen have flown from New York on a late-night shuttle to talk about turning over to one of them management of the Alice restaurants franchising operation. Hilly now is a consultant in the business, not an active participant. He enjoys the 1 A.M. urgency of this and rises to it. As always, he is impressive in business dealing, even when the ground is, as here, relatively unfamiliar. He listens, learns fast, makes up his mind at once, and, as stated, expects to stick by his decisions. Yet what one notices, with waiters bringing sherbets and soft drinks to trim New York business middleweights, is that the franchiser-producer is different from the artist-producer on WBZ radio of an hour before and from the man who talked astrology to Arlo at dinner. He approaches the same things from a different door; speaking now of Woodstock, that concourse of peace and sweetness, he says, "I could have made a million out of it," and half-seriously begins to think of the ways, as of course do the men with him. It is their nature and work, but probably what makes Hilly as producer produce is his gift of being victim and oppressor simultaneously, without strain, as well as his artist's gift of becoming others, so that if integrity means unbreached wholeness, or similar responses to similar stimuli in different situations, Hilly does not have integrity any more than artists do.

Raspberry ices, Tab, cakes, coffee, an entire bottle of J & B, apparently for me.

Hilly does not want to run the business but has an obligation to Arlo, who trusts him. "I never lied to him," he says to the new man, becoming him: "If you have a teenage son, you know what I mean."

The new man gets it. "Protect the image so no one is embarrassed by what's done—not Arlo, or Arthur Penn, or Random House, or UA. . . ."

Hilly's first movie is a hit:

"ARTHUR PENN HAS MADE A VERY LOVING MOVIE."

"ONE OF THE BEST FILMS ABOUT YOUNG PEOPLE EVER MADE!"

"HILARIOUS BLACK COMEDY!"
"MARVELOUS TO BEHOLD!"
"★★★½ ★ A VERY SPECIAL PICTURE!"

Teaser ads and the big film ads now show Arlo's face on coins and stamps with *"E Pluribus Arlo"* on them instead of "IN ARLO WE TRUST."

At 8:15 A.M. on the day after the smash premiere, the best reviews in, Arlo appears on *The Today Show*, Hugh Downs host; it is on transmission from Boston to New York. Backed by bass, drums, and second guitar, he sings in a sweet, twangy, put-on hill voice; his phrasing is offbeat, much like Bob Dylan, in fact. His guitar playing is good. ". . . eh-eh-eh"—hoarse— "everything. Y'Ah can't live without the love I left behind." The songs are country and city legends: mysterious narratives that sound like the Books of Chronicles and are sung in looping octameters or in serpentine Whitman periods filled with commas: ". . . and sing the song you sang before you sat before the king . . ." ("And I swear I will never translate myself at all, only to him or her who privately stays with me in the open air.") He plugs *Alice*, then sings once more, his other sort of song:

> I had a friend, a friend I could trust,
> went into the park and got busted
> doing the Ring Around a Rosy Rag. . . .
> Ring around, ring around rose,
> touch your nose and blow your toes. . . .
> I had a friend, a friend I could trust. . . .

2

"Great! Dynamite!"

Hilly is in the living room at 19½ East Sixty-second reading Julian Barry's still incomplete rewrite of *The $100 Misunderstanding* screenplay.

"In the book it's a Southern fraternity guy who wants to ball a colored girl to prove he's a man," Barry explains. "He gets no sympathy from that. . . . You need to like both him and the girl. Elaine made it all possible to do as a film, but she never gets into the balls of the relationship between the guy and the girl, and you have to. . . ." The screen version now involves three Indiana college boys on a film lab field trip to New York to make a documentary. He is pleased by Hilly's approval. The producer makes a few suggestions, and Barry replies to them. He asks for and is given a payment due, and then we walk out together (Hilly is on his way to Los Angeles with Claire). "I put it all in. I have to," Barry says about writing scripts for movies. "The stuff has to be good. I write it as if I'm going to die." He has a country place in Connecticut— we have a discussion about cesspools, and to illustrate an explanation he draws a diagram—and a studio apartment on Bleecker Street. "Okay, brother, let's go," he says as we leave the office. And fraternally and writer-like as we part: "Don't suffer so much."

Hilly's nails are being done by a woman in a white uniform in his newest office, called "the den"—a small room adjacent to Anna Justine's new bedroom. Anna is Claire's and Steiger's nine-year-old who is staying with her father for the moment.

"Nervous? I bet Arthur Penn two months ago we'd do forty million world-wide: what should I be nervous about?" *Alice* is doing well in Boston, New York, Los Angeles, and St. Louis. He stands, one hand in soapy water, a phone in the other. Judi lights his cigarette, then sits cross-legged on the floor to make calls on another line. "I'm trying to get my head together," Hilly tells his telephone. "I was in great shape until I became a millionaire. Now with two smash hits everybody's on my back for money, which I don't have. . . . Yes . . . You have been more than patient, but I've got to ask for more time." It turns out that he has been talking to his bank. "The nicest bank in the world," he says.

"Mr. Hillard Elkins—
"The following members of the cast and crew of *Oh! Calcutta!* feel that the type and variety of menu and the quality of food served between performances on Saturdays is not satisfactory. We would appreciate a change in this situation. . . ." Some of the signers add comments: "As long as you keep the *coleslaw*!" . . . "Fuck the coleslaw." Etcetera.

More of Julian Barry's pages. He brings them hastily from the Bleecker Street apartment, but now it is substitute work for material Hilly has rejected. He sits waiting in the hunting-lodge atmosphere of Hilly's living room; "Weighing the Deer" hangs over the mantel against paneling of distressed chestnut; lights show mutely on the phone console while Hilly concentrates. At last: "Much better."
Barry shrugs with pleasure.
In a moment Hilly gives a snort of laughter.
"What was that?"
"I'm into it."
Barry grins.
"Julian," Hilly explains, "is a New Yorker but has great sympathy for these kids."
While Hilly runs an errand Julian says, "He's great. I don't know if you're like this as a writer, but like I'll go from A to C and fake B to get there; then I leave B on the page. It keeps bugging me, but he stops there too. Then I know it's wrong. He's a great editor."

I have been trying to get some of Hilly's early life on tape. He provides the Panasonic Cassette Recorder, the tapes, and admonishes me to quit interrupting and filling pauses with encouraging sounds: "Let a guy go on, don't break the high. . . ."

". . . the kind of word-high you were on the day we drove out to the *Leaf* set . . ."

"I know. I'm hip. You're square: I'm hip."

Now the producer explains any neglect with "I've been on my honeymoon," and uses the phrase proudly to everyone. He has bought an eight-millimeter projector to show movies he and Claire took on a recent few days in Mexico. He can't get it to work. Bill Liberman solves it with a surly paternal affection by thinking it out, and Hilly is gripped by one of his moods of rocketing elation. "I told you I could fix it! Dis kid will make ha great movie! Ha great film!" He hammerlocks Bill's curly head. The projector develops another kink. "Dere's somepn wrong heah." On the phone to Norman Kean, *Calcutta* general manager: "Draw a check for five hundred dollars to So-and-so"—a member of the cast—"to be paid back at fifteen dollars a week, for his divorce. . . ."

"To the *Calcutta* Company—

"I appreciate your recent letter concerning the quality and variety of the food. Inasmuch as A, I'm involved in the restaurant business as much as I want to be, and B, we're spending as much as Equity requires on food, and C . . .

"We will, as of this week, commence the Saturday performances at seven and eleven o'clock and eliminate one piece of material from the early show, so that all of you gourmets can find your individual solutions to your dining problems. I recommend a tea shop I know in Chinatown. . . ."

"Hilly," Judi says when she has finished taking this, "Saturday's Rosh Hashanah. . . ."

"You are *working Saturday!*"

"What?"

"Don't give me that crap. You're going with a spade, you work Rosh Hashanah!"

After a moment they both grin, but it's hard to judge the real mood. (The office, except for one girl to answer the phone, will be closed on Yom Kippur this year, a Monday.)

Hilly wants to talk over extensive redecorating; the landlord's agent appears (the house is owned by a woman who lives in England; Hilly leases three floors of it and now wants to take over the basement and foyer. "He's putting all this work into a house he don't even own," says Jerry, the general contractor. "All this money and work; it's a work of art. He could make an estate like Jackie Gleason for what he spends, and it's rented." The same with the Eden, which is also leased. "Now that he's fixed it up the guy'll never sell it to him"), and we go into the basement, which was recently flooded by rain. "She won't mind," says Hilly. "I alter to suit, finish off in the same *verkochte* colors . . . a lucite frame"—to Jerry: "Putz, you can do it in lucite. If she doesn't like it, I'll change it." He ends, "I'll put it in writing."

"I have two other writings from you," says the dapper agent, stepping on his toes through the inch-deep flood. Hilly gets to an island and examines his expensive shoes. "I've been on my honeymoon"—in an absent tone, and to Jerry: "You'll carry me back." They come through the water, Hilly on Jerry's broad back; Jerry grins, but Hilly, a comedian, never cracks a smile.

Hilly and Claire are guests on *The Barry Gray Show*—WMCA: "The Voice of New York." A sign in the studio says, "A *dead* mike might be *live. Watch your language.*" Claire and Hilly wear matching long leather vests, big-sleeved ruffled-throated shirts, and bell-bottoms. . . . It is a two-hour talk show from eleven in the evening; Hilly has appeared on it a number of times and is himself occasionally the show's host if Gray goes on holiday; they are old friends. Talk is not restricted to the theater. ("Sure we've made tremendous strides," says Gray talking of Negroes becoming mayors of American cities, "but go tell that to a black cat.") Hilly describes his wedding: "UP, AP, UPI in my living room; the girl reporter asks, 'Is this the kind of wedding you always imagined?' " . . . They go back to 1947 and '48 to discuss the old Red Channels networks' blacklistings that brought down so many TV and radio careers. Everyone in the studio has a bad memory of those days, and each is aired. Hilly, then in the agency business (his involvement, really, was later —in the fifties), also fought for his clients against the creeping totalitarianism, and has praise for the William Morris Agency, his old employer and usually a favorite target for insults: "Abe Lastfogel and Nat Lefkowitz really went to bat for the blacklisted people. . . ." Later the producer attempts to clear up his position on the filming of *A New Leaf* (he has not been on the set except for a few particular occasions for weeks): "Howard Koch and I are presenting the picture. Joe Manduke is, and always was, producer of *New Leaf*—that was the plan from the beginning. . . . There was a . . . difference between Howard and Elaine May. She is a lovely, talented girl, but it was her first picture. . . . Anyhow, before the picture was shot it was clear we were going over. I produce on Broadway where if it goes over it's *my* money. . . ." It is his public statement to set against the columnists' and *Variety* stories that suggest the producer is no longer connected with the film.

Autograph hunters had been waiting for Claire earlier outside of the studio at Fiftieth and Madison: a shapeless woman with reddish hair and glasses, several white-faced dark-haired young men in shabby clothes—and Hilly bustled his wife through at 10:30 before the show. ("That's all, please, *thank* you!") Now at 1:30 in the morning they are still waiting beyond the plate-glass street doors, which turn out to be locked, so that if they can't get in she can't get out. The producer goes to look for the building custodian, and the autograph hunters crowd close and smile through at Claire. A thin, ill-looking boy shoves a blank card under the door: we are like fish, or they are like fish; Madison Avenue stretches emptily. "We *will* be out," Claire says in a friendly way to the boy through the door's crack, and he smiles to show that his eagerness strikes him funny too. The custodian releases us, and the movie star signs three-by-five index cards ("Put 'for Meyer,' please, Miss Bloom"). The woman gets Hilly's signature. "How is it working with Arlo?" she asks him courteously, while a boy points his Instamatic at Claire and she smiles in the sudden blue glare.

"I've never seen those before," she says in a cab. Apparently they are not part of the professional group that is based on the sidewalk in front of Sardi's armed with glossy photographs and felt-tipped pens.

At 2 A.M. they go to Julian Barry's Bleecker Street walk-up —two rooms, sleeping bag, a poster-photo of Lenny Bruce, a paper-globed center light that turns colors—and the producer picks up more pages of *$100*. Barry looks pressed.

"You know," Hilly says comfortably in the cab, which he kept waiting, gazing out at the cooling Village streets, pieces of screenplay in his lap, "I really sort of think of New York as a small town."

Claire won't stand for this. "Oh, come on!"

He turns it into satire: "I'm gonna take this town—bust it wide open and make it mine!"

A letter from Kenneth Tynan waits at home congratulating the producer on the success of *Alice's Restaurant* and praising his energies and abilities generally, a bouquet to which Hilly gives a sober nod.

Another day two film makers from India appear to try to sell Hilly a package: Hilly to produce a movie based on a short story about an English girl in India, Claire Bloom to star.

"Claire is, as I am, an admirer of the films you've done"— *Shakespeare Wallah, The Guru*—"and that's a big plus. On the other hand, I can't see that Mrs. Elkins would want to spend a great deal of time in India just now. . . ."

"Oh, no, no. Next year. We must get past our summer, which just begins now. Perhaps this time next year . . ."

The producer asks for a script and assures them that it will get a sympathetic reading.

Alice's Restaurant Response Brochure:
". . . *Alice's Restaurant comes onto the national scene pre-sold*. Across the length and breadth of this country, whenever someone sees an *Alice Restaurant,* he's going to recognize the name . . . welcome it as something familiar . . . feel comfortable about everything connected with that name, because he knows it. And in the restaurant business that's half the sales battle won. . . ." The people connected with the enterprise are described, including Hilly, the adviser, and a man who was executive vice president of Mahalia Jackson's Chicken System, Inc. Alice Brock herself will be Menu Consultant ("*quiche* Alice, beef and bacon drums, Alice's Restaurant casseroles, unique baked sandwiches. . . .")

After more delays the people who want Hilly to produce their version of the life of the comedian Lenny Bruce have marshaled actors, film, a more or less finished script, and much of the light and sound gear required for this "multimedia event," as their flier describes it. They are ready to show the producer their work. EPIC has paid most of the costs and lent the Eden Theater on a Monday evening when off-Broadway is dark. Hilly, Claire, the staff, press agent Sam Friedman, a number of *Calcutta* people, and guests appear at 5:30. (Playwright Julian Barry is also doing a version of the life of Bruce, but it is a different one, apparently.)

There are clips and stills from thirties movies: Andy and Judge Hardy, Fay Bainter, Beulah Bondi, William Powell, in montage with the numbers and patterns on film leader that flash backward like a countdown. Bojangles tap-dances; Judy Garland, a child again, is tremulous. While live actors mime fornication, an A-bomb takes over, mushrooming up to the plane. We hear Lenny Bruce with his anguished "Did you come? Did you come good? Did you come? . . ." Judge Hardy again, admonitory, man to man: coming up out of the depression, respectful, hopeful, going toward the Second World War in the sunshine on the MGM lot: "Oh, God, the movies really did screw us up," cries Bruce's own scared voice, speaking for the movie-struck, the hardest hit, generation. There are readings from his written work, and comic monologues acted out by the cast: the prison satire, the Transylvania sketch, and others. Lenny's childhood and family photos are projected. The mood darkens. . . . There is his Pope's press agent sketch; Hitler is handled by MCA. The actors do a number—"Are There Any Niggers in the Audience?"—a chant of opprobrium directed against everyone: audience participation. Then Lenny Bruce bombs humiliatingly at the Palladium, is sick in his dressing room after each show. More atomic explosions. Then the arrest in Las Vegas. We both see and hear his act in a supper club and on the Steve Allen TV show; he is arrested once more. "If you insult the Pope again, I bust you again," says a real sheriff. He becomes the saint of four-letter words, the oppression-fighter, iconoclast, funny revolutionist, champion of freedom from fear of words and other people's bodies. Then his San Francisco dirty-word trial is seen—TV news film of Bruce hiding, running fast up steps, down corridors away from reporters and cameras, his coat over his head, hat over his face, sitting on the defendant's bench in court with his forehead on his knees; he has grown a black outcast's beard, his eyes are deep-ringed with black, cheeks hollow, lips and nose prophetically sharp; narcotics arrests, and more news footage; later he kids hopelessly for a camera. The actors do transcript from trials, and then the man is dead. Over and over a hand-held camera climbs the outside stairs to a motel room in Los Angeles, glances over Lenny's litter of books, papers, bottles, food cartons, dirty clothes, then runs along the floor and lifts its gaze to the bathroom in a medium shot, so that we see Bruce dead in the doorway (he is forty-two), head in the bed-living room, the rest of him on his back on the white floor; tile and mirror flash back at us. He is naked and lies with his knees up and spread laxly, open, his black-bearded face turned to one side, though we see only the dark curly top of the head from this angle; he wears a wristwatch. The film is run silently except for the slight chatter of the projector. Once more the camera goes downstairs in this ring of rescued footage, looks back up; officials are descending—detectives, patrolmen, men from the coroner's office—brisk: hard light flashes from bifocals, bullet jackets, and belt buckles, which, with reporters joking against black palmettos, represents a standard horror in our black and white news. A jump: the balcony corridor upstairs; now Lenny, wrapped and strapped to a trolley stretcher, is being wheeled out of the nightmare room—he could not get his breath—and carried down, the camera accompanying. Remorselessly once more (it will be cut by some young movie-struck editor at the studio to about twenty seconds of the best footage): the hurricane room, the dead actor, his naked genitals (can't show that). Entirely naked, he is dead on his back of morphine poisoning, yet grudgingly so—blazing white in the news.

Hilly appears to feel that the moment for the work has passed. This is the key opinion. Everyone in the car on its way back to Sixty-second Street listens, nods.

Back from Boston, the Krishna-conscious are on the Lexington Avenue Local. They file chanting from car to car, turning a big two-legged sign sideways to get it through the doors (it has the "Hare Krishna Mantra" inscribed on it, their recommended process for God-realization in this age). A pair of large paper flowers blooms from the top of the sign. One boy, pale as flour, bears a denim bag over a shoulder and picks up scraps; as I watch he flips a pack of paper matches into it. I buy the magazine *Back to Godhead* for fifty cents.

Alice's Restaurant is a success. After two weeks on the *Variety* chart it is ranked sixteenth among the fifty top-grossing films, with a total New York gross to that point of over a quarter of a million dollars; it has more than doubled its previous week's gross, and its total gross for six theaters in New York, Boston, Los Angeles, and St. Louis is $383,354 for two weeks. Only *Hell's Angels 69* and *Staircase,* among films that have been on the chart for two weeks, are beating Hilly's movie.

VIII

Second Act Trouble / "It should mean something. . . ."

1

Actors Equity rulings require EPIC to file a preliminary cast breakdown, which will be posted in the Association's offices eventually; it is subject to change:

. . . Photos and résumés are now being accepted by George Platt. . . . *He will not see actors or accept phone calls at this time.* . . . All roles require actors who sing, unless specifically noted below.

The play takes place in the ghetto of Frankfort and various European cities at the turn of the 19th century. The action covers a time span of 40 years in the history of the famed Rothschild family.

The roles are listed and characterized; for example, "NA-THAN: from early 20's to mid-late 30's. Mayer's #1 son. Aggressive, yet personable and charming. Romantic lead with strong voice." . . . "HANNAH: zealous crusader for social rights. Beneath the veneer a Jewish princess. Romantic interest for Nathan."

The sons of Mayer as children: ". . . from 7 to 14 years old, the youngest three of whom double as street urchins." Mayer's other four sons grown up: ". . . all must have strong singing voices. Attractive Semitic types, but not of the stereotype mold . . ."

"Bock and I stopped doing songs three months ago while the second act was being finished. We're all involved in it, of course, and worried about it, but we're not getting together. If he gets an idea, he dictates it—the music—over the phone; I take it down; I give him back the lyrics. . . ."

Sheldon Harnick is a trim man with a halo of springy hair and steel-rimmed glasses. He and his collaborator, Bock, have had flops in their career of writing musicals, but with *Fiddler on the Roof,* which entered its sixth Broadway season in 1969 and which has companies in a dozen countries, they are in the class of hit-writing now that brings in a great deal of income. Harnick is modest about his success and simple in his manner of living; Bock appears to be the same. Both have Manhattan apartments and country houses. Harnick is more available than Bock, who is withdrawn except, it is said, among intimates. Harnick smokes cigars; Bock smokes a pipe. Bock dresses elegantly, Harnick plainly; the composer runs to leather vests, open shirts, and big-belted hip-riders; the lyricist to corduroys, turtlenecks, and berets. If they are modest about their success, they are also modest about their talents; in this sense and in most others they appear to be economical men. Yet there is about both—but particularly about the composer —an air nearly ineffable of paradise regained; it is more than merely obvious. They are successful. Roughly speaking, they are as Fra Angelico might have been in his monastery or Thomas Merton in his in the sense of being at one with men, if not by conscious trial and learned humility beneath them, and yet of being marked by a popular skill and their success with it; it is as if vows are easier to keep when you write hits. To note the national moratorium to protest the war in Vietnam on October 15, 1969, Jerry Bock and Sheldon Harnick, with writer Joseph Stein and producer Hal Prince, agreed to cancel that evening's performance of *Fiddler on the Roof* and, while the cast would be paid, to waive their royalties. The *Times* pointed out that the show grosses an average of $65,000 a week and that an average midweek evening gross was about $6,000.

"There should be a point of view," says Harnick concerning *The Rothschilds*. "It should mean something, and we're still without an ending"—in August, '69—"for the show. I'm deathly afraid—to paraphrase Mike Nichols—of bringing down the curtain at the end and having the audience say to itself, 'Why did you tell me this?' " It is the general problem. "I think the show needs a subtitle. Since we use the legends of the Rothschilds as much as the history, it should be called 'an exaggeration with music' or 'a singing lie,' so an audience will know it must not take this for historical accuracy. . . . In an earlier version Mayer is killed in a pogrom at the end of Act I. We said, 'Sherman, he died in bed!' so he changed it. The actor now who plays Mayer will be pleased to hear that he goes all the way into the middle of the second act." (In another year he will go almost to the end of it.)

"I only hope," he says, "that the second act problems don't have to wait to be solved, that the ending doesn't turn up on the road. It's my belief that we'll find the solution to Act II. Anyhow I hope we'll have done enough fruitful thinking and arguing at this stage so that it won't have to be rewritten on the road. The least amount of rewriting we ever did was on *Fiddler*. . . . Jerry Robbins can see a show in his mind in advance. On the other hand, on the road, with actors giving flesh and blood to the characters, it's easier to *see* problems; there are no distractions and hard work is possible."

We have barley soup and cheese blintzes in a dairy restaurant. You begin somewhere, so I ask the question: which comes first, music or lyrics?

". . . the way we—Jerry and I—get momentum: we both read and study, separately, the basic material. Jerry goes off and writes themes that come to him as he reads, puts them on tape, then gives me one or two dozen of them. I know the nature of the song I want to start with; I hear the tapes, and if I like one, I start there. I've found that form is best when it's dictated by the music. Then when I've used all the tape music I can . . . For example, we're working on a song now in Act II. The five sons are trying to persuade Gutele, their mother, to leave the ghetto. The brothers—'Mama! come stay with *me*: three months in Paris, three in London, three in Vienna,' and so on. It's difficult. I couldn't find words to fit music then—these specific words—'Paris, Vienna'—and the specific needs of the song. So then I wrote first and Jerry set it. I begin: 'Mama, please come and stay with me.' Jerry does some, then he calls, and dictates what he's done over the phone, I take it down"—Harnick is also a musician—"and so on. I remember that Jerry when he was asked once which came first, the lyrics or the music, answered, 'The book, of course.'

"We're improvising a lot of this now. On the road we'll see the show on its feet and know what's *not* working; hopefully they'll be obvious problems that require obvious solutions. Then, dealing with changes for specific problems on the road, the lyrics will come first."

Concerning the lyricist writing dialogue that overlaps the book's area and vice versa: "I'll write suggested dialogue to lead into a song and then if Sherman keeps it, feel I'm repaying a debt, since I've borrowed without credit the lyrics he works into his book text"—a graceful answer, since this is a sensitive collaborative area. "I took Sherman's opening lyrics and dialogue and reorganized them, sent them to Jerry, and he unexpectedly set both dialogue and lyrics, even the 'ladies and gentlemen.' The same thing happened when I sent him the episode where the French—Fouché—came into Frankfort." About the voices they want for the show: "Usually we need an actor who can act and also make a pleasant sound, like Jack Warden or Da Silva, but here we need men who can sing. Being a show about a subject that may prove boring to some, the real singing and music may compensate for any dryness in the story.

"A lyricist," says Harnick, "needs the patience and willingness to work in a highly circumscribed form. Sondheim, whom I consider the best, described lyrics-writing as carpentry. It's true. It's finding the right two- or five-syllable word."

2

Hilly borrows the movie, *The House of Rothschild*, from Twentieth Century Fox to run from his projection booth in the office. Sherman Yellen, Derek Goldby, Harnick and Bock come to see it. The new man, Leo Morgan, is present and, as an old movie man, answers most of the questions. Bill Liberman grapples with this projector, as he did with Hilly's small one upstairs.

"There's a good description of underwriting the peace bond," says Yellen. It was he who saw the old George Arliss film on television and suggested that the others see it. . . .

The credits.

Twentieth Century Pictures, before Fox; Joseph Schenck and Darryl Zanuck produce; a Nunnally Johnson screenplay, and he directs. Boris Karloff—before his monster period—is a wicked Metternich; Robert Young and Loretta Young

Hilly, Wolf Mankowitz, and
Frederic Morton in early discussions
about *The Rothschilds* in Vienna, 1963

Hilly and Sammy Davis, Jr.
at the auditions for *Golden Boy*
in London, December, 1967

Hilly, Jacques Levy, and Kenneth Tynan
discussing *Oh! Calcutta!*
PHOTO BY FRIEDMAN-ABELES

an Rachine and Raina Barrett
Oh! Calcutta!
OTO BY FRIEDMAN-ABELES

George Welbes and
Margo Sappington
in *Oh! Calcutta!*
PHOTO BY FRIEDMAN-ABELES

Hilly backstage
Oh! Calcutta! w
Raina Bar
PHOTO BY STEVE SCHAF

Boni Enten
in *Oh! Calcutta!*
PHOTO BY FRIEDMAN-ABELES

Hilly at home
PHOTO BY WERNER WOLFF FROM BLACK STAR

Hilly at home with Mitty, his blind Weimaraner
PHOTO BY STEVE SCHAPIRO

Left to right: Sherman Yellen, Claire Bloom, Hilly, Jerry Bock, Sheldon Harnick, Derek Goldby, George Platt at auditions for *The Rothschilds*
PHOTO BY SAM SIEGEL

Arlo Guthrie on location
filming *Alice's Restaurant*
PHOTO BY MUKY

Rehearsing dancers
for *The Rothschilds*
PHOTO BY MARTHA HOLMES

Joan Hackett and Hal Linden at opening day
of rehearsals of *The Rothschilds*
PHOTO BY MARTHA HOLMES

Jill Clayburgh and Paul Hecht at opening day
of rehearsal of *The Rothschilds*
PHOTO BY MARTHA HOLMES

Michael Kidd and Derek Goldby
rehearsing *The Rothschilds*
PHOTO BY MARTHA HOLMES

Claire and Hill
at London Airpo
PHOTO BY BRENAR
PHOTOGRAPHIC SERVIC
LONDON AIRPOF

Hilly, John Bury,
and Lester Osterman
at opening day of
rehearsals of *The Rothschilds*
PHOTO BY MARTHA HOLMES

Claire, Anna Justine Steiger, and Hilly
at the opening of *The Rothschilds*
PHOTO BY MARTHA HOLMES

Hilly, Claire, and Anna Justine doing
The Barry Gray Show at opening night party
(*The Rothschilds*) at Dinty Moore's
PHOTO BY MARTHA HOLMES

Hilly, Mayor Lindsay, and Lester Osterman
at opening night party
(*The Rothschilds*) at Dinty Moore's
PHOTO BY MARTHA HOLMES

Hilly, Claire, and Abba Eban,
the Israeli Foreign Minister
PHOTO BY NAT TILESTSON (MARTHA SWOPE STUDIO)

are the youthful romantic interest; Arliss plays both Mayer, founder of the Frankfort house, and his son Nathan, founder of the English line. It was made—someone works out the roman numerals—"in 1933."

"When did Arliss die?"

"In '32," Jerry Bock kids. He is a small man with woolly hair and startling green eyes; his normal manner is gentle, all but inaudible.

"Do exactly as your mother says and you will grow rich," says Mayer dying in the movie. Yellen, Goldby, and the others are solemn. Just rich? It touches their second act problem. Then: "In unity is strength," says the father.

"THIRTY FIVE YEARS LATER THE ROTHSCHILD SONS HAD ESTABLISHED THEIR BANKING BUSINESS THROUGHOUT EUROPE," a title declares.

"That simplifies that," says Harnick.

Arliss is good, everyone agrees, but the rest of the movie creaks badly. Goldby, asked if he has seen the film before this, says yes.

Bock says, "And you still want to do it?"

Drinks are needed, and I swagger by punching a button. "I am *serving* dinner," cries Robert furiously into the intercom; it is past eleven at night.

Hilly: "Who's this Joosh fella askin' for drinks?"—on the phone.

Bill gets them.

Nathan, in the next reel, threatens to go over to Napoleon because Bonaparte offers the Jews freedom. Yellen makes a note. Then Nathan requires a signed agreement ". . . to let the Jews walk with dignity. I'm fighting in the only way I can fight—with money!"

Later Hilly and Claire Bloom, dinner complete, appear. Hilly does the crass producer: "Okay, we got a show? I want it to be very naked, that's all. I don't care about Jewish, but it has to be naked and blond, blond. . . . Am I the only one thinks Stacy Keach is worth looking at?"

There are objections.

"I'll have a bialy, kid. All right, how's the work coming?"

"We have a big scene—eight minutes," Harnick begins.

"That was an encouraging report. I pledge one hundred dollars . . ." When the evening is over, I go along with *The Rothschilds* people and some EPIC staff members to a *Wurst* cafeteria. On the way one of the group says rather wistfully, looking up at a rich man's town house, "My analyst lives here."

"Don't say it. He's writing everything down."

Later Yellen and I walk uptown on the East Side in the hot night. For Yellen the period is one of work as well as of waiting, and it is difficult. Harnick and Bock, no matter how uncertain they may be of their art at any point in a project, must know that they are marked, are on the other side of success. But in terms of commercial success and all it can promise in America, this is Yellen's chance (his agent sent Hilly a couple of plays out of the blue; Hilly liked them). He is nearing forty. It may be that he feels he has fought hard for his career, with little reward in terms of his worth and little help. What odds does this chance offer? With some of the bitterness that attacks artists in the United States after too many years of compulsive diplomacy, of treating between the incompatible itches of needing to be good and rich, and failing relatively in both, with the near misses and disappointments, and though, like the rest of us, he had hoped as a serious solo man that his big chance would not be shared, yet there is never anything apparent even in Yellen's attitudes toward *The Rothschilds* project, the others connected with its creation, or toward producer Hilly Elkins that suggests that this musical can be anything but a hit.

It will be a hit is the promise in the air, though it may not be.

3

Derek Goldby on September 8: "I spoke to Jerry, and he's excited," he says, pleased. "We're to meet tomorrow. I'm to hear it. Then we'll play it for Hilly, and if it begins to look like a show, we can start to make moves. . . ." He works it out: "No, we can't possibly rehearse before November."

"I think we're probably on the way," he says on September 10. "I think we can get it into rehearsals in January. We've basically licked the problem of the second act, now it's a matter of filling in the show. Sherman did *very good* work.

"We'll start casting now. What we must get to, basically, is the assembling of a production team: choreographer, designer, and so on, so that they can start coming in on meetings. We won't get into major casting for about a month.

"There are still unwritten songs, but you can deal with un-written songs. There's a great difference between that and wrong play structure. . . . Basically, what's happened is a simplification of the second half of the story: Nathan's rise in London, his courtship of the girl—all are dealt with now in a shorthand that leads up to a family scene, which is vital. The sons say, 'We did it on our own.' The mother says, 'Non-sense, you had your father's help! *He* did it.' It's a kind of hubris that they get into.

"Gutele's stand helps me to accept the show. What Sherman and I had in mind was something more radical. With the peo-ple we have that wasn't possible. What we've got now is a romance but, hopefully, one in tune with our times. . . .

"I'll work on the script. There's a lot of rewriting to do, and then planning the physical shape of the production. You do that in your imagination, projecting into what you'll do in rehearsal: when we get into that, I'll want to know what to do more or less. With only four or five weeks' rehearsal you must have a strong vision of what it's going to be like. What one really does is direct the thing in one's mind before one directs the actors; but I have a strong visual imagination only if I'm hooked on the work. . . .

"It'll have to be a large theater. We'll be talking about key roles—perhaps one name person. It'd be nice to have a couple of pivotal people signed up in the next month."

He stands at his door in sneakers, khakis, and blue work shirt. "You'll probably never see me again as relaxed as I am now, since we are really getting into it." He looks as if he is ready to work and says, sounding pleased, "Next time you see me I'll be a neurotic figure"—pronouncing it "figger."

A preliminary cast meeting breaks up.

"All right. The chorus isn't going to be lovely," Goldby is saying. "It'll be a character chorus. . . . They're arrogant, chorus people. They're so pleased when they get a part, they're arrogant. Okay"—counting—"we have fifteen in what we'll call featured roles, including the children. Then we'll need"—counting—"fourteen chorus with acting ability and that leaves ten chorus to sing and dance: right? Making a grand total of a cast of thirty-nine: right?"

"How does that shape up with other musicals?"

"I don't know. Who cares? At least this will give me something to talk to Hilly about when we meet tomorrow. We must get him to put his cards on the table and commit himself."

"I insist it goes into rehearsal by January," says Yellen firmly. "I'm committed to other things."

As he had predicted, Goldby is wound tight; he discusses his own endurance and energy in the same objective way he went over cast a moment before. Increasingly, the creative part of the burden of making the show will be his. The meeting was in Hilly's living room and the producer, coming from one place and on his way to another, stands briefly with Goldby at his own elevator: "I like the hair," he says to the tired man, who wears it long: "Don't like the socks," which gets a grin.

4

I try Bock for an interview, but he dodges it. He is on Long Island, or he is in New York and cannot be reached. I ask a mutual friend to intercede. It can't be me; yet New York in the heat is a dark place, and paranoia erupts everywhere. I sneeze at Fiftieth and Madison, and a friendly woman says, "God bless you." She stops to give an example. "Where I used to work was a woman. We never spoke; we were enemies. For three years we never spoke. And then, one day, I sneezed, and she said, 'God bless you.' Can you imagine? Three years she couldn't speak, but she had to say that. . . ."

The marquee on Loew's Sheridan across the street from St. Vincent's Hospital where Dylan Thomas died: "DEMOLITION BY D AND D DEMOLITION CO INC . . . ANOTHER DRACHMAN PROJECT," and destruction of the theater has begun. Late at night a World War Two survivor, full of wine, wearing an outfit of checked shorts, white shoes, black socks, and yellow polo shirt, supports himself against a door to watch a 1970 girl—was she seventeen?—stamp past before the shell of the theater and go on. "Woudja like to hear a Canadian duck?" he asks when she is past hearing, gives an arty raspberry, and murmurs, "Sweet thing"—seeing apparently that she is not. A few days later, almost as if in consequence, one of the unsupported walls under which she walked collapses, and kills a retired architect. Finally one hot dawn a woman or girl screams down into the well of Village back yards, against which my ground-floor bedroom abuts, ". . . in the *United*

States of America!"—all I catch, struggling to stay asleep:
". . . the United States of America!"

5

As a matter of record (in Frederic Morton's book about
them), the sons of Mayer Rothschild used their wealth and
position where they could to help the cause of early-nineteenth-
century European Jewry, whose condition then, as it would
be a hundred years later, was a terrible one. But the emphasis
that develops from the collaborators' interest in social significance can alter honest priorities. The acquisition of power
is brutalizing. Yellen wants to show the brothers as capable
of becoming that and at the same time wants to like them as
men of humanity and good will. That is, in order: they must
be at core incorruptible; they must demonstrate the ghetto's
fertility and deadliness; they must make conquests brutally.

It is axiomatic on Broadway that a dyed-in-the-wool Broadway audience does not wish to pay to see a show in which the
principals are unlikable or even in which likability—niceness,
good will, strength, intelligence, humor (humanity)—is not
number one on the list of a character's qualities. *The Rothschilds'* second act problem, except as a technical way of
speaking, might never have come up if a probable historical
priority had been accepted—using the same example. The
ghetto brutalizes and makes for personal ambition (it also
makes revolutionists with social attitudes, and also kills people
young; it did neither to these brothers); with success unselfish
interests develop or not (they did in this case); the people
involved may be likable or not. It is hard to see how they
could remain so.

The first order obtains in this musical collaboration, and the
cloth of the work must be cut to it; when the convention is

breached, it is contended, people keep their money in their pockets, and the result is a flop. The principals shall be worth writing about. After that let them be tough, even commit an unethical act, since we know they are good and that right comes of right. Exceptions such as Rodgers and Hart's *Pal Joey* prove the rule to Broadway veterans.

The American musical may be the last artistic sanctuary for the sincere notion of goodness with its dependent virtues as an element of the total human consciousness with an existence of its own, like an old-fashioned idea of God. (It is often argued from the viewpoint of "evil," with Hitler adduced: faith in goodness following.) The real trouble in this exacerbated summer of the second act, a trouble that will persist to beyond opening night, lies in trying to make persuasive an order appropriate to the craft that is not appropriate to life.

It cannot be said that the Rothschild boys at the turn of the nineteenth century, struggling to get out of their prison, were not good, ambitious, and tough in that order; but history being what it is, the order should be open to doubt. That may be the heart of second act Broadway musical problems generally: the order is almost never open to doubt.

6

Hilly, addressing a tape machine, discusses producing on Broadway. "The problem with budgeting Broadway shows is that no matter how hard you try you never start out with the show you end up with. It depends on a variety of things: on what kind of cast you have, whether you're paying a percentage of gross to your cast members, what your director, your writers are getting. *The Rothschilds* is a heavy show. That is, it is a complicated show scenically, and it has a large cast, and it's heavy in the costume department. My attempt is to cast it without superstars, of whom there are very few anyway; and I would cast it without stars if that were possible, because I think it's the inherent value of the property that will make or break the show.

"In today's market a show such as *The Rothschilds* costs between 600 and 750 thousand dollars to produce. Up to this point, aside from whatever that budget is, there's some 125 thousand dollars that's been invested to date: scripts, fares, travel. . . . Can I do that for you, darling?"—to Claire. Robert is serving supper in the den. "Further on budgeting, you have certain fixed costs. They obviously include what you've spent to date: your advances, your expenses in putting it together. Once you decide on your production people, you have fixed fees in your production budget and certain continuing charges in your operating budget. You allocate, depending upon your particular philosophy, a given amount for advertising; you set your cast and know your costs in that department; and once you've set your department heads, you can get together with them and your writers and director and your script and begin to estimate what your below-the-line costs are going to be. You allow a contingency for your mistakes, their mistakes, and your future mistakes. You allow for loss on the road, previews, and you cut that down so it resembles something more realistic, at last, than what you first ended up with. Then you file it with the SEC and pray a lot.

"You don't incorporate, you form a limited partnership. It's a rather archaic system, but it gives certain tax advantages— at least this year—in the event of total"—Hilly says "tot'l," one of his few regionalisms—"loss, which is what theater financing is predicated upon. You have more loss than gain. You want a tax advantage if you lose your money. That's why people are patrons of the arts."

"Always?" asks Claire, who has been trying to load a Polaroid camera.

"That's the way it's done on Broadway. In the old days when you didn't have taxes, a producer put up ten thousand dollars and you had a show, a show that today costs 250 thousand dollars."

"Is it true," Claire asks, "that some shows are put on deliberately to lose money?"

"No. Some people may invest money in shows because they need a tax loss and don't care about losing it. . . . Let me get the phone. . . . There's a category there"—in my notes for questions—"called 'getting a theater.' This year you merely walk up Forty-fifth Street and say, 'I'll have one of those, two of those' . . . 'cause they ain't nothin' to put in 'em, man! What you askin' them damnfool questions for? . . . Why is Broadway in an economic slump? Well, because it seem the people wanta watch other people *fuckin'* on the stage. That's made a lot of producers uptight, because they don't know how to do that; theah ah some of us who have a natural inclination in that direction."

Abruptly solemn: "Broadway has been very much, with some notable exceptions, a rear-view mirror. It's been reflective of the society rather than involved in setting trends: it's been involved in following them. It's in a tough position because it's alienated over the years the younger audience, and it's frustrated and disappointed in large measure the older audience.

". . . Well, anyway . . . you can't get away with the same old shit, and that's what people have been trying to do for years—the same cyclical thing we talked about. . . . Yes, will you, please, Robert? . . . Stakes are getting higher, the odds getting smaller; there's only one reviewer. . . .

"Raising money for a show: There are many ways to raise money for a show and none of them are any fun. . . ."

The tape is turned over; Hilly tests the machine: "Now is the winter . . . *Now* . . . Now is the—can't get it. Now is the . . . Now . . . *Now* is the winter of ouah discon*tent* . . . *Now is* *the wintah of ouah discontent!*"—Olivier. "Okay, blue eyes, you wanna knuckle shanwich? . . . Evuh been stung by a dead bee, Hairy? The bee comes right up and stings yuh. . . . A-N-A . . . C-I-N: not just one but a combination of medically proved and tested ingredients recommended by *your* physician. . . .

". . . I think there's going to be such a revolution in entertainment because of the media situation—I don't mean mixed media, I mean transmission media—that it's very difficult to predict what live entertainment will do. I think that there will be more and more productions that emanate, for better or worse, from a regional level—particularly the West Coast. I think that there will *be* a theater.

" '*The Rothschilds*—the second act problem solved?' I'm holding my real response till I hear it all together—for a variety of reasons. One, because any intrusion at this point would impede the progress, and it's much easier to deal with something that's been done than with something that's being done, and the freshness of my perspective will be retained only if I don't get inside the material now. I was able to see *Golden Boy* hundreds of times without losing spontaneity. I honestly don't know how one does it—I mean I *swear* I don't, but without that ability you're of no value.

". . . There are as many ways to produce as there are producers. Truly. I . . . *admire* David Merrick's way of doing it. It's of no value to me. It's of no *interest* to me, except in depressed periods. As there are no qualifications for a producer, I don't think that I really want to set any up. I'm a meddling producer. I usually start with the idea, then assemble the units—the elements—and make it happen. I try to assemble the elements I really believe will be the best; but compromise is your full-time partner, because you get what's available, you get what you can attract, you get what you can afford, and all too often you get what you deserve. . . . I have a couple of qualities. One is tenacity. The other is a fortuitous lack of foresight, because with any degree of foresight one would either go into another business or . . . go into another business. I am proud of what *I* do most of the time. I have another quality, which is mine alone, which is my taste— certainly open to *attack* this season. Whatever critical mistakes I've made I've made by not following my visceral instincts, and so"—broadly—"I will follow them to the grave if necessary!" He adds, "It's infinitely more fun, and it's not much fun, to make your own mistakes than the disaster of making other people's. Everybody should have a chance at their own. I believe that the more one knows about every aspect of what one is doing, the better one is at it. That may or may not be true; it's true for me. *Or* it seems to be true for me. That's about it. . . ."

"Hold it! That's it!" cries Claire, taking a Polaroid flash picture.

"There's a noisy broad on your right. Uh yeah, I dig what I do. And every now and then I'm surprised that I get paid for it. And every now and then I'm surprised that I *don't* get paid for it. But uh, there's nothing else I'd rather be doing."

"What are your politics?"

"Well, I was born a liberal, went through my Communist period, gave that up. I'm now a Republican on the way to fascism. . . .

"Okay, I'm a *Democrat* on my way to fascism. No, I'm a strong believer in totalitarianism provided that I can pick the totalitarian." (Claire crows delightedly: "I believe it! *Yes!*") "Not given that choice I'll settle for democracy."

"Are you a capitalist?"

"Not yet but working very hard toward that goal. I'm an enlightened, liberal, capitalist nigger-lover. No. Um, I detest categorization and labels. I really do. It's not a very original statement, but it's quite true. I think I am progressive in my outlook. I would not be happy, if I were to be successful in my efforts, to have someone decide to divvy up the house for five people; I would think that was a bad move. I have operated as a functioning capitalist under dire economic straits. When things get better, I hope I shall be able to continue along those lines."

". . . unions?"

He clears his throat. "I think that unions in the theater and elsewhere miss their purpose when they eliminate work. I don't think that's the point of it. And I think the rear-guard action against what is an obvious technological revolution in all phases of our society is, ah—is insane: unproductive. I think that people should be well compensated for their efforts. . . . Darling, that black Polaroid stuff gets all over things. . . . But ah, sorry, Robert . . . but not in terms of featherbedding, creating jobs that don't exist, the union deciding what the requirements of a show are. I mean, we've come a long way from the days of the White Rats, and you"—looking at Claire's photograph of him—"*haven't* come a long way from the days of the White Rats."

"You don't like it."

"The background is great, the foreground is kind of washed out."

"Well, but you can see how nice it is if you only look."

"Ah yes. I'm sorry. . . . The White Rats was the predecessor of Actors Equity. And there was a time when there were no hours, companies were abandoned, people were not paid, there were no bonds. . . . It was a terribly chaotic, unfair, horrendous situation. I think the definitive moment came for me when I was doing a benefit called *Broadway Answers Selma.* You may have seen the program in the office; if you haven't, you should look at it; it's quite impressive. It's one of the most exciting benefits ever done. And while organizing it I got a call from Actors Equity, who said I wasn't using enough Negro performers. . . ."

"It's unbelievable!" Claire says.

"I hung up on the fella. It's like . . . it was for Selma, Alabama, where I had *marched*. I mean, I don't want any medals, but leave me alone with the spade shit. . . ."

"*Did* you march in Selma?" I ask.

"Of course. Yes, I marched in Selma."

"So tell me these things."

"What's that got to do with the price of . . ."

"I asked what your politics were. . . ."

"Politics? . . . Got nothing to do with politics. I don't like people getting pushed around. It's not political, it's . . . quite another thing."

"What else have you done to keep people from being pushed around?"

"Not much. I've done a lot of benefit things . . . formed a group called AHAB. A lot of us were down at Martin Luther King's funeral. It hasn't really gotten off the ground yet, but the basis—Artists Helping the American Black Community. It involved a group of us who were down there . . . spent many hours talking to Bobby Kennedy . . . people like Bob Culp, Bill Cosby, Sydney Poitier, Sammy, myself, Nancy Wilson. . . . I do a . . . few things."

The next question is lost, but the answer is not:

"Well. I have a great regard for talent, and I have a great antipathy for schmucks, and when they come in the same package, it's a difficult choice."

"When did you grow your whiskers?"

"Sammy and I decided to grow 'em until *Golden Boy* opened, at one point; and then we decided to grow 'em till it closed; and then I decided I didn't care whether he shaved or not, I liked my beard. So I kept it."

Extended silence.

"We've worn him out, honey!"—in a W. C. Fields voice.
"I knew we would!"

7

The producer was born on Eastern Parkway in Brooklyn
forty years ago at the beginning of depression times. His father
held a variety of jobs but was always, in part kidding, part miserable memory, a lawyer, a doctor, a rabbi. . . . The boy was
fierce, the dominator of schoolyards we all knew, teacher's despair and pet, the inventor of deadly games who could also cry.
He ran with a gang, "was knifed a couple of times," learned
about Italian food, played doctor, went to the beach, which was
near enough to be part of any Brooklyn boy's life. He went to
Hebrew school ("Religiously, so to speak"), and long before
he decided to go straight (he became an "A" student in high
school), was "turned onto heavy reading" by a friend with
Look Homeward, Angel; in exchange he introduced the intellectual to girls and sex.

"I spent the entire summer of my fourteenth year stoned.
Pete Hagan rye. It was very cheap. Once I got stoned on a
bottle of kümmel because we were baby-sitting, and I broke
the fucking cork and I couldn't close it, and chugalugged it.
It was then that I peed through an entire set of the Sunday
Times edition being held up by my friends on a street corner
of Avenue N in Brooklyn. . . . That was the last time I was
drunk."

He spent a brief period in a reformatory holding institution
called Youth House, got hit by the garbage truck. . . .

He saw his first dramas at the Flatbush Theater—*Saint
Joan,* he thinks . . . *Oklahoma!* He sold papers and magazines.
At thirteen or fifteen, depending upon when he tells it and the
circumstances, he auditioned for the All-City Radio Workshop
and was admitted. During the summers—one summer at

least—he was a combination counselor and drama director at a Farband Labor Zionist Camp. He and his best friend, Arthur Black, wrote their senior high play, directed and starred in it. He did professional radio work ("A-N-A-C-I-N . . ."), raised $8,000 and started a summer tent theater (the first of its kind) in Belle Harbor, Long Island. ". . . I lived the summer on Velveeta cheese sandwiches. I was a combination producer, star, and janitor. And a group of us got together and did everything from silk-screen posters to playing the parts to building the sets." A storm knocked down the tent and ended the season.

He married at nineteen, got a job as an office boy at the William Morris Agency—a conglomerate of agencies for theater, film, TV, writers, artists, etc.—and moved quickly into the theater department, where he displayed great natural talent and did well. He also made basic contacts, and began to learn theater finance and production from the inside. Hilly was drafted into the army, got into a TV film-making unit, came out, joined a small agency, divorced, remarried, and got into personal management. As written elsewhere here, his money clients were Steve McQueen and Robert Culp. Ultimately, wanting always to be in production (Belle Harbor had been the great time), he sold out (in 1959), and, after a brief stay with the purchasers as a vice-president, left, as former-owner vice-presidents do, and came east. He divorced and married. He had some money (though he would go quickly into debt anyway); he was one of the theater's great salesmen; he knew everyone; and though people did not quite trust him (probably because of the flash of his style, possibly because his ethics were Protean as well as deeply honest), everyone loved him (though some did not like him).

He at once began to produce flops: *Golden Boy, The Best Laid Plans, This Winter's Hobby. . . .*

Golden Boy was a heroic flop. It wrung, after an endless

out-of-town tryout period, good reviews from reluctant re-
viewers in New York, but in the last analysis made no money.
It was good work and clear disaster, in which the producer
showed, at last, his full strength. As a flop, it was a great hit.

HILLY (on tape, concerning the events that followed the
disastrous Boston reviews): ". . . At that juncture it was apparent to me that there were three choices. One was to close
the show, which was not bloody likely. The other was to bring
it in the way it was, knowing it wasn't the show we had started
out to do. It would be successful, because of Sammy, perhaps
more successful than if we fixed it. Fixing it was a gamble. It
was also obvious that you couldn't cure what I considered to
be cancer with a Band-Aid, and consequently it required, if it
were to be done at all, if it were going to be an involvement of
any kind of energy, it had to be total. And I called two people.
I called Paddy Chayevsky and Bill Gibson, both of whom came
up. . . . It turned out to be a strange situation. Paddy wasn't
really willing to commit himself to it. Bill, for reasons I didn't
know at the time, wasn't—didn't really want to; he'd inter-
rupted the book he was writing called *Mass for the Dead,* but
he felt obliged to. He'd been a friend and pupil of Odets—he
was with Odets when he died. . . . Bill agreed to come up and
see the show; and he did, and we agreed that it was terrible.
And he said, 'Well, I don't know what I can do, but I'll go back
and see.' We played the show. A week later I got a call saying,
'Would you like to hear a first act?' Bill drove down. . . . We
assembled in my room, and Bill read a first act that had us in
tears, and we asked him to please go on. . . . And he did a
second act. . . . Prior to this I had told Peter Coe—Sammy had
a party; we had parties almost every night, and I had . . .
good night, Judi . . . and I had signed a contract with Coe
whereby he was to direct for a maximum of ten out of fourteen
weeks—we were on the road for twenty-two weeks—and I

pointed out to him that the contract was signed for London, where we were going to have a short tryout, and didn't he think it was a little unfair to leave, and he felt the show was in excellent shape. I told him *I* didn't think the show was in excellent shape and that I was going to change the book, and he said, 'Now, you mustn't touch my show.' And I said, 'No, I won't touch your show, but I will fix my show,' and he was there with his wife, and I was sitting there with my friends. . . . You were there, weren't you, Dad? . . . His voice kept getting higher, and he said—he had a beard; I didn't at the time— 'Don't touch my show.' Gibson had done the book . . . and there was a . . . chemistry between Bill and myself from the first moment we met, which was still as unlikely as that between Claire and myself to many people who know us separately and not together; and I'd gotten Peter back to hear the book; and he heard it—Bill read it through from beginning to end— and he said, 'Well, I don't find that much different. You don't need me to do it; get any hack to do it.' Bill got up to his six feet three and a half, started to walk out of the room, and as he passed me I said, 'Call him'—I have a lot of funny conversations with people—and he said, 'Okay,' and he went out and called Arthur Penn. We had never discussed it before that moment. And Arthur came down to see the show with Annie . . . Bancroft, thinking about Annie going into it, came back afterward. And then Bill *again* read the book from beginning to end, and Arthur said, 'It's remarkable; 's marvelous,' and we talked for half an hour, and I said, 'Let's stop the bullshitting —you gonna *do* it?' He said yes, and that was the end of it. Or the beginning of it. . . . I then . . . George and I had breakfast with Peter downstairs—Platt to make notes—as a result, Peter left the show. . . . And we went into rehearsal—in Detroit, and . . . interesting: must show you the set of reviews by Elliot Norton. First one he wrote; then he wrote, not a review, but a Sunday double column about the intestinal fortitude of the people involved in the show who were not willing to accept an easy win, and we were going for a home run on a different basis, which I, you know: totally unsolicited and rather remarkable thing. . . . We opened in Detroit to bad reviews in a newspaper strike, worked for one week rehearsing different material and playing different material, building an entire new set for new scenes, and the following Monday night we opened an *entirely new show,* which was unsolicitedly rereviewed and got raves. There was only one problem; the score didn't work. The score was written for the old book, so we started rewriting the entire score, and recostuming. . . . The show was budgeted at half a million *dollars;* it came in at three-quarters of a million dollars; I had signed for the extra quarter of a million. . . . Our choreographer—it was the first time a black choreographer got a Broadway show—he was very good: Donald McKayle, but he couldn't cope with the speed; he was a concert-trained fellow—couldn't cope with the speed, and the pressure. There were a couple of dances in that show that were really outstanding. The opening number, which came in at about this period, was phenomenal. . . . You never saw the show. . . ."

"No."

"Has Christopher got the record?"—Claire.

"No."

"You should hear it. It opened with no overture. It opened on a black stage, a pin spot picked up a boy, boxer—chu-chu; another pin spot picked up another boy who came in with a rope, going skitsukasuka-skitsukasuka; another pin spot on a boy with a bag: tonga-tonga-tong: rhythm; then all those rhythms worked together—electrifyingly; the audience was rooted. We had twenty minutes of shit following it, but no one knew; it was the most exciting opening scene in the theater;

and the fight was unbelievable. The setting up of the ring, which happened in full view of the audience, drew applause every night; and the fight was phenomenal. It was the most exciting thing. It was done in a very unconventional style. It was not choreographed. It was set as a fight. The movements were set out of reality and then the music was composed to the movements, so that every move was on a beat, yet it wasn't a dance; it was real—every move of the wrist, of the leg, was scored after it was done. It was a phenomenal experience; it really was. Ahhh . . . And there were other things. There was a scene where Sammy was alone with a girl—a bridge scene; they did 'I Want to Be with You,' and they finally ended up kissing, and it was called the assassination scene because so many threats were received. It seems silly today: the first time a black man and a white girl ever kissed on the stage, where it was intimated that they went to bed together. . . . And interesting side notes: We had a piece of artwork that I spent months getting—Saul Bass did it: brilliant piece; it won two awards—didn't sell any tickets, and . . . I'll follow that end up, because it's an interesting side story. . . . In any event, I called So-and-so in and he came to see the show, and he had a choice of getting a percentage or cash, and he thought it was going to close in two weeks, so he took . . . twenty-five thousand dollars. . . . He lost about a hundred thousand by taking that deal. People like Buddy Morris, who was the publisher, stuck behind me all the way—but *all* the way; and part of the answer to your other question about living is that he loaned me a hundred thousand dollars during the course of production, which lasted four years. . . . Alan Livingston, who was then president of Capitol Records, stuck all the way through. . . . And we kept working. Word-of-mouth was just dreadful. We were in trouble, 'd never make it, and so on. We came to New York, and we previewed. We set a record for previews. We previewed for—what did we preview for? I think we previewed for ten weeks, after twenty-two weeks on the road—which is longer than most shows *run*. It was at the Majestic—best theater in New York, which is what I promised Sammy. And we made changes up until opening day; in fact, we were unsure about one situation, and we called Elliot Norton again to come down, and he said he would on two conditions: one that he paid his own way, and two that he tell us the truth, and we said okay, and he came down and he saw it. Sammy had gone from the violinist in the early version to a pianist, which we thought made more sense, to a medical student—trying to keep the analogy of the hands. And Norton said, 'It's a marvelous piece, but what the . . . I don't believe he's a doctor, or student, or a surgeon. . . .' So the three of us went down to Sammy's dressing room. We said, 'Sammy, we just talked to Norton. You're no longer a doctor.' He said: 'Then—what's my *problem*?' We looked at him and laughed. . . . And about three days before opening Sammy was getting very fatigued, and I pleaded with Arthur to give him a day off, but Arthur said, 'We haven't got it.' I said, 'You better give it to him, or he's going to take it.' The Saturday matinee before we opened, quarter of a million dollars over budget, fully sold-out house, Sammy didn't show up. And I went out and made the speech, and everybody left. We rehearsed all day with the understudy, Lamont. In half an hour, on Saturday afternoon, the banks were there, the Shuberts were there, suppliers were there. And Buddy Morris offered to buy anybody out who was unhappy, and so it held together. Sammy finally called me—about three o'clock in the morning, and I said—out of a deep sleep, I said, '*Hel*lo, Penrod, you comin' home?' And he said, 'Yeah.' And I said, 'Okay, rehearsal's ten o'clock.' He had no voice. And we went for the curtain. That was on Sunday. We opened on Tuesday, and it was . . . totally anti-

climactic. I mean the success was anticlimactic for me. Dick
Schaap, who was then a young feature writer on the *Herald
Tribune,* wrote a piece on it, which was a lovely piece. He
called it—from the party: he called it 'The Death Watch.'
Essentially he said, 'They all came in and said hello to Sammy
and Hilly, and avoided talking about the show'—Sardi's? No,
Sammy wanted it at Danny's Hideaway . . . terrible place for a
party. He said, 'There were a lot of people called Sam and Joe,
and 90 percent of them were called Baby.' And he said, 'Then
the reviews came in, and everybody went over and told Sammy
and Hilly how they knew it was going to be a hit, but not
everybody was happy, because some people can't stand the
sight of no blood.' And so the show was a hit. And . . . another
thing: before the show opened—sitting at Sardi's and Vince,
who had been through the five years of preparation and had
carried me through a good portion of it, said, 'You know,
tomorrow night, you're going to come in here after the show,
and two guys sitting across the room are going to nudge
each other and say, "That's Hilly Elkins. Tsk. *Lucky* son of a
bitch." ' And that's the lovely kind of . . . story of our business.
And Sammy and I did go in about midnight—to Sardi's and
took the ovation we knew we'd get, and went to the party to
wait for the reviews. And that's the story of *Golden Boy.*
Except they then started to shoot out the glass in display
windows and send hate mail; and in the advertising we changed
from the Saul Bass black heart. What? Yeah. No, don't, don't
help me, don't fool"—cutoff. "Okay, Robert, you can now
move things. Almost every week we had to replace windows.
Milton Green took some photographs in his studio, which was
in lieu of the artwork: Sammy—it's down in the office—with
Paula Wayne. And there was a point at which sales were
going off. Well, Sammy was doing a television special—a
series, a motion picture, and the play, and the pressure of

that schedule finally got to him. He got sick and . . . started to miss performances, and finally we had to let him take a couple of weeks off . . . and the sales went down to about twenty thousand—cost us a quarter of a million dollars, his two weeks off. It was the difference between paying the show off and not. And I did a campaign on his return—two-word campaign: 'Sammy's Back.' Billboards, signs, ads—fortune. And we're coming into the summer and all the shows were dropping, and I changed the artwork to tits and ass—six broads and Sammy —and our gross went from twenty thousand at the bottom in the middle of the World's Fair summer to *ninety-nine thousand*. He was an incredible draw. Smashed every house record heretofore existing. And then Sammy, being totally exhausted, said, 'Lemme go.' And . . . so I did. . . .

"Anyway, we talked about doing the show again. I had an obligation and a contract, and I wanted to get the backers out, even though they pleaded with me not to do it. And Sammy said no. This went on for a long while. He wanted to go only to the Palladium, which had never had a legit show in its history. I finally got the Palladium. We spent eight hours, from one in the morning till nine in the morning, at Lake Tahoe. And it was the most open session we ever had. It wasn't totally open, but it was the most honest session we'd ever had. Sam and I fenced a lot, but we knew we were doing it; we knew when we were doing it, and it was part of the relationship. . . . We had some concert tours we were going to do together, and Sammy got sick, and on the sellout houses, instead of making fifty thousand dollars I lost seventy—a few things like that. And I was the sole backer of the show going to London, and there were a lot of problems with that. We went to Chicago. Bill Liberman went out to do advance sales. We built a *million-dollar* advance sale for six weeks at the Auditorium Theatre, which had not been open for seventeen years.

Our first week broke every record in the history of theater. We did a hundred and eighty-six thousand dollars. And we *lost money.* Sammy got ill. I figured he was rested and well enough to do Chicago and London with no problems. Didn't work. He went to London, where he was *king,* really king, could do no wrong. He was loved. . . . And he got sick, didn't make it, missed performances, and at one point I had a choice of losing two hundred thousand dollars by closing the show or losing two hundred thousand dollars by running the show, so I ran the show. . . . Builds up the obligations, half million dollars . . . and didn't quite accomplish my purpose. . . . But you might say we had a nice trip. And unbeknownst to me Elliot Norton had gone to London and reviewed the show. I had it tot'lly rewritten, the whole show. New song. New second act. And he said, 'Finally Elkins has solved *Golden Boy.* It's a brilliant show.' "

Producing "The Rothschilds"

IX

False Start

1

For the role of Mayer: Donald Pleasance? Richard Kiley. Marty Balsam. Chris Plummer? Suzanne Pleshette for Gutele. Maureen Stapleton? For Nathan, the starring son: Paul Hecht, Ron Leibman? Dustin Hoffman, Gabe Dell, Alan Bates. Eric Porter for Prince William, or Ian Holm, George Rose, Max Adrian. Victor Spinetti? For sets: the Eckarts? John Bury? Richard Pilbrow for lighting. Pat Zipprodt for costumes . . . Auditions for casting will begin at once; rehearsals are set for January, 1970, the New York City opening for the April following. A budget is drawn: "Confidential: Estimated Costs of Production as of September 21, 1969 . . . Scenery, Lighting, Costumes, Design, Construction, Purchases and Rentals: $253,500 . . ." A subtotal of $597,300, to which are added returnable bonds and deposits, advances made by the general partner, Hilly, of $31,300 ($2,136 is for telephones and wires over a period of six years), plus "Contingency for Production

143

Costs and Out of Town Tryout Period of Eight Weeks" of
$200,000, brings the total estimated budget at this point to
$878,720, not a record but close to it.

The first backers' audition is scheduled to take place in the
producer's living room, Bock and Harnick performing, so that
potential production people may in their turn consider the
show's quality and chances; also, a theater-owning Shubert is
to be persuaded that the musical has the kind of moneymaking
potential he wants for his Majestic or the Imperial, Hilly's two
first choices. By late September the tension required to carry
the show into production has begun to be generated. . . .

"Judi's getting her hair frizzed." It is supposed to replace the
Afro wig. Ominously George Platt says, "Wait till Hilly sees it."
A man appears in the office. He is known to no one and carries
a brown parcel under one arm. He was just passing: "I came
in on the *spur* of the moment"—in a Viennese accent. Who is
he? George handles this. "I have come from Havana, where I
was a booking agent. May I see him? You are too busy. I
thought maybe you could send me to someone."

It is difficult to look at the man who represents failure:
Hilly is tied up.

"Yes, you are right. *Right,*" he says. He is trying to open
a package of cigarettes, but since he won't put the parcel down
he cannot. "I remember also when I was too busy to see
people." He says it as if he is not really here. Then, politely,
he disappears. Was it a bad omen? What was in the bundle?
There is a memo on Hilly's desk: "Bribe garage guy."

Judi appears and presently is saying to director Jacques
Levy on the phone, roaring: "I didn't have to there!"

"He'll either do ten minutes on it or he'll ignore it completely," Bill Liberman says of her frizzy hairdo and the
producer's response to it as they go upstairs for a staff meeting.

I learn later that Hilly was reasonable.

2

Bock sits up straight at the piano. Harnick, an unlit cigar in his hand, prepares to perform. Yellen, looking dour, perhaps astonished, sits on the crowded sofa glancing now and then at Claire Bloom. Goldby wears a red tie. A potential choreographer, Grover Dale, is present, so is the Shubert (Lawrence Shubert Lawrence) with some others who are aides or friends. There are prospective investors and their wives, most of the EPIC staff. . . . "Has everybody got a drink or whatever they'd like?" Hilly asks. But this is not a party. Bock, silent, lights a cigarette and sips water.

"Thank you all for joining us this afternoon," Hilly begins in a slight English accent. "This is the first time the score has been played for anyone not directly connected with the show. Of course, it is brilliant. I don't say that about everything I produce. It's not *true* of everything I produce. . . ."

And: "Here's the show. . . ."

Harnick takes over, cigar aloft, hand trembling slightly. "We open and try literally to convey the eighteenth century, of something glittering and gay, at the end of which the sharp contrast for when we go into the Frankfort ghetto. A little . . . just twelve bars . . ." He begins to sing in a deep true voice as Bock plays. The artificial years are auctioned off: " 'A Marie Antoinette of a year . . . a God is dead fun in bed year . . .' Lights low, a smattering of snow," says Harnick, creating the scene: ". . . three little urchins, not cute kids—little horrors: little German urchins. There was a custom: 'Jew, do your duty' . . ."—a bow to the Christian; children made it a Jew-baiting game. He sings the number, and it is apparent at once that the people in the room are caught by it.

" 'You'll go to hell, Jew. . . .'

" 'Hear ye, hear ye . . .' The ghetto is closed. We go to

Mayer's shop . . . a notion of what he's living through to provide adequate motivation for what follows." His wife-to-be,
Gutele, sings a love song, which so evidently moves the
listeners that the lyricist risks kidding: "After that Mayer
punches her in the mouth. . . . No, no"—assuringly. The team
appears to gain confidence; the roomful of money and influence clearly is attracted to them and the work. Together they
sing the money-changing scene. We are compelled. It is good
stuff; everyone is beginning to feel appropriately exercised
upon, serious when one ought to be, or grinning, inspired in
fact by music and rhyme in gliding combinations of that which
is expected next to that which is a surprise. Bock cries out the
lyrics of "Sons," head back, clutching at the piano keyboard.
The boys grow up, Bock and Harnick their parents. They want
everything, everything! Lawrence Shubert Lawrence smiles at
last. Napoleon's wolfish troops now, and the creators' French
is up to it. Act I.

Act II, incomplete, will be carried off rather than presented,
so that the letdown is not great. Hilly watches, flushed. Yellen
pulls on a pipe. Claire is attentive, Fred Morton nodding,
approving. They have waited six years for this; here at last
are Nathan Rothschild and Hannah Cohen in love. What had
seemed ridiculous in manuscript ("She turned my pound and
shilling world to a world of milk and honey"), now sung,
seems significant. When the grown and successful sons beg
their widowed mother to leave the ghetto to live with one or
another of them in their palaces, there is no doubt that the men
in the room think guiltily of their mothers. (Both of these
songs will be dropped by the time the show opens.) "That's
the last written number we have," Harnick says, sweating. "Not
that there are other kinds. Sherman, do you want to take over
from here?" After Yellen describes the missing pieces of the
story, Harnick declares, "There are three or four songs missing.
You've heard about 85 percent of the score. . . ."

"It's great! It's terribly important."

Congratulations.

"Fine." Harnick is exhausted; Bock drinks water thirstily.

"Fine, my ass: it's great!"

". . . all in the nude," Yellen is saying, "so we'll have no costume problems."

"Sheldon, you're getting better and better," says Hilly in his deepest voice, delighted. He is about to leave for the West Coast. "I'll pick up the rest of the financing there"—for all to hear, as if there's nothing to it.

When the guests have gone, the principals confer.

"We'll know in a week whether Pilbrow"—the asked-for lighting designer—"will do it."

"Gee, that's tight," says Derek.

"If he doesn't like the book," Hilly begins, grinning, and Bock: "We'll change it, we'll change it!"

The names of coins are needed. "There's a museum of coins right here in New York City," says Harnick.

Bock kids: "Yes, it's called the Jewish Museum."

"No, wait. Our next move," says Goldby, rising. "Wait. Can I give you a stage picture? . . ."

"He was *gloating*," Platt says later in the office.

Bill Liberman replies, "Well, it's good!"

"I think it's good too, for the moment. *Good*," says someone else.

George is grinning ferociously, as if vindicated. "I was watching Hilly watching people react. So-and-so turns to him, and Hilly's gloating! 'See, you prick, I told you it was great!' "

A second living-room audition is held for backers, and for John Bury, who is Hilly's choice for set designer and who has been flown from England to hear it, and others (Milton Greene, musical director of *Fiddler on the Roof,* among them;

he wears a small sea captain's beard and smokes cigars confidently). The mood is altered. If the first audition was not a party, this one may be. The theater owner has returned with more guests. It is pleasant to have the power to bring relatives and acquaintances to these semisecret hearings. Big and bluff, Shubert said jokingly into the intercom at the street door, "Friends." And the secretary above, her voice crackling: "Fuck that, who is it?" The elevator, trying for the fourth floor and filled with its gay party, staggers from third to first and back, overloaded, stubborn, everyone roaring, though Robert, learning of it, will be upset. The living room is jammed. The valet brings chairs, and we sit on the floor, on windowsills or radiator covers. Bock today wears a leather vest, Harnick a red turtleneck sweater and corduroy jacket, again with a cigar; Goldby wears brick-colored jeans. . . . At the appropriate moment, with flair, Hilly enters, Claire beside him. He is pink, the smile shy under the mustache; his costume is the one he sought in Boston but could not find—a black suit—a vest suit—with silver clasps, a lavender open shirt with sleeves like pillowcases. "I'm sure this distinguished company can amuse itself for a few minutes more. There *will* be refreshments."

A photographer begins to flash pictures.

"Oh, really!" Harnick groans.

"There's a wedding after this!"

Claire serves red wine; Robert passes a platter of Swedish meatballs.

"Some of you are concerned. The wine and the meatballs are not on the production budget; they're on the house." Hilly then makes general introductions. The big brown-bearded Englishman is John Bury. He will do the sets, Hilly says, "all things being equal." Then Goldby; Pilbrow (not present) for lighting. "Mr. Greene will direct the music. . . . My guess is that the production will cost between seven hundred and fifty and a million, and it will be a bargain at that. My further guess is that it will be financed by ten folks putting up 10 percent each. The album will be done by Capitol Records." Its representative rises, bows. "Which is the best news they've had in years. That's all I have to say. Darling, don't push the meatballs. We'll have 'em for supper tonight."

Harnick takes over.

He and Bock will do this a couple of dozen times before the show is staffed and financed; they will be doing it, to raise capital, after rehearsals have begun. It is hard work, but no mechanical substitute has been found that serves: tape doesn't work or closed-circuit TV; the backer wants the creator right there in front of him. "Last time I did this I had a cold," Harnick says. "I don't know what my excuse is this time. . . ."

It does not go as well, perhaps because this audience had heard good things about it. The men smile grimly at Yellen's line, "Loans to relatives degenerate into gifts." Harnick has a joke for Bury: "The second act curtain goes up on a veritable fairyland," which the designer appears to enjoy.

"Does he want to do the costumes too?" Harnick asks later. The potential backers are gone. Goldby and Bury are conferring.

"He's a *starke,* Sheldon," says Bock. "Let's let him."

" 'I sculpt. I don't draw,' " Hilly says, quoting him. " 'I work in space.' . . . We don't want sets that say *musical, musical.* . . . A little cream, Robert, thank you. The fewer minds interpreting this, the more show we'll have. . . . I think the next two weeks will tell us from your point of view: 'Yeah, we have it; we can lock in and go,' or not. . . . I really haven't bothered you yet."

Bock says hastily, "No, no. The more notes we get now, the better."

"I've felt best advised to hold myself back. It would serve no purpose to nit-pick now."

"In another two weeks . . . I don't know if we'll have the whole score, but we'll have another number. I'd estimate by mid-November we'll have a show."

There is talk of the prodigious estimated budget.

"Hilly, where does the waste come in?" asks Yellen.

"I'll tell you. You hand me on January 29 a perfect book and score that won't be changed, and I'll bring it in for five hundred thousand. But don't try it and we'll stay friends. . . . These guys *know*. You play a piece on the piano, it's the greatest musical in the history of the theater. You get an orchestra into a theater and you wonder why in fuck you spent five minutes on it. You learn about the collaboration with the theater you're in, among other things."

"Have you got a rude message for Trevor?" asks Bury of Goldby. The two Englishmen have not met before.

"I don't know him that well. We were at Cambridge together. Well, yes. Tell him next summer I want to do a show at the Royal Shakespeare."

Bury describes his recent travels and work. ". . . taught the bloody Japanese to make tunics for my *Hamlet*. *Thousands* of men making things at colossal speed." He is currently doing the sets for a play still on tour in England. "He's terribly charming, but he's drunk half the time. He's all right till you cross him, and then he's petulant like a schoolboy"—referring to its famous star.

"Oh, like So-and-so?"—another star.

"Much worse than So-and-so."

Later Goldby says, "I've been out of England two years, since *Rosencrantz*. I'm unknown there. They don't think of me for jobs now. They think I've copped out to the American

commercial theater. . . ." He advises the designer on negotiating. "All I can say is, insist on what you need. . . . I'd be
devastated if we lost you altogether. Hilly wants you and Richard. We have no one else in mind. You did *Oh, What a Lovely
War!*, didn't you?"

When the producer appears, Goldby says, "I went through
the basics of the show with John, and he threw out some marvelous ideas. . . . This thing about *projection*: look, we both
feel the show could be done without it."

"Let me say this. I love projection. I have great guys doing
it for me with *Calcutta,* and they're doing a feature for me."
It is the introduction to capitulation. "*But* your point is, Derek,
that we are doing a show that is theatrical and its devices
should also be theatrical, and it's turned me around." He looks
at Goldby, at Bury. "*If we can do the show without projection,
we're better off.*"

"Unless we do the coming of war with it," Bury says.

"Well, I finally said to John, 'Go away, mull it over, and
see if you *need* projection.' "

"No, I feel strongly it's a better show without it."

"I find I'm sympathetic to Derek," Bury begins, "and he
likes my ideas. . . ."

"I don't fly people over from London because I don't want
to make deals. We'll find the best possible people for you."

Bury's agent is mentioned.

"Give him all your ideas"—meaning money.

"If I call from London and say I can't do it, it's not because
of anything that happened today. I want to do it." The Englishman, dealing with Hilly, has grown more English—"bloody
this and that"—whereas Hilly, at first very English with Bury,
moves back into American with an increase of "fucking this
and that," which he appears to have discovered amuses the
other. In addition, he is letting the other know who he is. . . .

"I *can* work with Richard," says the designer at length. "We disagree on lighting sometimes. He tends to be . . . overcolorful. If he works on this, I'll definitely design with his lighting in mind."

"I understand both what you're saying and what you're not saying"—solemnly.

"I *did* mention to Derek that there are one or two places where the script works against the sets. Also, one tends to be seduced by the ballroom or the opening scene. . . ." He wants a grand plan of the theater he must work in. Hilly declares that he has the Imperial but wants to trade it off for the Majestic. "It has one balcony, which is divine. Very intimate." He will send plans for both. . . . Later, Bury gone for his plane, Goldby gets on a phone in the office. "He's great. He put his finger at once on at least two things about the show. . . . Oh, he loves it. In fact, he's going to give up a show to do it."

George Platt complains, "This will cost a fucking fortune, flying these Englishmen back and forth."

3

Casting auditions begin. At this stage Hilly keeps away. He will see the principals and help make final choices, but as per his usual hands-off policy he does not wish, apparently, to cramp the creative style of the others.

Goldby will want for the reading something classical, he says, or something from Restoration comedy. Bock and Harnick have made a list of musical numbers, from which they expect to learn essential things about singers. Everyone must come prepared to sing "Sophisticated Lady" plus a song from "an opera of your own choice." Actors trying for Mayer Rothschild are to have prepared "Brother, Can You Spare a Dime?" and "Blow, Gabriel, Blow." If an actor wants to be Nathan Rothschild, he will sing "I Got Plenty o' Nuttin'," "Younger

Than Springtime," or "They Didn't Believe Me." William-Fouché-Herries-Metternich: "any patter song from any Gilbert and Sullivan operetta" as well as "Falling in Love with Love." Gutele: "Can't Help Lovin' That Man o' Mine," verse and chorus. The rest: the two basic numbers. (The formula will be simplified later: a rhythm number and a ballad.)

The Eden stage is bare except for the single bentwood chair at the center of it and one overhead light. It is a scene that has been done so often in Hollywood movie musicals—casting the Broadway show—that it seems familiar. The house lights are up—glowing balls of cut glass; exits, draped in gold-fringed scarlet, are lit; there is a light on the piano's music rack in the pit; the stage, with its sable *Calcutta* cyclorama, and the lights make the place a pleasant womb even without performance. A sign has been taped to the outer lobby door: "Rothschilds Auditions Inside." Musical director Greene is ready at the piano. Stage manager Greg Taylor greets actors at the door and shows them to the basement lounge to wait. Stage manager John Actman escorts them down the aisle, introduces them, and helps the ladies make the big step to the stage.

"If Derek had his way, he'd audition every actor in New York City," Platt says. "He wanted to hear them from eleven in the morning till seven at night. People scream about singing in the morning because their voices aren't settled yet." Platt, in charge of announcing and setting up auditions, calls the present method "shotgun," meaning broad invitations through agents, plus a few invitations to names, for whom specific appointments are made and unhurried periods of time—usually twenty minutes—set aside, no waiting. These are Equity calls and run for from five to ten days, not consecutively, and speaking generally the auditioners who appear are competent. Union rules require a producer also to hold open or noninvitational calls for males, then for females, then for singers if their function is separate, which is not the case here. The choreographer holds auditions for dancers, and again there are particular rules (no cement floor, for example). After that there is usually an open call for anyone, Equity or not. Call-backs are governed by rules too. Principals may be called back, which is to say reserved and recalled for a further hearing, four times, chorus three times, after which an eighth of Equity minimum weekly salary must be paid the actor for each call-back. (A reason actual production songs are not used in auditions is that then rehearsals are considered to have begun and full salary must be paid.) At first the field is broad, with few restrictions. ("I want character people, no WASP types," says George to agents. "I don't want dirty types either.") An actor, learning from his agent that he is to sing "Sophisticated Lady," phones, a secretary reports, to ask if he may come in his drag clothes. There is another agent's letter suggesting what he calls offbeat casting for Gutele Rothschild. ". . . You see, she is black. . . ." George Platt's code is "CB" for call-back, which means possible, and "CBL" for call-back-later, which means unlikely but worth stringing along. "Thank you" means no. (As a matter of history, two finally cast principals, Hal Linden and Keene Curtis, both of whom won Tonys for their performances, were heard on the first day of auditions. I was not there.)

"Gentlemen, this is Merwyn Goldsmith," says Actman.

"How do you do, Merwyn," Bock and Harnick say.

He checks in with Greene at the piano. " 'Half a million boots went sloggin' through the mud,' " he sings. Then "Sophisticated Lady," the release being a severe test. He does a speech from *Volpone*. At last he is given a scene from *The Rothschilds* to take to the lounge to study.

Norman Smith.

"I *think* it's a good morning," he says uncertainly, and sings

"Brother, Can You Spare a Dime?" " 'I was the kid with the drum!' " He wears dark clothes and a tie and sings well. " 'Once in khaki suits, gee we looked swell, full of that Yankee-doodledee-dum!' . . . A little key change in there," he says of the difficult release in "Sophisticated Lady" ("Is that all you real-ly want?"), having sung it properly. If it is badly sung, which is easy to do, Harnick or Bock will stop the auditioner at once; only the seven notes are needed.

"Do you have any acting piece that you can do off the top of your head, Norman? Straight acting . . ."

Few are prepared for this.

"I'm on *Secret Storm*. Would that help? I play a multimillionaire bastard." He is given a scene to study in the lounge. While they wait, Harnick sings the seven notes. . . .

"Gentlemen, this is Ann Wakefield."

She must stand near the piano, she is warned, or she will be unable to hear it.

" 'Words! Words! Words! . . . You blighters . . . !' You're right about the piano." Then she embarks on her Gershwin. "Jane, Jane . . ."

"Ann."

"I'm sorry. Ann. Are you American, by the way?" English. "Good!" Goldby cries. Platt gives his private sardonic laugh. "You were one of the fair ladies, weren't you?" Yes. "*Jolly* good." "Yes," she says, "jolly good show for England."

An actor returns to read a scene with assistant stage manager Actman. Mayer Rothschild is presenting a rare coin to William of Hesse in order to gain his patronage. No. "What I'm looking for is something where you give me a high energy level." He is sent off to study Nathan ("A dynamic, volatile sort of person, the dynamo of the family," the director says), and *sotto* to Harnick: "Do you still think he's an actor?"

Possibly.

A tough professional European actor with a slight accent

sings, glances arrogantly through pages of music, casual, skill-ful. He does a bit of Albee to be American, some *Twelfth Night*: "If music be the food of love"—sounding uncannily like Olivier. Then a joking little tap dance. He is a CB. . . . George complains that on-the-spot studying is leading to back-ups. Actors sing, study, return to do a scene with a monotone stage manager, leave photos and résumés unless George al-ready has them from their agents. The production people have lists with the actors' names and hour of tryout; each writes his comment beside the name. Before a CB or CBL, though the decision is the director's, Goldby confers with the others, which Platt feels he ought not to do. Turndowns on the basis of music will be made by Harnick or Bock without conference or with a gesture behind the back of a seat: "Thank you very much indeed, *thank* you," Goldby will say. And Bock is effu-sive over turndowns, smiling brilliantly, waving his notes to say good-bye, thanking the failed candidate almost with pas-sion. . . .

"How do you do, Joe?"

"Hallo! Hallo, Derek. Look, all I've got is a song from *Camelot*." But he also does "Poor Little Buttercup" well, and everyone is amused. "Joe, do you know anything just off the top that would be more sustained?" Bock asks. He does "Fall-ing in Love with Love." He tells them what Chaliapin said when called for a morning rehearsal: "I can't shit before eleven." At breakneck speed, yet distinctly, he does the Queen Mab speech: " '. . . smallgreycoatedgnatnothalfsobigasaround-littlewormprickedfromthelazyfingerofamaid . . .' "

CB.

"Brother, Can You Spare a Dime?"—someone else.

"That's Al Jolson up there!" cries Harnick.

The actor does an eccentric dance step, flings himself flat, head hanging into the orchestra to hear the inaudible piano.

A thin boy in a long embroidered vest and white shoes sings without pep: " 'I got plenty o' nuttin' . . .' " He cups an ear for Greene's piano, then does the "Sophisticated Lady" trick. "Stop! You've negotiated the rapids!"

"Gentlemen . . ."

" 'Fish gotta swim, bird gotta fly. . . .' "

"You'll miss my ending!" cries another man in despair, stopped midway. "I swear I knew all this perfect. . . . Is that all?"

The auditioners wait in the newly decorated basement lounge for Taylor to call them, pace, and study their music. Some, who have come with accompanists and vocal coaches, work with them, singing in undertones, or confer on vocal problems. Bringing help makes it expensive for the actor to prepare an audition. Most are nervous and, this being a professional environment, show it freely: Bock and Harnick are imposing show-business figures capable of generating awe. Some, apparently, are as cool and smooth as milk.

"Do you bother warming up for these?"

The present road company Tevya in *Fiddler,* Robert Carroll, replies, "I did a little on the train up"—casually. Taylor appears, introduces himself. "Hi. Do you have a pianist? Right. She can go up this way and down the far aisle where the piano is. Milton Greene is there. . . ." He leads the performer up the other stairs. Two men wait at the empty lounge bar addressing each other in its mirror. A man in amber glasses who looks like George C. Scott sings Gershwin to himself; he shares a coach with a girl doing "Show Me" under her breath, and the portly plain woman moves soothingly from one to the other. "Have you *got* all that?" the girl demands of the man desperately. "I *know* I'll forget the lyrics!"

As it grows late, the production people tire, become laconic.

"You're skipping bars, dear." No CB.

"Sons of Burgundy."

"Lovely!" cries Bock, rejecting the man. "Good! *Good* sound!"

Robert Rounseville appears direct from his *Man of La Mancha* matinee, still in makeup, gives George Platt a bear hug and kiss (he is an old client from Hilly's agency days): "Gentlemen, I have great respect for your project, otherwise I wouldn't be here. I read the book—however many years ago that was—and was enthralled by it. . . . Now, you guys are going to have to put up with an improvisation. . . ." He does his notion of Mayer Rothschild: on his knees, from a whisper to a roar, possessed, hurling bits of song and poetry and half-invented speeches about freedom and hope out into the audience, finishing with "The Impossible Dream."

Applause.

"Crazy," says Rounseville. "*I* enjoyed it—like going to the bathroom in public." Then, peeling off beard, mustache, and eyebrows as he paces the stage, he sings an easygoing "Falling in Love with Love."

Another day boys are auditioned, along with grownups; four of the five Rothschild brothers will appear as children (the youngest brother does not appear on stage until grown), and three of the four will double as the anti-Semitic urchins.

" 'You charm the husk right offa the corn, Ma-ame!' " a boy sings.

"Fine, Jeff!"

Everyone is more relaxed with the children.

Dewey is introduced. "Okay, let's hear a voice," Goldby murmurs. "Yeah, uncork one," says Harnick.

" 'When that red, red robin comes bob-bob-bobbin' along . . .' " He keeps his hands on his trouser seams like a soldier.

"Good. What else did you learn?"

" 'Smiles,' " he whispers. " 'Smile through your fear and sorrow' "—making the r's into v's.

"Don't you know a happy song? You don't look happy."

Immediately he sings "Kids." His voice cracks.

"He's one-dimensional," Greene declares.

"You know you have a very New Yorky accent?" says Goldby. "Could you lose that?"

"You want an English accent? Like you?" He does a Jud-y, Jud-y, Jud-y Cary Grant voice. "Jolly good!" cries Goldby. "We'll see you again. Try and get rid of that accent. . . . He's a jolly good little actor."

"If we give you the part," Goldby says to another boy, "do you promise not to grow?" He has a "rough quality" the director likes. None of the boys has as yet gotten his voice above a whisper. Now, however, Mark Hall changes that, singing loudly and professionally in the Artful Dodger's Cockney, " 'Consider yourself one of the fam-i-ly.' " Mark's brother Brian is here too and ("Please, for God's sake belt it," says Goldby to himself) belts out his song—" 'So keep on *smiling* . . .' "—like a trombone, and the creators of the show look pleased. "Do you know any lines?" He does lines from *Mame*. Does he know funny lines? He does. Goldby offers him *Rothschilds* speeches. The boy leaves his photos—a montage of himself in several roles—and a résumé and gets a CB.

The résumé is typical of the professional boys:

Member of SAG, AFTRA, AEA. Born 1959. Height 5' 6"
Stage: MAME, AS YOU LIKE IT, OLIVER (Tokyo), CAR-
    OUSEL, etc.
Commercials: *Ideal Toys* (1968 Clio Award), *Woman's Day
    Magazine, Pertussin Cough Medicine*, etc.
Voice-overs and dubbings: *Ideal Toys, Film strips, Frosty O's,
    Foreign films*, etc.
Training in: TAP, MODERN JAZZ, ACROBATIC, MUSICAL
    COMEDY, VOICE, DRUMS, TRUMPET, PIANO.
Other interests: *All sports, animals, photography*, etc.

(*Has 14 year old brother who looks similar*)
Agent: Fran Dilworth.

Attached are statements made by theater professionals—
Janet Blair, Elaine Stritch, the musical director, and the dance
captain of the *Mame* national touring company ("Brian Hall
is a natural and talented young actor. . . ."). There are also
notices from the Cape Cod *Standard-Times*, the Salem *Evening
News*, and so on, and finally the photo montage: Brian in
Mame, Brian in a baseball cap, Brian in a pair of glasses carrying books. . . .

A final boy. Platt twists in his seat to watch him descend the
aisle. "Here's a big kid! My God, that's a big kid!'

"How old are you, Alan?" asks Harnick.

"Fourteen, believe it or not," the boy says miserably.

Grown-up actor Ron Leibman is next, who will come close
to getting the role of son Nathan. It is not, in my opinion, a
good role (only Mayer and the four-part role are good in the
show), but Leibman wants it. He is a first-rate creative talent,
now in rehearsal for an off-Broadway play, *Transfers*, for which
he will get good reviews. He brings tension and insecurity to
his audition (he has never sung in public), leaps to the stage:
"See the actor shake. See him being scared," then picks himself
up, as it were, and hurls himself into a love song, frightened by
what he finds himself doing. He is good: a big, wide-open, un-
trained bass that conveys the man; he mops his eyes with a
handkerchief; singing the love song, he says emotionally, he
thought of his wife, Linda Lavin an actress and singer, which
made him cry. His tension makes his talent storm into the
auditorium.

"Have you brought anything rhythmic?"

"My heart." They praise him. "No, I'm *lousy*," he says with
passion, and then sings "Lullaby of Broadway" well. The cool
professional performers are, as Harnick says, competent; so

many of the singing voices, as Bock puts it, are "covered." Leibman is raw, scared, and exposed, so that the talent finds its passage. It is an old difference: the academy on one hand, the independent artist on the other. After this, his straight acting bits—comic and serious—are an easy triumph.

4

John Bury, the English stage designer, cannot be released from a prior commitment and is unavailable to do *The Rothschilds* for the April, '70, opening date. "I'm glad," says Platt. "Maybe we'll get an American and save twenty-five thousand on the budget."

There is talk. Hilly may "jiggle dates." No. "A cock-and-bull story," says Liberman.

Hilly wants the Englishman, and he takes little trouble to hide the fact that he wants a new director. He and Goldby are at odds, quietly so, for the most part, though shouting has been reported. Their temperaments and talents do not suit; there is an incompatibility that may reflect, at least in the case of *The Rothschilds,* the incompatibility of Broadway with certain other kinds of theater—large-scale show business on one side, for example, easygoing repertory on the other, for another example. Hilly mixes art and money, Goldby wants to try; it's not going well. Also, the director, idled by his EPIC contract for two years, is less and less a name to conjure with, and this does not serve the producer's needs either. It may be that he can wait him out. Furthermore, there is the show itself, with its stubborn second act: will it be "locked in and ready to go" in time for winter rehearsal?

"Finance is war," Grover Dale says. He is the choice of the moment to be *The Rothschilds'* choreographer. He is thinking his way through the script in order to uncover its essential meaning and find a direction for his work. "Okay. War is conflict, and there are two conflicts here. The outer struggle of achieving fame and power, and the inner one—the moral conflict. My own basic instinct for wanting to do this show is for the *money*—for the royalties, if it's a success—and I saw that this, *The Rothschilds*, was about me: about my feeling that I should be an artist, about that pull between wanting to do the good stuff and wanting money and fame. Then I saw that the staff . . . us"—Harnick, Bock, Goldby, Yellen, himself—"we *are* the Rothschild brothers—and Hilly is Papa: Mayer!" He can use these feelings, he says, to help him create. "It's perfect, really!"

5

"A lot of things are going to happen this week," Hilly says pleasantly. He is shaving with care, working on the sideburns, getting ready for an interview. Claire is shopping. "We're reshaping this whole company . . . manpower changes . . . decisions on exact production dates. . . . Paramount and I are not going to do *$100* together. So-and-so said it's vulgar. 'Putz,' I said to him. 'It's about a black hooker and a white boy and they fuck together for fifty minutes!' 'Well anyway,' the guy says, 'I want Bill Cosby to do the screenplay'! . . . I'll put the movie together in the next few months, and I might finance part of it myself."

An actor in the San Francisco *Calcutta* company has been arrested on charges of "genital contact and lewd acts." There is also a warrant out for Hilly's arrest. "A procedure only." He descends to be interviewed.

Another day. Hilly has a cold. He sprawls like a pasha in his yellow terry-cloth robe on top of the huge bed. Bock,

Harnick, Yellen, and Goldby are expected, and the word is that something is up. The airconditioning is off, which is unusual in itself, and the room is warm. Judi, told to get the Mayor of San Francisco on the telephone, finds he cannot be reached.

"Ducking the call," says Hilly. "Okay. Cool . . . You didn't know I was a sex offender, did you?" he asks a new secretary who sits at the foot of his bed with her notebook. "My friends have known for years." He makes the announcement: "I'm postponing *The Rothschilds*." A heavy-lidded look. "June rehearsal, open in September. It means I'll do *$100* in March—roughly." The ostensible purpose of this morning's meeting is to record the principals' votes in the matter. In fact, the producer's mind is made up. One of the reasons put forward for the delay is that designer John Bury is worth waiting for.

Platt brings chairs from the hall and places them in a tight crescent facing the producer's bed. Harnick, Bock, Goldby, Yellen file in, sit in the small chairs, and, like fathers visiting in first grade, are at once disarmed.

"Mayer's death scene," Hilly says, grinning. "*Well*, my sons?"

But the others are not in a kidding mood.

Harnick will be reported to have said afterward, "That's the way I like to hear you talk," as if applauding a show of firmness he had doubted.

Choreographer Dale says, "The postponement is frustrating and aggravating. I've dropped all my thinking about the show. They haven't completed my contract, and I'm pissed off about that. . . . There was a meeting today, and I didn't show, because I want to feel part of it first. I'm back on other work. . . . The forward motion on this has stopped."

"There are crises in this production you'll never know about," says Yellen. "Difficulties with personalities. Probably

you wouldn't use 90 percent of it if you knew, but you won't."
He talks freely about the creative side of things. He worries,
for instance, about the "importance" Dale wants to give the
show's dances. "I beg Jerry and Sheldon: don't make it more
important than it is." Generally: "The first act works. The
second act works, but only conventionally. . . . So far it hasn't
bridged the gap between a good conventional musical and a
landmark one like *West Side Story* or *Fair Lady*. If I thought
the delay would do that, I'd be all for it. . . ." He is doubtful,
too, about the director now. "Will he be strong enough to control, say a Ron Leibman?" Does he understand the peculiarly
Jewish sense of alienation from one's environment? He thinks
he sees what the producer is up to but feels that the director
must have his chance. The writer is angry at Hilly, as he often
is, and talks about "the delicate balance" in collaboration, how
Hilly "with tricks and force-outs" makes for secret meetings,
cabals, alliances. Others are also angry at the producer, apparently, feeling insufficiently consulted upon matters important to the production—the postponement, for example, or
the choice of color for posters and ads (a red borrowed from
a Plaza menu): the creative principals were not asked their
opinion. . . . The producer will send them into production with
a cloud over them; and so on. It is a difficult time, a long
winter looms, and no one is particularly happy.

Goldby and actor Leibman are at Sardi's against a wall
under the ranks of stars' caricatures. "I just turned down two
thousand dollars a week!" cries Leibman. "If I don't get this
part, he'll be a bloody pulp on Avenue C"—the director. "This
is a terrible guy! He drinks his bath water. . . ." Goldby smiles.
"I think that for you to hire a lesser actor is a mistake," Leibman says. "For *you*. I don't necessarily mean it has to be me.
. . . I know Hilly doesn't pay that well. . . ."

When the actor is gone, Goldby says of his own situation and the postponement, "At a certain point you *can't* throw in the sponge." He talks of doing an off-Broadway play in the interim. "There's something by Edward Bond. . . ." He seems damped.

"We didn't really feel he had compelling reasons for the postponement," Harnick says. "And we thought we had a choice. . . . Anyhow, now that we have the time we know we can use it. . . . And Hilly has had the show for seven years, and suddenly I think he's anxious—seeing it as a reality. . . ." The writer agrees with the producer that Bury and Pilbrow are the best and worth waiting for. "But it's hard on Derek."

"What disturbs Bock and Harnick, I think," says Fred Morton, "is a certain volatility in Hilly—this sudden decision to postpone without notifying us. . . . Harnick and Bock have more muscle than Derek, but of course legally Hilly has a lot of muscle. . . ."

Auditions proceed, but their pace limps.

" 'Fish gotta swim, bird gotta fly,' " a girl sings from the Eden stage; she is plump, perhaps pregnant. Bock, in a blue vest, sits very straight on the front of his seat, extra-attentive in the difficult time, elbows propped on the chair ahead, cigarette aloft.

Platt whispers, "There probably won't be any more auditions until the first of the year."

"I was a stand-up comic until a couple of years ago," says another actor, ". . . commercials . . ."

"Yes-s!" Bock cries when he has finished. "Thank you! Good-bye!"

Stage manager Taylor declares gloomily, "On a day like this

it's a curse to have perfect pitch," and bangs his head against the padded lobby half wall.

"My agent said you *wanted* an accent!" an Israeli says, and Goldby replies with severity, "Well, your agency was wrong."

The movie actor Eddie Bracken auditions. He looks almost as he did at the height of his popularity, which was in the forties. He has kept his hair, and it falls forward over the familiar steep Greek nose just as it used to; he is slim and smartly dressed. Harnick, Bock, and the rest rise respectfully. "Hell, I never need music!" he says in the peppy Henry Aldrich voice, an actor's carrying voice. "It Was Just One of Those Things." He sings confidently, does an accomplished tap routine for fun, reads a few lines, not well. A factotum waits in the lobby and a car in front of the theater. . . . The lounge is filled. Men and girls audition, a few little boys, their mothers hovering. Second Avenue is dark by now. They climb awkwardly onto the stage, face the handful of men, who seem somehow hard, coarsened by the long day (they are put out by the new delay in production); they sit near each other but not together, heavily professional, exacting, courteous; all on the stage are threatened by them, but the girls seem particularly threatened.

Idly, in the difficult winter, I acquire an introduction to a genuine Rothschild (Morton says he is "tangential" or perhaps distaff), feeling that is appropriate. He is elderly, has houses in Kenya, Cortina, Syracuse (Sicily), Santa Barbara, and an apartment in New York where he is presently in residence. "You want to—what?" he asks with a French accent on the phone: "Look me over? . . . You see, I have an Americanism." He had been described as a fascinating man, and I report this. "I am, I am," he declares with a chuckle.

"I had been saying for years to Edouard," he says in the

hallway of the apartment where a Titian hangs, "I *want* the Titian. I want the Titian and the Ming rabbits. And before the sale went on at Christie's he gave them to me." He is tall, young-looking, elegantly dressed. He describes his apartment, which has furnishings from several Rothschild and royal houses, as plain. There are yellow chrysanthemums from his California house, where he will be going soon to get away from the New York winter. He maintains a hospital in Kenya, and its head and fifty of the staff have just been his guests. He is exhausted. He has two African houses, and giraffes come in the morning to drink from the swimming pool of the one in the country. Each year he brings ten Kenyan boys to America to go to school. He and Kenyatta are friends.

"I consider it to be an invasion of my privacy," he says of the musical based on his family's history. "Anyhow, it's certain to be mediocre." He saw the play *Plaza Suite* recently. "Of course, I laughed, but I hated it: it was mediocre and middle-class. I like the upper and lower classes," he says definitely, "but hate the middle class." He has tickets for *Oh! Calcutta!* "I will enjoy that. Like all old men, I love pornography." There has just been a peace march and rally in Washington. "Good for you!" he says to the writer, who went and who also picked up some inexpensive liquor. "Are you Jewish?" Yes. "That was Jewish," he says, "not American—to go and do good and also to get your gin."

In 1933 the Mayor of Cortina politely asked his permission to have the George Arliss *House of Rothschild* shown in the local movie house, and he said yes. "I didn't much like their ducking into the cellar to avoid paying their taxes."

In a tour intended at last to ease the interviewer out we wind up before a lean old Crucifixion writhing like a tree root on the wall. "An El Greco," he declares with well-bred satisfaction. "There are six El Greco sculptures in existence." He recalls the names of the other owners. Most are kings and princes.

Their leader carrying a pink conch, the Krishna-conscious march in Greenwich Village; the thick smell of incense trails from them, and they offer incense sticks for sale. They head west to MacDougal.

"ARLO GUTHRIE WEDS IN BERKSHIRE MEADOW," says a *Times* headline in an earlier warmer week and shows him and his bride photographed in white, flowers in their hair.

"Start the New Year off with a Bang!" advises the *Oh! Calcutta!* ad with youthful salacity.

There was a new kind of national theater in the offing. We heard of massacres by Americans of Vietnamese women and children. Billy Graham announced from his home in South Carolina that all wars are sinful, some justifiable; still he had not made up his mind about Vietnam, and we waited for this decision. "What Does 'Massacre' Mean to You?" asked a syndicated newspaper feature called "Words in the News." "What" it was asked, "is the specific meaning of this word in capital letters: 'The MASSACRE (MASS uh kur) of March 16, 1969, may be only one betrayal of American ideals.' . . . Pick a word that seems close in meaning: A: wholesale slaughter. B: assassination. C: senseless murder. D: a purge. . . . This incomplete word is close in meaning to MASSACRE," the sardonic quiz goes on. "Can you fill in the blank spaces correctly?

"b − − − h − r."

Theater representing as it does something real without itself being so and without requiring anything real of its audience, the hearings in reference to the butchery became public theater, and, as at a play, we saw that we could be punished, deterred, and absolved without anything actual being involved. At last, on the first day of the new year, Billy Graham moved carefully near the edge, and on network TV between halves at the Orange Bowl football game prayed for guidance that we might know the rules and penalties in life as in football and avoid violations of rules, so that we would be able to reach the goalposts of peace.

X

Intermission

1

The tone at 19½ East Sixty-second has changed, perhaps because it is no longer a bachelor establishment. There is, as there often is, a turnover in staff. Elizabeth the maid-cook who needed Hilly's talents for curing sciatic pain, Judi the outspoken secretary, ex-TV producer Morgan, Norman Kean who is himself a producer and his assistant Dale Burg, along with a few more, will leave EPIC's stage, and others will be hired. Efficiency is the word in the new year. Bob Malina and Manny Azenberg are taken on as company troubleshooters, the latter specifically as general manager for *The Rothschilds*. Azenberg worked for David Merrick and, more recently, both worked for Madison Square Garden. Malina, who is apparently serious, knows law; Azenberg, who is apparently a joker, knows production. Both understand theater. One of their jobs will be to control Hilly's lavishness, at the same time trying to pare down his colossal debts (nearly three-quarters of a million dollars) without standing in the way of acquiring new debts for new productions and for the producer's way of living. (An interoffice memo puts at seven and a quarter million dollars the amount required for all projects as of the end of the year.) The basement of the building, under Jerry Simek's supervision, develops into a working area as efficient and comfortable as officers' quarters in a submarine; the old third-floor rooms are now a honeycomb of tiny cells. Bill Liberman and George Platt move out of Hilly's office, and the producer returns to sit behind the big desk, the console at his elbow ceaselessly tuned to WQXR, the New York station for classical music. New photographs are on the cork walls, mostly of Claire, and new framed posters: *Alice's Restaurant, Oh! Calcutta!* If the top of the house is not out of bounds, it has at least become a more private place, and the offices themselves are noticeably less flashy with expletives. Rarely now is this writer pressed by the staff with the history of the producer's former sex life and other adventures. The atmosphere is cooled rather than altered, but the coolness is definite: Hilly is married. A trace of regret, inadmissible, hangs in the air.

2

"Dear Mr. Elkins," writes a girl who wants the role of Kitten in *The $100 Misunderstanding*, "How are you? Fine, I hope. My name is So-and so, I'm only 15 years old but I can pass for 14. . . . Sorry I don't have a picture. . . . I'm only 5′ 2″, 117 lbs and my measurements are 34-24-34. If you'd like to call my number is . . . Soulfully yours . . ."

A *Fortune* magazine piece on prepared-food franchising appears, and there with Hooker of Minnie Pearl's Chicken System, and Brown of Colonel Sanders' Kentucky Fried Chicken Corporation, is the producer.

EPIC must soon go into "sub-showcase" with *Alice's Res-*

taurant—"the underbelly." Bill Liberman tries to make it clear. Premiere showcase is one or two small New York houses and single art houses in places like Boston, St. Louis, Philadelphia, and so on. Then there is the golden showcase, which in New York consists of about twenty or twenty-five theaters in which the film will play simultaneously, still at high prices. After that it's belly showcase: sixty or so houses in New York; then, apparently, there is a general distribution. Occasionally, the right movie revives or, withdrawn (as *Alice* will be), is sent back in altered form to go part of the route again. Bill regrets that the film was not ready for distribution earlier in the previous summer to take advantage of school vacations, and that United Artists did not exploit its good reviews.

There is still no contract for choreographer Grover Dale, and his agent writes angry letters.

A new project.

"We're doing Abbie Hoffman's *Revolution for the Hell of It* as a movie—starting next week." Hoffman and seven co-defendants are still on trial in Chicago. *Oh! Calcutta!*'s Jacques Levy will direct it; it is not documentary, not fiction, yet both: "something new," Hilly says in high excitement. The director has been in Chicago with a cameraman and will stay until the end of the trial. He is then to go to San Francisco, where former co-defendant Bobby Seale is in prison. "We're going to sneak Jock into Bobby's cell!" Hilly says. He does not know how. It doesn't matter. "We'll do it!"

A new project.

Hilly will do an off-Broadway play. It is called *The World's Greatest Play* (the hero's name is Hero) by Israel Horovitz. He expects to do it soon: March.

Though all signs point to the fact that *The $100 Misunderstanding*, Hilly directing, is being eased into the wings, the producer insists: "It goes in April."

Quietly, he has acquired a co producer, Lester Osterman, with whom he did *Candide,* for *The Rothschilds.* Osterman is rich and owns theaters. Raising money for the show in a depressed economy is already showing itself as a problem, and this move ought to ease it. Hilly is in the saddle at once: "Get him for me."

"He's having lunch."

"Get him for me where he's having lunch. Why should he enjoy?"

The Rothschilds schedule is now "locked in." Rehearsals start July 6. The show will open and run in Detroit in August, go to Philadelphia for September, open in New York on Hilly's birthday, October 18. He may revive the production of *Candide*; half a dozen other projects are being approached, discussed in meetings, a few set afoot, most dropped.

"He's a poor businessman for himself," says an analytically-minded associate who has known the producer for years and worked for him from time to time, "that is, an unorthodox one, often a careless one. What he is is a moneymaker, an *earner.* It's nerve. For example, he'd open *The Rothschilds* at twenty dollars if someone else was charging fifteen dollars a ticket. It's as a result of that nerve they're grossing forty-five thousand on *Calcutta.* Yet he spends more than he makes. If he feels bad, he buys ten suits, a dozen pairs of shoes—peanuts . . . But he's a great agent, a genius, the very best in our business, and a charming and lovable kid. He takes *anything* and makes it the greatest thing in the world and sells it. But he's a poor judge of people. I work for him, quit in protest, start again, quit. . . . He can't fire anybody. *I* had to fire So-and-so. He was getting two-fifty a week, and no one had asked for him since he was hired! I said, 'Hilly, you need that for rent!' He works five projects at once, and he can go right around the clock working. Then, of course, he has to handle everything right down to the paperclips. If you do things and don't tell him, okay: he's happy; otherwise, he handles it. . . . He's always *at the moment*, wants to work with people who are right up front and of the moment too: hits. *The Rothschilds* is old-fashioned now. Eight years ago when he first got it it was *the* thing, like *Fiddler*. *$100* was hot when he got it, but four-letter words are old-hat. Now he's hot on Abbie Hoffman—always something sensational. But he also makes sensational mistakes. It's a good step he's taken with Malina and Azenberg. He might put his own money into something, which a producer should never do—three hundred thousand, half a million—and lose it. Then he'll be sunk—out of operation. In this business unless you stay in operation you're finished for good. . . . Do you know Hilly got Metro, *on the phone,* to give him one hundred thousand dollars so he could get the Hoffman movie up and shooting? . . . He's a genius. His own life would make a movie."

3

Bob Malina wears sideburns, Manny Azenberg a guardsman's mustache. The manner of both displays casual authority. "What can I tell you?" asks Azenberg. "We're in the bunker down below. In case a bomb drops we're safe." Hilly appears both spurred and quieted by their presence, their advice; Platt's and Liberman's areas of authority are now circumscribed, but on the whole the office goes on as before.

"We must reassure them in Australia," Hilly is saying about the *Calcutta* company there. "We'll tell 'em we'll use G-strings. . . .

"A police inspector called. He wants to subpoena the *Calcutta* script. I said, 'For God's sake, you can go and buy a copy for $1.75! I'll give you a copy!' " Claire Bloom is in the office. "Put down I came in and kissed Mrs. Elkins," says Azenberg to me, doing so. "Also, put down 'shit.' Someone said 'shit.' "

Claire asks, "Did you see that David Susskind made the Ten Best Dressed Men list?"

"Don't tell Hilly. He'll do fifteen minutes, and we don't have time."

Hilly interviews girls for the vacant secretarial job.

"Tell me about yourself."

"I'm looking for a secretarial position that's active, diversified, and that I can sink my teeth into. And somebody nice to work for."

"Well, you can't have everything. People eventually get to the bottom line and find that I'm ah"—gently—"a son of a bitch. . . . Do you work well under pressure?" She does. "Are you a prude?" No, definitely—with spirit. "I don't mean in terms of *our* relationship, but of language around here and so on. . . . The hours are erratic. They're impossible when we go into production, and that's nearly always. It won't be *every* Saturday, but when I give you a Saturday, you're eternally grateful. We start out with utter chaos and the idea is to turn it into a smooth-functioning organization. I can tell you: bored you won't be. . . . We have worked together for a long time in this office," he says to the attentive girl. "We're friends here, not associates. . . . I give the impression of being a creative, disorganized type. I'm neither creative nor disorganized. The only thing that makes me wonder about your intelligence is that, having had the job described to you, you haven't walked out. But you come from Brooklyn, and you're probably a masochist. . . .

"I'm not buying the rights to the Chicago trial!" he says, taking a call. "No one can do that. They'll be making books, and they'll be making things out of this, and they have every right to. I'm buying Abbie Hoffman's book. The movie does not concern Chicago, though that will in fact be part of the ending of our film. The exclusivity refers to the material in the book. That we have a right to and that we'll get. Make it clear to Metro. . . . We're going to get Jock Levy into jail with Bobby Seale. We may not get him out again, but we're going to get him in." The job candidate waits, sitting straight, her bag on her lap, while Hilly takes one more call ("Hello, Jack, how's your beard?"—to his West Coast lawyer), then turns to her: "Anything else you want to ask?" She is worried about those Saturdays, so the producer gets it "clear in front." She will work an average of two Saturdays a month, *not* nine to six, ". . . but when we're in production, in rehearsal on a play or in production on a film, when we're out of town and down to the nitty-gritty, it's seven days. Hopefully, you'll be so interested you won't want *not* to be involved." EPIC will make up its mind within twenty-four hours. The girl leaves. Hilly consults with Jerry concerning a loose screw on the knob of his and Claire's bedroom door, also a matter of the trim on the sauna. He shouts at the next candidate waiting in the outer office, "Welcome to chaos!" and later puts a blue *Gymnasium* student's cap at a steep angle on his white locks and sets off with Azenberg to inspect a theater he may lease.

"HIRI I ZOTIT TONE JESU KRISHT QOFTE ME JU TE GJTHE" —a Greek Orthodox church on West Forty-eighth Street is being converted into two small theaters; the motto hangs aloft exposed to the sky. Hilly and his general manager are shown around, stepping over beams. It would be good to bring *Calcutta* here, escape from the confinement of the East Village, but bad to change a known location. Green rooms and dressing rooms are sketched on the air by the builder. "You know what that says in English?" Azenberg asks, studying the motto: "Don't invest in show business." Two workmen are quarreling on a girder, and at last one turns his back, jerks down his welder's mask, and sets sparks showering into the cold air.

"Never mind him," says the builder. Later Hilly muses aloud. Perhaps he will build a theater of his own. (The one he has just seen will be called the Playhouse Theatre, and in it, the following year, he will produce an Ibsen repertory with Claire Bloom.)

A photographer from a national magazine appears at 19½ in the afternoon. Malina is on the phone talking deals. "What happens when you smile?" the photographer asks Hilly cajolingly. "Don't ask!" cries Malina.

"The room lights up," says the producer.

The manicurist has come from the hairdresser's next door and settled into her work while the other men in the room glance self-consciously at their nails. One of the two new upstairs servants, Sylvia, appears with coffee. A second photographer arrives. He is from *Show* magazine; the feature they are doing on Hilly—it will be a good piece of work by Jane Wilson—will predate the magazine's death by only a few months. The new receptionist, installed in the first-floor foyer and instructed to announce people before sending them up, announces Sandra; and the barber enters in a state of irritation. "Will you tell them downstairs that anyone who looks faintly groovy be allowed in?" Her picture is taken too; she objects at first, still ruffled. The photographer is delighted by everything.

"Hilly, I want to talk to you about your hair," Sandra says. "If I cut it so it won't stick out, it'll grow out in three months and look the way it should. . . ." She becomes accustomed to the cameras. "Take enough pictures? I hope I didn't fuck them up too much. I *hate* to be photographed." She goes upstairs to Claire and later will cut Bill Liberman's hair. (Bock is using her now too.) Hilly dictates his schedule: ". . . towel dispenser, Sammy Davis, Lester, hat . . ." He has at last given his notes to Harnick, Bock, Yellen, and Goldby: a scene with the kids is too cute; the important song "Mama, Come Live with Me" is "cutesy," and so on; they are sound suggestions, and it is reported that the creative people welcomed them. When Sandra is through for the day, she announces that Claire has agreed to go on her brown rice diet, which has pleased her. It is January, yet Hilly has had the office airconditioning on for an hour and people are starting to shiver. "What do I owe you?" Fifteen. Claire has paid her own $15. The producer hands over $30 for himself and Bill. Sandra, gay, moving slightly out of line, grabs a handful of flesh at the producer's waist. "*Wot's* this? Are you pregnant, Hilly?" . . . Claire comes in after Sandra has gone, and they compliment each other's haircuts, embrace, and discuss Sandra's diet. Both may go on it.

"We're sneaking Jock into a Black Panther cell," says Hilly, taking a call. "How? Ah! If we knew!"

4

The Senate Small Business Subcommittee on Urban and Rural Economic Development is hearing testimony in its probe of franchising. Is the system good for the investor (and franchiser) or not? For the general economy? For both? Minnie Pearl will appear, and so will Jackie Robinson, Pat Boone, Joe Namath, and others, including Elkins. They want to talk to celebrities apparently. At first, the producer was to be "sandwiched between Pat Boone and Minnie Pearl," but he persuaded them to let him be a morning lead-off witness instead, pleading other engagements.

Hilly and Claire fly down the night before and stay at the Washington Hilton for its famous breakfast. The young assistant to the committee chairman calls on the couple in their suite, and they go over the producer's prepared testimony ("After glancing at the distinguished list of witnesses scheduled to appear before this committee, I was both flattered and puzzled—flattered at being included and puzzled as to what contribution I, as a fledgling franchiser, might make to such a body of expert testimony . . ." etc.), and the assistant shows Hilly the introduction the chairman will use, which sounds like an MC bringing on a club act: ". . . It is also a pleasure to note that Mr. Elkins is accompanied by his beautiful and talented wife, the famous actress, Miss Claire Bloom."

"We close with the bank today," says Hilly on the plane going home, "for a loan to set up financing for three films, to pay debts, and to have money left over. . . . Manny and Bob are following through magnificently. Of course, it puts us in a very different kind of operation." He will invest in his own productions indirectly through another company. The producer cat-naps, Claire does a crossword puzzle provided by the airline. He wakes up: "We're arranging to get press credentials for Jacques to see Bobby Seale in San Francisco and shoot some film. . . ." Any sort of journey—in a cab, a plane—is a chance to pull threads together, sum up: "*$100* goes in March. The Horovitz play , , , Did I tell you the billing: 'Hillard Elkins Humbly Presents The World's Greatest Play'?" What about the valet? "He left in ignominy before he met violence. We sold him, traded him for two pitchers." Apparently, in fact, there was a kitchen scene of violence that involved Hilly and Hilly's father, with threats, a little scuffle. . . . Judi, as said, is gone too. Her move "into production" was a step toward dismissal, as far as can be understood, though when it came to it the secretary quit. This is a vexed matter; there was friction on several levels. He and Claire discuss a proposed trip to Australia (they will come home around the world), where the producer will see personally to the *Calcutta* franchise, which is meeting state opposition.

As we land, Claire gives herself an objective, actress' once-over in her compact mirror. "Tell me when I frown"—pressing a finger between her brows. And later, about her hair for a TV appearance: "Do you think it will be all right?"

"You look sensational."

"Really?"

"Sensational."

"I think so too."

These are objective remarks between professionals.

                                    5

Claire and Hilly are to leave in less than twelve hours for London, the first part of the world tour, and 19½ crackles as almost never before. Klein, the dapper agent for the land-lord, is here on a matter of rent. The present rent is more than $15,000 a year, and the owner proposes to raise it to $22,500. Hilly claims he has put $30,000 into improvements. They run back and forth over it. Malina recapitulates what Klein appears to want; Klein nods: "Want me to justify it?"

"I want you to *forget* it."

Hilly outlines his terms.

"He asks me for lunch," says the agent. "I get a quarter of a cup of coffee."

"Language is a subterfuge for communication"—the producer. "Will you do it? Okay? *Okay?* . . . If you were working for me—and you will be soon—what would you pay? All right . . ." Hilly will ask the owner herself while he is in London, and Klein departs.

A merchandiser, who has recently moved his office to New York, arrives for an appointment. "As of three months I'm in New York in business, Hilly, and I'm swamped."

"The statute of limitations ran out?"

The other handled licensing for *Golden Boy* and has also

worked for Merrick. "Westmore wants to do an *Oh! Calcutta!* line of cosmetics."

"Well, I have a whole new look in mind: genital spray, invisible talc for naked bodies. . . ."

A line of *Calcutta* terry-cloth robes is "definitely in order," sweatshirts. . . . Hilly and Malina kid about it, but the merchandiser is like a dog on a scent. He will import Rothschild wines from Austria, both to promote the musical and advertise the wine, which he will then sell. "On *The Charge of the Light Brigade"*—a recent movie—"I had the General Cigar people come out with a Charge of the Light Brigade cigar." He merchandised *Coco.* "*Before* it opened I worked with Cecil Beaton, developing ideas based on his sets, the colors. . . ."

"Save it till I'm back."

"I'll be in London next week. At the Dorchester."

"I'll be at the London Hilton."

"Why do you stay at that place?"

The producer likes the view from the top. "Besides, I'm secure enough to stay anywhere. . . ."

Okay. ". . . Listen, remember what I did with the girl in gold pants? I can give you so much on *Rothschilds* you won't know what to do with it."

"*I'll* know. But anything on *Rothschilds* has to be gilt-edged."

"*I* know. I want your scene designer to use Du Pont fiber, for example. I need a working script. I want to know where wine is used, where there's a drape setting. Think of this: I would love to come out with a color: Rothschilds Red. . . .I'm in touch with *Vogue, Harper's.* I want to get textiles involved: Bloomcraft Fabrics. . . ." There is a "firm commitment" with a liquor company for an *Oh! Calcutta!* cocktail. Swank wants to do *Oh! Calcutta!* jewelry. An *Oh! Calcutta!* game "for sexually mature adults" is being developed. . . .

Hilly grins. "An *Oh! Calcutta!* candy bar?"

"You think you're kidding?" and while the producer takes a call he muses frowningly. Later, the other gone, Hilly grinds the heels of his hands into his eyes. "I gotta get my head together." His New York lawyer appears. "You're spending *one day* in Israel?" A day and a half. "You don't like Jews?"

"I can take 'em or leave 'em."

The day builds instead of easing toward the end of it. There are more appointments. Hilly sees playwright Israel Horovitz with the musical group, The Open Window, that did *Oh! Calcutta!* They may do music for *The World's Greatest Play.* Hilly listens hard to the discussion, learning. Later, if the project goes, he will give their words back to them in functional form; this is an act at the heart of producing. . . . Jerry Simek appears, to rehang a framed *Alice* poster, which had fallen down. "When it's 6 P.M. here, what time is it in Australia?" 9 A.M. The couple will be in Los Angeles by March 6 and in New York again on March 10. "Maybe an extra day for Osaka . . ."

A *Rothschilds* audition is being held in the Hotel Manhattan for theater-party agents, and Hilly goes by limousine. There is coffee and Danish on a sideboard in a cramped second-floor meeting room. Co-producer Lester Osterman is officially introduced (he is supposed to raise 50 percent of the money for 40 percent of the producers' share of the profits). Bock and Harnick go to work. There is a new love song (Gutele and Mayer) and a song about selling bonds and outwitting the villainous Metternich. "What they're going to fight for is power to help the ghetto *and* to make money, and, as in the Arliss movie, to pursue dignity," Harnick explains. Hilly sneaks out. There are only a few hours until departure and more meetings are scheduled, foremost among them one at the Hotel Pierre concerning selling a share of EPIC itself. Hilly's masseur waits for him and Claire, and, as night falls, Sandra comes back to give final trims. . . .

It now seems that Hilly is a moneymaker past stopping. Bock, Harnick, Yellen wait. Others, projects ready, wait for him, for a signal. He lies naked on a table in his bedroom. Blind Mitty is sentinel at the top of the stairs. The masseur wears a smock and an old-fashioned pencil-line mustache; he has a weightlifter's forearms. The producer, soaked in Nivea oil, is attacked. "A caption for this cartoon is 'You really know how to hurt a guy, don't you?' " Hilly gasps. Kagen, the masseur, cracks the moneymaker's arms, smashes his ribs, pounds and pummels him. Hilly kids in agony. "I once turned around and bit his hip." But it is true, Kagen says in a Charles Boyer accent; he winks heavily, very French. No time. Hilly has no time. No time to shower. "Alco*hol*, then"—reaching into his professional bag—"that awful *stuff*, Hilly?" Sandra waits. The millionaire waits in the Pierre. (Manny is there too, waiting for Hilly.) Hilly will shower after all. The choreographer waits for his contract. Lawyers, accountants, tax men, colleagues and co-workers, actors, safecrackers (the Eden will be robbed in a few weeks), agents, guilds, writers, valets, dogs, cabbies, pilots, men's stores, Rothschilds themselves are waiting as it grows late. The producer takes his time at top speed. He and his movie star wife will go eastward with the earth, turn up in the sunset: Hilly once got into trouble as a boy and was, as has been said elsewhere in this book, put into a place called Youth House in Brooklyn. He had forged and cashed a check for $500, signing his father's name, and spent it at once like a lord, taking cabs to school, breaking bills of large denomination for his twelve-year-old boy's lunch. He told the cops he'd found the money in a handbag, the handbag on a subway, and told them, of course, that he wanted to be a rabbi or a lawyer, having given up on medicine, and couldn't afford a record. But he was taken out of school anyway one day and, pale, wearing his father's suit, had a hearing, and wound up in the holding institution. He stayed a week and was paroled in his father's custody. He recalls an escape attempt and that a boy broke a leg in it, and that another boy sang "Is You Is or Is You Ain't My Baby?" all night every night, or so it seems to him remembering.

XI

The Avalanche: February–July, 1970

1

In February *The Rothschilds* open-call auditions again become urgent, at the same time begin to seem as if they have gone on forever. Though the producer is known for reversing himself and famous for delays ("You're a perfectionist"), this production has moved to a point near no-return, and a universal if unexpressed belief is that it will get to Broadway on schedule sometime in the fall of 1970. Bock and Harnick, seated short of midway dead center in the theater (Harnick paces the aisle from time to time; Bock, a Dutch burgher in corduroys, clogs, smoking his curved pipe, is sedate and keeps his seat), are curt, though still courteous. A fast expression of gratitude, the auditioner trots obediently off, and that's that.

"I brought something else a little more rhythmic. . . ."

"I *think* not," says Bock.

" 'But my heart isn't mine to give,' " sings an auditioner, " 'Fanny . . . Fanny, Fanny . . .' "

"Very nice."

"Lovely," says Harnick. "Did you bring anything that's on the robust side?"

"Robust?"

"Open, vigorous."

"How about 'Lotta Livin' ' from *Bye Bye Birdie?*"

Goldby is in England, and Bock and Harnick have taken over tryouts. It seems that multitudes have come to sing. Some are called back, few are to be chosen. The list is narrowing. "Sophisticated Lady" rings out again and again. "Johnny One-Note," "I Wanna Get Married" . . .

"Do you have laryngitis?"

"No. I just didn't have time to vocalize first."

A young man with woolly shoulder-length hair like a merino sheep sings powerfully, " 'For Thine is the KING-dom and the POW-er and the GLO-RY! ! !' " and must sit sweating and panting on the apron of the stage for a moment—". . . little dizzy. Okay in a sec"—before doing his ballad. Soon the actual call-backs will start. At the office uptown George studies lists of names and photos, résumés. Consultants that specialize in finding, grading, and producing talent for auditions have been put to work (they will themselves run auditions, if asked, for a fee). One—Shurr-Hartig International Talent—is greatly distinguished by its cable address, SHIT-New York. Derek Goldby cannot be located for the moment. Hilly's new secretary, Barbara Platoff, understands that Goldby is in Paris "waiting to see Edmond de Rothschild," but neither she nor anyone else knows why. Platt has had a good deal of experience in conducting auditions and is in official charge of this one. He catalogues mistakes actors make. "They come late. That's worst. They say, 'What do you want to hear?' or 'What key shall I sing it in?' or 'I just got out of bed with the flu' . . . 'I only learned today I was going to audition.' They're lying or their agents are fucking off because I got word to them long before." It infuriates him. "They're supposed to be professionals dedicated to their work! They should just get up there and sing, for Christ's sake!" . . . Now George wishes Hilly were back. "Then the shit will hit the fan," he says with grim pleasure. "We gotta clean up this casting by the end of March. I could cast now with the people we've heard—people right on the nose." He feels that Goldby is too leisurely, perhaps unsure, and that Harnick and Bock protect him. Contracts must be started. John Bury, the set and costume designer, and Richard Pilbrow, who is to do the lighting, will come from England in April with designs. General manager Manny Azenberg will get bids for building the sets and costumes and bring in a team—stage manager, carpenter, electrician—with which he has worked before. . . . Hilly, traveling around the world with Claire, called from Singapore to announce that EPIC has been enjoined from producing *Oh! Calcutta!* in Australia: "They've read the Grove Press book and think it's vulgar. Also, it's being used as a political issue during their national elections."

Projects simmer during the producer's absence. Levy's film of *Revolution for the Hell of It*, still uncut, needs a script written around it. It is timely, and MGM, in financial trouble itself, wants it out quickly. "They've been trying to get in touch with Hilly for two weeks to tell him to hurry up, and"— the old complaint—"contracts aren't even signed." Another day, George gets another round-the-world call from Hilly, and reports to the office at large, "He's rested and rarin' to go to work."

Among other things, the producer will find on his desk the realized *Calcutta* game (designed and manufactured by Egg Cream Engineering International); it has four sequences: "Take It Off," "Fantasy," "Adventure," and "Position." Among the choice-cards is one for perversion. Instructions: ". . . all players are now ready for intercourse simultaneously if that is their desire. This may or may not occur. If an odd numbered

player exists then he or she will assume a position for mastur-
bation. If any orgasms occur then you have won the game of
Oh! Calcutta!"

Hilly and Claire return.

"Dynamite," the producer replies, when I ask how the trip
around the world was.

2

Elaine May and Walter Matthau hang drying in long strips
—dailies, they are called—at the Elisha Birnbaum Image-
Sound Studios. Dry dailies are being wound and rewound
behind closed doors to synchronize with sound strips. Jacques
Levy, redheaded, stocky, mustached, wearing a cowboy outfit,
studies uncut footage of *Revolution for the Hell of It*, and Hilly
drops in now and then to see this rough work.

Levy's plans for the film are complicated: color, black and
white, real people playing themselves, actors playing real
people and fictional roles, documentary footage, interviews,
etc.

A girl named Jeannie, who may have a major part in the
film, tells the camera in color how she was first turned on to
personal freedom (dropping out), then much later into the
Movement. As always, they are mystical, these discoveries,
the equivalent of being saved: ". . . at one point we got
undressed . . . the rain . . . I was totally naked, makeup
washed off. I had to face myself, and I was really fucked up
then. . . . Oh, the guy had a good sensual experience, but
not like mine—not mind-blowing. . . . I never wore makeup
again."

"Great!" cries Levy in the dark room.

Shots in hot hard color: "Bullshit" on yellow flags. "Free

Them All!" The police appear in tailored uniforms. It is a bright icy Washington day. "Bullshittt!" girls enunciate at the police. "*Sieg Heil!*" . . . Blue helmets, plastic masks, billics at crotch level; shots of cops making movies of marchers, news movie-makers making movies of us. "Revolution, revolution, rah-rah-rah!" Suddenly a girl in a beaver coat is being arrested by three policemen, the camera coldly observing the brutality: her arms are pinned high up behind her neck; she blinks at us red-eyed, her mouth gaping with pain. . . . A bus goes by in front of the camera, and there is a flash of bright blue. ("An Antonioni shot!" cries Levy in the dark.) The police, black and white, are mountainous; a flying wedge comes at us, realer than real in the bloody color. A cameraman is wrestled to the ground. Our own film images somersault and topple into blankness. (Levy's cameraman was pinned across a car by police, a baton against his throat; he saved his camera but missed shooting the last minutes—the cops actually coming at him—and Levy is irritable about it.) Sound goes on: "We're moving! We're moving!"—in panic to the shoving police. The images return. On-the-spot interviews later: a girl tells of another girl, her friend, being clubbed; the blood; she starts to weep. A boy: "They see it their way, we see it our way. That's what it's coming to."

3

Desks in the basement office have been cleared for Bury's model, and the designer, big-girthed and bearded, his gentle nasal English voice murmuring soothingly, hovers above it placing cutouts of ghetto Jews and courtiers. There are the houses, rough and black—a miserable place—and the dark gate, always locked; here are the market carts, the interior of Mayer Rothschild's shop, details of it microscopically rendered, treasure chests, palace columns, gorgeously painted backdrops suspended from balsawood sticks. . . . Bury will go through the script for production people both to show what he has done and to permit cost estimates in a preliminary way. Co-producer Osterman is present with his associate, Richard Horner. Goldby is here, back from Europe. Bock and Harnick are expected. The staff is here. Hilly is here too in a consciously modest capacity, easing into someone's office to take calls or upstairs for meetings, though later, fascinated, he will shout, "No calls!" when others get them. Bury sweats as he works in the close quarters, big hands careful with objects made of matches and toothpicks, bits of gold filigree and paper. ". . . It is deliberately not realistic," he is saying of Prince William's palace. "It is seen more as the resident of a ghetto might see a prince's palace. . . ." He chooses characters from the throng of cardboard cutouts, sets up a scene, shoves some toy cannons around for Napoleon's invasion. "There's a whole chandelier problem to discuss," he says warningly. "They take up fly space and are expensive. Of course, I know chandeliers are dear to my director's heart. . . . Nathan's pillar at the Royal Exchange. *And* we have the little figger. No, that's not Nathan. Ah! Here he is. All in black . . . twenty-five rather complicated costumes for a two-and-a-half-minute scene? I'm sure it'll be well worth it. . . . A minimum of . . . Where's our poet? A mauve poet . . . The arbor." Bury's American assistant, Fred Voelpel (he is himself an established designer), hands him the fragile objects. "Lights down . . . *and* the clinch . . . Mayer dies at his desk. . . . *Now* the chandelier . . ."

Bock and Harnick arrive. A sound man is here. Production carpenter Arthur Finn is here (one of the Azenberg team), whose job it will be to install the set in a theater, take it out, see it trucked from city to city; he is short, hard-looking, white-bearded, and wears a bristling white crewcut; his responsibilities are considerable; Charles Gray, the team's stage manager, and others: all gaze at the small stage and the dolls seriously: what will work? What can be modified or done away with to save?

"Heavy," Azenberg says of the set consideringly. "Of course, he did what the script called for."

Harnick worries about how much of the show will have to be played upstage.

"It's a question of feasibility," Goldby is saying about actors themselves moving portions of the set onstage to save machines.

Finn, ceaselessly jingling coins in his pocket, says they must build in June. "There's less overtime, and we'll get good bids then."

Choreographer Grover Dale descends the stairs but lurks in the background. His contract is not signed.

They discuss theaters. Some will hold such a setting easily, others will not. They are going to the Fisher in Detroit, which is all right, as is the Forrest in Philadelphia; the Lunt-Fontanne, which has been signed for after all instead of the Majestic, has less space.

Bury says, "We don't want to get into a situation where we can't see Dad in his study in Act II. He's sitting up there the whole of Act II. . . ."

The designer, who is also doing the costumes, has brought along those too, in sketch form, and they are passed around. The group breaks up into meetings, money is discussed. The cheapest of the costumes will cost more than $700. An estimate is made of $120,000 to build the sets. Hilly looks saddened. He presents the sum to Bury, gives it a beat, uses his up-from-under look, and says, "John, we must find a way of bringing it down to eighty thousand. . . . Wait. . . . Let's *talk* about how we can bring it down."

"I'll start," says Manny. "If these were not built"—the

permanent backdrop of ghetto houses. "John, I'm being a manager now. . . ."

"I'm not a painter," Bury says firmly. "If these are built, you can light them in dozens of different ways, and they're always exciting. . . ." The point goes back and forth; at length the designer makes his stand. "I would resist largely not building the back half of the show. This is my language. If you ask me to paint, I can't. . . . If you want to make a very rich effect and say this is a prince's palace, you can do it with a few effects and two dozen gorgeously dressed ladies, or the other way round, and you're all right, but this . . ." And Hilly finally backs him; they will not tamper with the basic set element, which, as in most of Bury's work, is three-dimensional —"built."

"All we can do is nibble at the edges."

They discuss ways. There is some kidding but not much ("Take the food out of the carts"; "What if we did it with three brothers instead of five?"). And Bury at last: "Having said it's built, I don't care what the hell it's built out of. Sixty pounds of polyethylene and a couple of spray guns, and you're away."

"Wigs!" Hilly exclaims suddenly.

They are cheaper in England and on the West Coast. They discuss this. "Think a *little* bit," the producer says finally in a slight English accent, cautious but definite, ". . . the first twenty rows: of *not* quite being overwhelmed. . . . I *love* it, John. . . ." And Bury, carefully yielding in turn: "I'll talk to Derek."

Yellen appears when most of the rest have gone on to other appointments—lunging down the steps into the redecorated basement. He had not been told about the meeting, he says, and is angry. Bury starts to go through the show for him. "To be pedantic: would they use barbed wire on the ghetto gate?" Yellen asks.

"No, I suppose not."

"Are those the actual colors?"

"More or less."

"It's black," the writer says.

"We wanted to set up a Brueghelesque situation against the sort of fantasy that's going to come up in a minute."

Yellen seems to want literal scene shifts, Bury to let moods and scenes linger, overlap. "How will we know we're out of the ghetto?" Yellen demands.

"One either does it for real or does it with suggestion."

"If it's a *philosophical* solution," he says a little grudgingly, "and the ghetto looms throughout, all right. . . . And we didn't want this particular palace to look quite that palatial."

Bury does Napoleon invading Hesse: cannon and smoke; paper Rothschilds, father and sons, return from Denmark successes. If smoke lingers, Yellen worries, and they appear not to notice, they will look silly.

"Well, you must decide how much it's worth—the image of their not knowing."

Yellen gazes at Act II's London. He does not much like the mottled sandy-silver effect. He is lean and dark-jawed, usually gloomy-looking, now deeply so; he puffs steadily on his pipe. "Where's the Georgian?"

"You say 'gray London' in the script."

"Sheldon does."

Later, not entirely without malice, Bury refers to the Nathan-Hannah sequence: "It's really a sort of *Major Barbara* scene, isn't it?"

Yellen grins unyieldingly around the pipe. "Don't push it." He finds the costume drawings beautiful. "The set comes as a surprise. I had a very different conception." The two men begin to get along. Bury generalizes.

"The use of this sort of textured building is that it's incredibly sensitive to light. It can come up, or burn, look springlike, or somber. It's a sort of sounding board." Yellen admits only that it's drab. "Well, when you see it up close," says Bury, "you will see that it's rich—like an oil painting. It has depth, the way glazes in an oil painting give depth. In any case, if it's too drab, you can go to work with a spray gun, but when you paint a set you're committed to it."

He is not much concerned with the belated signing of contracts, speaking of the young unsigned choreographer (". . . a veddy superior young man who shook hands and went away"). He has not signed his own contract yet. "And *I've* come all the way from London."

"It may interest you to know," Yellen says blackly, "that I haven't signed mine, and I've been on the show four years."

"It's sculptured," Hilly declares. As a producer, he is proud of having produced this set. "Now do you see why I postponed the show to get him?"

4

Call-backs are both the same as and different from initial calls. The auditioners are good and have been told so already by the people hearing them, so that even when a job is badly wanted the turndowns are not as injuring.

Both in leather, Hilly and Claire have come to the Eden on the scooter, put their helmets on a seat. Claire reads *Madame de Sade,* glances up occasionally at the stage. Goldby is in charge once more. The creative principals and much of the staff are here; now actual casting may get done.

"I'll stop you when I want you to go into the next character, darling," says Goldby to an actor trying for the four-part role.

The actor becomes English for the German William.

"Hello? That's lovely. We don't need any more of that. What's next?"

French. A good accent for Fouché: a big carrying professional actor's voice. The lines by Yellen sound fine. "Lovely!" Goldby cries at length. "Just hang on a second. Don't go 'way."

They confer.

"Good!"

"I don't know if he has the dignity."

"He has urbanity."

"Is he masculine enough?" Harnick asks finally.

And later Yellen offers his explanation of the turndown. "The faggotry shows through after a while. You begin to hear his voice and not the words. We'll probably wind up with something in that line though."

"If you're a smart actor, you know three thank-you's mean you don't have the job," Azenberg says.

The day wears grindingly on.

"Darling, are you English?"

"No," says Hilly *sotto,* "she's from Brooklyn like the rest of us."

"*Enjoy* yourself more"—Goldby to an actor, himself slouched in his seat smoking as the afternoon gets heavy. "There's something I like. . . . I like his look."

"To use Jerry's expression," says Harnick, "he's one of them, not one of us."

"Oh, really? . . . Well, I don't see him as James. Oh, make him a CBL. I said 'Enjoy the scene,' but he didn't change at all."

" '. . . How weary, stale, flat, and unprofitable seem to me all the uses of this world!' " an actor cries. " 'Fie on't, ah fie! 'Tis an unweeded garden. . . .' "

"He's very nervous," says the director.

"He has a winning quality"—Harnick.

Yellen says, "A fantastic reading, but nervous . . ."

" '. . . That it should come to this—but two months dead; nay not so much, not two . . .' "

"That energy could be converted into something interesting," Bock muses. "It's Kalman breaking through with all kinds of things. . . ."

"You're a what's-it artist," says an actor at once, asked to do comedy. "You paint something and people say, 'What is it?' . . . I can do Phyllis Diller." He is sent to study brother James.

"To me, just from looks," Bock says of still another, "he's on their side." The reference appears to be a distinction between Jews and non-Jews, or at least between Rothschilds and their then contemporaries. "But he's so deft."

Harnick says thoughtfully, "I could accept him on our side."

"John, thank you. Thank you very much indeed. Thank you." Out.

Another:

"I like him."

"I see him as a brother."

"He's . . . feisty," Bock says, rolling his shoulders like a boxer to illustrate.

"It's dismal"—Yellen later about hearing his words read. "The only time I liked it was when Hal Linden read, and he went beyond the lines. I could learn something new from him about them."

Bury and Bill Liberman have worked out an "availability chart" at 19½.

"You look for a forty-year-old lady who can play a whore *and* an elderly peasant woman," says Bury with pleasure.

"Four soldiers here; swap them for three servants . . . look for similarities, work out costume changes in terms of when people come on and go off, so that they can double: get it worked out on a chart in time and place, and you have a production. . . .

"I had no idea how expensive things were here. . . . And this flying of the Atlantic with a few pieces won't do. I must bring myself close to a total commitment and come over to live. . . .

"I was told Broadway musicals wanted spectacle and none of my Brechtian empty stages, but I come here with spectacle and find it's too expensive!"

A call from Goldby.

"Hello, Derek. Oh, fine." He is studying the chart. "We're down to 144. . . . It's going to be a drag ball at the end—all your kings and emperors and three girls. . . . You've got *one* female pogromee. One other large female laughing would be good—smashing. . . . The main thing is, you've got your charts now."

The stage designer, decisive himself, wants firm decisions. "I mean, I came here for decisions. Sherman says, 'I won't change this.' Sheldon says, 'What about that?' Jerry says, 'We must all stick together.' Manny taps me on the knee and says that I must make my own decisions and go ahead. Well, that's all very well. . . ." He talks about the meetings that followed the first one with its coffee and pastry. "You missed the nasty parts. You were there the first day for the congratulations." He seems cheerful about it himself. "Just write: 'John Bury packed his bags and went home.' End chapter six."

It seems firm that Grover Dale is out: no agreement was reached between his agent and EPIC, and a new choreographer must be found. Replacements are considered: Eliot Feld, perhaps, or Howard Jeffrey; Donald McKayle, who did *Golden Boy*. It is uncertain. . . .

Press agent Sam Friedman, who has been in the hospital for surgery, is now at home and calls to his office get through to him there, so that his business goes forward. Fortunately, most of his contribution to the production lies ahead. The pace shifts into higher gear. Raising the money, which had once seemed a minor problem, becomes major. The economy is not what it was, and the postponement has made difficulties. Hilly the money-earner is not doing it at this point, and he stands at the base of a harassing climb.

Dancer-choreographer Eliot Feld begins attending auditions. He is small, dark, intense.

"I *want* eight male dancers, ideally, and eight girl dancers," he says. "I could do it with six and six, for example, with big costumes and other people filling in. *Or* eight males and six girls. But then I'd need one to cover, because girls will stay out. . . ."

Feld watches small boys audition. It distresses him. "Oh, my God! I'd like to kill his mother. . . . *There was nothing childlike about him!* This is totally out of my area, but that's so totally inhuman what he's doing up there!" (" '*Me?* I'm sittin' pretty!' "—a boy in brown-and-white Atlantic City-looking shoes putting over a song.) "Of course, his voice changes in September. That's why his mother's mad; she'd cut his balls off."

Hilly has appeared in the theater; he makes directly for the dancer, with whom he must deal quickly in the matter of hiring, since time is short; the choreographer, according to EPIC, negotiates firmly. "How are you?" Feld asks at once, firing first.

"Okay, except for you."

"It's mutual."

They confer at the back of the theater. ". . . Your reality isn't necessarily the same as mine," the dancer says.

"How much can I *pay* this putz choreographer?" Hilly asks later in the office.

"You can't do more than 1 percent," answers Azenberg. The general manager, who still plays for the Madison Square Garden baseball team in the New York inter-theater league, wears sneakers and khakis and leans on a Louisville Slugger as if it were a cane. "We played the *Calcutta* team. 'Traitor!' they were yelling at me."

Hilly says concerning some hidden matter, "Gentlemen, we're on the brink," without enthusiasm. "Get me Jack in California and Jay Frankel, and we'll blow this thing wide open. . . ."

"First time up at bat I knock it out of the ball park." He shows his swing. "I was batting .420."

"That's because you play against fags."

"They play good."

Sheldon Harnick drops into the office, and Manny holds forth about dance rehearsals.

"We start July 6, open August 10 in Detroit. . . . We don't think of this as a big dance show, and five weeks of rehearsal seems to me very valid."

"The Muscular Dystrophy people have asked if they can get a closed-circuit TV performance of *Rothschilds* prior to opening for a quarter of a million dollars," Hilly declares, and Harnick chuckles involuntarily. But it is a rare ray of light and in fact will not work out.

A stack of loan agreements is on secretary Barbara's desk, which, when signed and in force, will enable EPIC and LOPI (Lester Osterman Productions, Inc.) to spend the money they are raising for the show before it is fully financed. . . . Their

SEC-filed money-raising prospectus requires general partners Elkins and Osterman to list theatrical experience and accomplishments, as well as to warn prospective limited partners in a larger way of the hazards of the investment. Particularly in recession time, the confessions make gloomy reading.

The Rothschilds will have to run on Broadway for twenty-two weeks to capacity houses in order to return initial contributions. EPIC and LOPI must point out that 90 percent of the shows in the 1967–68 season failed to run that long, and of the ones that did "it is not believed that any played continuously to full capacity audiences."

Finally, the producers are required to make a declaration as to past performance. For Hilly, only *Oh! Calcutta!* shows a gain to date, but it is a substantial one, and the show is still running and earning. Osterman's sole money success out of six listed productions, including *High Spirits* and a revival of *Dinner at Eight,* is the U.S. production of *Hadrian VII,* which closed in November, 1969, and which returned a gain of ten cents on each dollar invested.

The Rothschilds Company is proposed as a limited partnership capitalized at $850,000, or 50 units of $17,000 each. Fractional units may be issued, but investments of less than $500 are not supposed to be accepted. Hilly and Osterman are to raise 50 percent of the total each as things stand. They are the general partners in the partnership, with authority over the use to which the raised money is put, within the bounds their prospectus defines. The backers are limited partners, whose power in the production is, generally speaking, limited to being hopeful. . . . With general manager Azenberg's help, the production will in fact come in for less than the proposed $850,000.

"I called Sammy," says the producer another day. "He said he won't invest, but he'll be here."

A silence. "Byron said nothing?" Manny asks.

"Byron was hemming and hawing. I'll push him."

"I'm going to have dinner tonight with So-and-so," says Platt.

Another pause.

Hilly taps the desk with a pencil. "Anybody else?"

"Let me call Eddie Jaffe right now."

Approaching investors becomes the accustomed office background. All other matters go forward, but most are colored by the pressing need for money. "Barbara, I want Elliott Gould regarding the twentieth. . . . Get me Hal Linden. . . ."

He shuffles bills, is astonished by the amount of one, and pretends to eat it. He then pretends to set fire to Malina's tie. Both Nathan Rothschild (Paul Hecht) and Mayer Rothschild, his father (Hal Linden), are close to signing, but there is a dispute about billing. "Each one think he's the most important part of the show," says Hilly on the phone.

"There's no star part. Nathan? Mayer?" says Manny. He is just in from another ball game; there are hand prints where he gripped his knees taking leads off first and second. "First billing means first billing—on ads, cards—that's all. It's over." He shrugs. "They're like children. Hecht would blow the whole thing. . . ."

Backers' and casting auditions continue through May, as does the exacting work of contracts. Bury will come to remain in June, and the building of the sets must begin no later than the fifteenth. (Feller Scenic Studio in the Bronx got the contract.) Feld is out, and Michael Kidd, who has been in Hollywood for several years, is about to sign to be the show's choreographer. "He likes the script," George says, "and he'll do it, but I don't know about the price. After all, it's one or two dance numbers. . . . We gotta get somebody this week or we'll lose the dancers to summer stock." There are sounds heard of what's to come. "Nothing to do at nights?" asks an announcer on Detroit radio. "Going to stay home and do your stamp collection? Boil water?" He laughs a little. ". . . Go to the Fisher Theatre this summer. They will show *The Rothschilds* by the authors of *Fiddler on the Roof.*"

By June 1, Kidd is "all but signed." Bock and Harnick labor, going over their work repeatedly at backers' auditions for people who are more reluctant to part with their cash than they have been in years. Guest lists for these are drawn up, revised, invitations sent or phoned; a typical one, headed "Those who have accepted," includes both a Van Rensselaer, Mr. and Mrs. Edward Sarnoff, and the owner of the delicatessen where EPIC phones daily for its lunches. George says that his butcher was in for a $17,000 unit, but that instead he's invested $500 (the lowest permissible subunit; in practice, the producers take almost any amount). "From filet mignon to hamburger," George says.

Bill talks to Sam Friedman about requesting a ticket agency on Forty-sixth Street to move its sign. To pedestrians walking west on Forty-sixth from Broadway, the sign is seen to cover the Lunt-Fontanne side marquee and its *Rothschilds* board. (The agency will comply eventually.) Friedman now goes to his office. Bill talks to Hilly's New York lawyer: "So do what you can about it," gets off, and announces, "The market's down again today." He reports to Hilly. The producer stares.

"Am I finished? Is that what you're going to ask me?"

Hilly nods. They find time to do a short sketch.

"I had a dream that I was fired again."

"That was wish fulfillment, only it was my wish."

"It's why I'm being strong: to feel loved and wanted."

"You're loved and wanted. *Now* will you get out?"

"Well," he says a moment later on the phone, "if you decide you want a rooting interest in the show, I want you in on it. . . ."

Platt on his phone continues the search for actresses for Gutele. "This is not a Jewish lady! This is not Joan Loring. . . I'm not yelling. . . . This is not Joan Loring doing *Awake and Sing!* . . ."

Hilly is saying on his, "Charlie, you wouldn't want to be out raising $850,000. That's my worry. . . . Charlie, I will discuss it with Michael. . . ." Azenberg and Malina are in the office. Hilly carries on conversations with them and Charlie simultaneously. "What do we do with the truck and bus ads?. . . Wait a second, Manny. Are there any other points we want Charlie's opinion on? . . . Okay, Charlie, have a nice weekend. . . . Will you get off my fuckin' back on that one? . . . You'll queer the deal for two lousy house seats?"

It is time to pick up Claire, who has been shopping. Hilly lifts a closed louver, squints through at the weather, then departs with an umbrella. Someone has sent the actress a dozen yellow roses, and they are on his desk.

Most of the major casting is completed by June 6. Derek Goldby has had what he describes as "general character talks" with Hal Linden and Paul Hecht, now signed . . . "at dinners and so on. . . ." He will not do his actual blocking until early July. "I do very little. Some directors do a lot to get the play on its feet. No, I haven't made notes with which to talk to the actors." He does not, as he warned some months before, want to talk about his method now that he is deep into it.

Richard Pilbrow, the lighting designer, is in the country with John Bury, and there are meetings. Pilbrow lighted Goldby's *Rosencrantz* both in London and in New York, did *Zorba* in the U.S., and has a long list of credits in England. He will stay briefly, go back to England, and return in August just before the Detroit opening. His work is in a generalized state now; when the set is on the stage and actors in costume are in front of it, then he will make of his imagined pictures "electrical-mechanical" ones . . . "light compositions." He does not mind being in a book. "Wonderful! There's many a show one wishes there had been a book written about. . . . Oh, no. I'm delighted."

He is a young cheerfully smiling man with straight long hair going gray and a beard and mustache that make him look like James Joyce in Paris. At no point during the production will anything appear to ruffle him. Both of the English designers, hard-working and professional as they are, show something of the detachment of men translating foreign disaster, as well as an air of the liberation shy men feel in talking another language well, saying some things in it that they mightn't say at home.

Charles Gray, the stage manager—a clean-shaven aristocratic-looking Princetonian, as unflappable by trade as the Englishmen appear by nature to be—attends these meetings in the basement office, as does Mike Thoma, production supervisor—a competent, dedicated theaterman. From first to final curtain during rehearsal and performance Gray and Thoma hold between them the backstage command, conducting there as Greene will in the pit, while directors and producers watch from in front.

As production draws near, Azenberg, who teaches a class in practical theater at NYU, becomes narrative occasionally for my benefit. "Now we're reaching a point where there is literally no time," he says.

Bury examines muskets and swords that litter the general manager's desk. "Yes. Good for officer French or officer Hessian."

"Scabbarded?"

"Yes, scabbarded."

"Look, this is the center of gravity of the stage," Pilbrow is saying. . . . "We must *nominate* three or four windows that have lights in them so that it doesn't look like a New York skyscraper. . . ."

"What's the situation with airconditioning up there?" Gray says on the phone, arranging for rental of a rehearsal hall. "That's a problem in July. . . ."

"I talked about using a winch," Bury is saying, "but he started rubbing his hands with glee and talking about electromotive force. . . ." Scenery and costume supervisor Fred Voelpel begins, "Dick . . . does one call you Dick or Richard?"

"It *is* Richard, actually," says Pilbrow cheerfully. "But I don't mind being called Dick in moments of stress."

A major purpose of this meeting is to discuss with Michael Kidd, the finally signed choreographer, his preliminary ideas and begin mutual accommodation between dancer and designers, since sets and costumes affect movement. Kidd arrives. He is a small, square, tough-looking man with curling hair. When he listens, he does so completely, unsmiling, thinks over what he has heard right on the spot, taking what time he needs, then replies plainly and to the point.

5

A dancers' audition, June 9:

"Has everybody got a card for me?"

The dance captain is Pat Cummings, who has worked with Kidd before; he will demonstrate the movements Kidd devises, rehearse dancers himself, and otherwise assist the choreographer. Today is for the girls, and a great number is on the stage of the Lunt-Fontanne. They wear leotards, tights, and hair bands; some are in dancing slippers, some in sneakers, a few in bare feet. The leotards are cut to the waist, so that their legs are long and their muscular behinds revealed. They work out against the whitewashed rear wall of the theater, doing splits and calisthenics. A girl in black leg warmers sits, places her hands on the stage, stands casually upright on them, flips over backward onto her feet, and looks as if someone else had done it. Unbleached-muslin shrouding on the theater seats has been rolled back from the first rows.

"Girls! Girls! Come on stage, please!"

They move from the wings.

"Back up, please."

"Good morning. I'm Michael Kidd."

He introduces the others, then says, "I'm assuming that since this is an open call some of you are unfamiliar with the audition procedure. . . . Pat Cummings will show you the steps we want. . . . Relax. Take it easy." And, when it is fully explained: "Let's go ahead and give the audition, and it will be an experience at least." They laugh. "Back up in line. . . . Sort of loosen up. . . ."

"It must be agony for some of them the first time around," says Manny aside. "He's a *mensch*," he declares of Kidd; "the way he introduced them to it. . . ."

"How many will he pick?"

"Four."

Almost eighty have answered the call.

There is an upright in the wings, and production pianist Sande Campbell plays Strauss waltzes. Cummings leaps from a rear corner of the stage, feet scissoring neatly behind him in a series of cabriolets (the leap of the he-goat), stops, and turns, showing no apparent increase in respiration. "We must start eliminating rather rapidly," he says, "because there are so many of you ladies. When you stop, you'll be told, for example, 'Numbers one and three remain.' Those who remain go to the right of the stage. . . ."

The piano. Four-girl teams do their cabriolets, one behind the other, and Kidd chooses: "Numbers two and three remain. One and four, thank you."

It proceeds steadily, the rejected girls leaving the field at once. At last Kidd gives a gentle Avenue A whistle, fingers in his mouth. "Let's try it a little faster, just a very little bit faster."

Occasionally all four are asked to remain or all thanked and dismissed. In ten minutes the eighty have been reduced to forty or so. With elimination, the choice becomes more exacting. Kidd moves to the front row. "Remember, ladies, there is very little time for us to see you. Try to draw our attention to you in a nice way." A nervous laugh from them.

Later, Cummings demonstrates a more complicated series of movements, leaping and turning, arms raised: "*One*-two-three, *two*-two-three, *three*-two-three, *four*-two-three!" Twenty-five girls remain. They try it. "We'll take it two by two, ladies. Side by side."

Lester Osterman appears, the short, portly co-producer as usual in business gray. He is affable, at the service of his "people." He sits with Kidd. Goldby arrives. He is in sneakers; he wears horn-rimmed glasses. He lights a cigarette, sinks silently into a seat, draping his legs over the seat in front, then disappears with only the cigarette visible, held aloft.

The girl in black leg warmers, who had survived the eliminations with apparent ease until now, and a highly colored blonde are dismissed. Two more; they go jauntily off, kicking high.

"Girls, I want to tell you at this point that you are all good dancers and that we have to use other reasons now," Kidd says. "Size, height, and so on. If you're perplexed at being turned down, it's not because you're not good dancers." And when he and Osterman and others in the audience share a laugh, the choreographer at once addresses the stage. "Sorry.

We're not laughing at you, ladies. And please make jokes about us. . . ." Kidd demonstrates the next step himself, leaping fairly agilely to the stage to do so.

Six.

They line up.

Cummings shows a leap and mid-air turn.

"Don't worry about your elevation," says Kidd. "Just a feeling of flight: heads up. Lift your chests high."

Finally it is decided to keep all six for the moment. The men will be seen the next day, and six of them will be chosen. The choreographer later describes the day's turnout as "light." He has come to expect at least two hundred in an open call for a show of this kind. "There are people who make a career of auditioning. They don't expect to be taken, but they can't not try."

In the afternoon Goldby rehearses a group of small boys in an improvisation intended to show their potential as Rothschilds and in order to do some more eliminating. Disorganized shouts are heard from the balcony lounge. Press agent Sam Friedman, looking well, wanders into the theater, meets Bock, oddly enough for the first time (theatrical class lines being what they are), gets down to business with Kidd: "Mike, would you like to do some writing for me?—'Why Broadway Again?' "

"If I can think of something plausible."

Goldby returns with his boys, having assigned each a Rothschild identity, and lines them up on the stage: "Amshel, Solomon, Nathan, Jacob"—three groups of four. "And two spare Jacobs." Fourteen boys are on stage. "Okay, now remember, you interrupt, but you don't drown him out. Don't be *too* gentle." He comes into the orchestra and says, "This will give you some idea of their personalities."

The boys haggle shrilly, with gusto, one team moving up as

the first finishes, selling each other cars, catcher's mitts, the Brooklyn Bridge, occasionally hitting each other. . . . Half are eliminated. Paul Hecht and Chris Sarandon, grown-up Rothschild sons, climb up and stand beside the remainder to compare looks.

"Would you believe it?" Goldby asks.

"Pretty good."

Bock has the boys sing "Row, Row, Row Your Boat" as a round. Kidd sets them skipping around the stage to fast music, stages a swing-and-miss fight, gets their names straight. Five are chosen finally, but due to contract problems and prior commitments only one will be cast, and more will have to be found elsewhere.

"Well, we cast the boys today," Hilly reports to Manny at the office.

"*Ach!*" cries the general manager. He stands against Hilly's brown cork wall, arms wide, and does a falsetto scale—being a boy auditioning. "*Der liddle pischers.* Did you get one he can go both ways, you should forgive the expression?" He uses a drawing pin as a rapier to stab at the cork, puts on Hilly's blue crash helmet. "Hilly used to be six feet two till he started wearing this." And to an unsmiling Malina, who needs Hilly's attention: "For once in your life be brief. . . . Okay. We'll start negotiating for the boys tomorrow."

Hilly gets Claire on the new intercom to discover her reaction to a film script.

"Did you pick it up?"

"Yes."

"Did you like it?"

She replies in a crackling static-filled voice, "I'm afraid not."

"Don't you like being wanted?"

"Yes."

"What are you doing in the tub?"

"It's the best place to read the script."

6

"Producer HILLARD ELKINS won't mind me telling his wife, CLAIRE BLOOM," says Earl Wilson in his column, "—sorry, honey, you'll have to wait your turn about Hilly producing the Strindberg classic 'Miss Julie' (about a lady and her footman), starring you, because he's got such a mess of work . . . 'Oh! Calcutta!' is a year old. . . .'"

The Sunday *Times* ad shows the *Calcutta* lady on a birthday cake with one candle and the line, "O.K. Everybody. Now Blow!" The slogan was Hilly's idea. "He wanted 'Over the Hump,'" says Barbara, "but everyone thought that was in poor taste."

New York was warming up for another summer. Billy Graham would be in town again for a five-day crusade, at Shea Stadium this time instead of Madison Square Garden. One year later, with My Lai, Kent State, and Jackson, Mississippi, between: "We have allowed the word patriotism to get into the hands of some right-wingers," Graham told the *Times* interviewer. "I don't guess anybody loves the flag more than some of the people that are against the war." The *Daily Enquirer* ran an anniversary story: "JUDY GARLAND IS STILL NOT BURIED." The Krishna-conscious were moving farther uptown and to the east to encounter on Third Avenue the hip ones who stand on corners, fill bookshops, and stand in line for movies that are as expensive as Broadway theaters were a few years ago. Because of the whimsical cruelty that is both the humor and truth of the hip, the Conscious Ones risked mild danger—love beads snatched, a kiss stolen, witty questions—

but received wished-for attention as, in robes, salmon-dyed sneakers, and pigtails, they patted a drum, chanted, shuffled. . . . Graham prepared for "Honor America Day" on July 4. He was co-sponsor with actor Bob Hope. "I called Bob . . . and said, 'Bob, let's keep it up away from the war. This is not prowar or antiwar. Let's make it for all America.' " Alice Brock came into the EPIC offices and complained bitterly about the quality of the food served in one of the restaurants called by her name. In any case, it looked as if the chain would not catch on. Circus-cut poodles were dragged limping along gutters by wealthy men until the bowels of one or the heart of the other would move. Progress had been made on all building, but bombs began to go off in some of the older skyscrapers.

7

"Except for the problem of raising the money—I'm not talking about that—but from the managerial point of view everything is great," says Manny Azenberg. "The show's committed. It would cost more now not to do it than to do it. . . .

"The major contracts have been settled, right? Also, all the principals, except for the women. We should be right on budget. . . . But I don't worry about money; that's all upstairs. I need forty thousand dollars by Friday for scenery and costumes? I need sixty thousand by Monday?—they say I'll get it. Actors get paid, musicians get paid, stage hands get paid. . . . I don't worry, I don't promise: everything correct. I do nothing on my credit." The general manager is confident that he can bring the show in for less than its budget and talks about "real" dollar costs of production: ". . . spent, cash, good-bye . . ." It ought to be around $640,000, as opposed to the $850,000 total capitalization. "The money will be raised; Hilly may have to give away points to get it, and I hope he doesn't have to. But the show's committed, and there's absolutely nothing at this point that's in crisis. . . .

"You want an analogy? . . . You start a musical it's like an avalanche. All you can do is contain it, because you can't stop it. I look upon that as my job: to contain it."

"The show's pretty well cast," says Goldby. "The book is in *very* good shape—ready to go into rehearsal. We're still missing two or three songs; maybe a couple will come after Detroit. No doubt some things won't work in Detroit and may have to be replaced, but we can go."

Joan Hackett is supposed to play Gutele.

Actresses still are being considered for Hannah. One, Jill Clayburgh, was recently in a play in which, George thinks, she was naked except for a covering of whipped cream. "Some guy licked it off," he says in a commemorative tone.

"We go into rehearsal on Monday," the producer says. "I'm around a hundred thousand-odd short, but we're going ahead." Hilly is pledging his own money. "We're doing it the aggravating way for fun. . . . I am tired: in the crunch on several matters. . . ."

He and Malina phone-confer with Osterman.

"Lester, I gotta come up with it. There's no if. . . . Hey, I'm not keeping any secrets! If the two guys I'm talking to pull out *and* Capitol pulls out, I'm in trouble. If either one comes through, I still have problems but I'm not in trouble. . . . We're talking about eighty-five. . . ."

Azenberg finds a sheet of paper after the call.

"Take a bigger piece," Hilly says to him. "This is in the

bag already. . . . The butcher is five hundred-something. Me for a unit"—$17,000—"Schwartzman for a unit . . ." They list it all. "Okay. Is that it?"

Manny totals it. An agonized pause . . . "We got any other possibilities that we know of?" He announces the total.

"That's crazy!" Malina cries. "It should be a hundred and ten!" He adds it. "A hundred and two. A hundred and two! It's a hundred and two."

"What about Frankel?"

"If Capitol said you'd be virtually capitalized, let's finesse Norman."

"I've got a shot. . . ."

"I've got shots too, but I'm not counting on them. . . . Pablo!"—into a telephone. "Seven o'clock tonight, your place. Groovy." Off: "If Capitol says yes, we take Norman's one-half combination. It gives us $158,000, and I don't owe Lester any favors. . . ."

The producer says later, "I'm not unhappy. You know I work well under pressure. I'll get the money. Now my stomach's all right. My back doesn't bother me. . . . We're going to do Ibsen in repertory with Claire. She may do both roles— Hedda and *A Doll's House*. She has qualms, but she's very excited; she can do it. . . .

"I'm a hundred and a half short." Hilly looks at me. "You want to put it up?"

8

It is July 6 in the morning. Rehearsals are to begin, but first there must be a semiformal occasion: a greeting, introductions, photographs for publicity and eventually for the souvenir program, and a read-through of the script. Hilly has

arranged to pick up Osterman and go with him to the rehearsal hall on Broadway. "Lester's collateral is good and mine
is not," the producer says realistically, sprawled in his cab.
"I've used mine in other ways. I accept that." Osterman, he
explains, raised his 50 percent by guaranteeing its return. In
exchange, those investors who used the advantage accepted a
reduction in value of each $17,000 point they had bought.
Hilly, on the other hand, will have to increase the value of
points to get his money. He is calm enough about it at the
moment. Osterman, scrubbed, contented-looking, gets into
the cab. He owns race horses and has recently been to see
some run. "We made enough to pay for the evening."

There is the morning of the first full-cast read-through, as
described.

Act II is run through after lunch.

"I want you to remember what I'm going to say now right
through to opening," Goldby says when it is all over. "Even if
you forget with the front of your mind, you'll know what
we're doing with the back of your mind. . . .

"The show is about power. It's about money, if you like.
It's about persecution. But what the show basically says is
that if you persecute somebody, then he will fight back with
every weapon at his disposal. That is really what *The Rothschilds* is about. The question of whether they're right goes
unanswered. It's a serious show. . . ."

He talks well about it and at length.

". . . Read a little history, get into the period: study your
costumes. We're getting into an area which is not, for Broadway, usual. Think about the costumes and how they'll feel
early on. . . . Another of the things to be concerned about
is words: diction. We have to understand everything you're
saying, and you've got to have respect for the text. . . .

"I'm saying a lot of solemn things. I don't want you going

into this feeling too solemn, which is why I say keep this in the *back* of your mind. . . . We're all very happy we're doing this show.

"We'll take a break. I want to chat with a number of you. . . . Tomorrow we'll start work."

9

Properties contributed to a production are paid for with a program credit, a photograph of the product in use on stage—preferably on or near a star—and, often, free seats. If the show is a hit and the product is visible and recognizable—a Pepsi bottle, for example—then a good return will have been made on a small investment. . . . This give and take has been organized into a business by a company called On The Spot Productions, which EPIC has retained in addition to the merchandiser who will handle the exploitative side of things and a few hard-to-get items (Celanese Corporation's gold-looking show curtain, Con-Tact's blood-red flocked paper for posters, the Rothschild wine, etc.).

Propertyman Frank Love, Bury, and his assistant Voelpel, Platt meet at On The Spot's offices. Samples have been provided.

"We can scuff it up, spray it down," says the merchandiser, watching Bury examine a satchel.

The designer, crowded in the tiny office, runs through his list: prayer shawl, Hebrew Bible ("find real one—old"), arm bands with yellow stars on them. . . .

"I have a bag that's coming back from another show—Gladstone type; and it's currently in town. . . . I can get the prayer shawl. . . . The arm bands would be costume?"

He produces a large cardboard box filled with fake coins. Bury wants variety: ". . . brass discs, washers . . ."

Platt warns, "Actors put 'em in their pockets and walk out with 'em."

Certificates—bonds—are needed; these with other items go on the propertyman's lists—things that cannot be promoted by On The Spot.

". . . wallet. Greasy and flappy, so that when Mayer takes his papers out, they'll seem very precious. . . . In *all* these Jewish props you've got to feel he's had these things all his life. Right . . . Babies! We need five babies or half-babies for sons. . . . Muskets, sabers . . ."

"Lay in an arsenal," says Voelpel, referring to the certainty of changes: "I see weeks of trouble from Michael Kidd."

". . . cigars . . ."

The merchandiser passes some out. "We audition cigars here," he says pleasantly.

". . . broom to sweep up after the pogrom . . ."

" 'What more do we want? What more do we need?' "

Joan Hackett sings, standing by the upright. Greene plays. The actress' tape recorder is on a folding chair, listening. Sheldon Harnick sits on another folding chair reading the New York *Post*.

" 'We have enough—we have enough. . . .' I'm forcing myself."

Four of the five brothers stand by.

"See that?" says Greene, indicating a musical note.

"Is that . . . ?"

Later she sits in a corner attending to the tape. The brothers then sing, responding to her question. " 'We want *everything*' "—thundering in the small room (the company will move from these rooms to the Lunt-Fontanne in a week), and Joan Hackett says, "You sound terrific."

"It's those breathing lessons."

"I think I prefer," says Harnick mildly, having lowered his *Post,* " 'a-nother' to 'uh-nother.' "

Hackett's tape goes on in its corner: " 'What more do we want? . . .' "

"Now the Rothschild boys," Paul Hecht announces, "straight from their smash engagement . . ."

They sing once more. Greene, tidy in the seafarer's whiskers, politely corrects something. . . . Harnick rises. "That's an eighth note—a full crotchet."

"Now, let's do the entire thing," says Greene. "Let's see if I can work out a modulation."

Harnick says, "We have to modulate back."

"That's right."

They do it.

" 'A-nother,' " Harnick reminds them. "And it's a matter of styling. The anger isn't at first. It builds after the interlude to an angry finish." Then he thinks and decides to try it softer and softer instead, each "everything" quieter than the one before to a whisper.

"Yeah," says a brother. "It's a cyclical song that way." And Hecht: "I think it's better soft."

"Joan Hackett quit Saturday," declares Platt a few days later. It is a mystery why to the writer, one that is never properly solved; someone had said that she was not Jewish-looking; some guess that the role was not big enough; her scholarly approach slowed rehearsal pace. "It was stop-press in the paper on Monday. We have selected a replacement," he goes on in a measured tone, "a girl everyone wanted all along except Hilly, and he's giving in. Leila Martin." A certain amount of auditioning continues, particularly for male dancers. "It's because we got our choreographer late."

Since Hilly is still short his share of the capitalization, co-producer Osterman has offered to put it up. Understandably, he wants in return a fifty-fifty profit arrangement plus, not so naturally from Hilly's view, first billing on posters and ads. The problem is tested and tried in a variety of ways, for example, alternating the billing: Hilly first on posters, Lester on ads. Though the producer has agreed in a general way to Osterman's terms, he is still trying hard to raise his own money.

John Bury sits in an outer passage of Ray Diffen's Stage Clothes on West Forty-eighth Street waiting for cast members, freed from rehearsal, to arrive for costume fittings.

"They're all going on about the poverty of the ghettos," he says looking over a book of drawings and engravings of the time that shows Frankfort ghetto-dwellers as well turned out. Dummies bearing stars' measurements stand in corners (Carol Channing, July '65: 34½ inch bust, 23½ inch waist, 34 inch hips). There are plumber's-pipe clothes racks, a gray poodle, scraps of sculpture.

"Oh, leaning on me fabrics," says a bearded boy in striped trousers and love beads mildly. "That won't do." He unrolls some cloth. "Danielle Darrieux's negligee. She wants hers in lavender."

A dancer appears, goes into a fitting room to change. Bury regards her in the mirror, turning his head this way and that. Ray Diffen, tall, wearing a purple-striped shirt and graying shoulder-length hair, glances in from his office, nods, retreats; he looks something like John Gielgud. "I just don't understand," says his fitter around a mouthful of pins. "I said put the black frill on the overskirt, and where'd they put the frill? On the underskirt!" She has a candid Liverpool accent.

Two more dancers have been released for fittings.

"Well, I'm getting back into shape," the boy says. "I notice it in my legs."

"Are you working out?" she asks.

"Well, it's disparaged. If you do a plie . . ."

He is marched in in his peasant costume to stand beside the girl in her peasant costume (one green puffed sleeve, one arm bare, an apron with roses, her feet bare) to see how they will go together.

"He looks so sinister with that black hair," says Diffen.

"Oh, he is sinister," the girl says.

The boy turns his hand into a gun and shoots her in the head with it. They never stop observing themselves and each other in the mirror. Diffen holds a necklace around her. "You don't go all funny if we put brass on you, do you?"

Bury examines Prince William's coat and waistcoat, mounted on dummies. They are magnificent garments (Diffen will charge around $1,000 for them). The woman who sewed them watches anxiously as the designer backs off to squint, pins on gold braid, then removes it. "We've got a line of buttons, don't we?" He checks his sketch, comes to a decision. "Take the pocket away."

"No pocket at all?"

The frail bearded boy, a tailor's tape knotted around his neck, is tracing a pattern; he wears a denim apron and a ring on his right forefinger. The tracing done, he at once begins to cut the rich cloth rapidly with large shears.

"We're in deep water," says Bury, referring to the progress of his work. "I'm trying to steer a middle course so we look all right in Detroit." He is not happy about the American way of production with its chronic changes, the consequence of which is changes in set and costume. "In England the set and props and costumes are final at the outset. Director and actors work within this. Here we're always changing.

"Kidd, all right. He came in late and said yes, yes to everything, because he had to feel his way through designing his dances. Then he finds he needs something: a trick fan or something. But Linden, rehearsing, says, 'Well, look, I want the scales over here instead,' and Derek says okay. But the scales are designed to go in one place! If the method actors"—he illustrates with a Thinker pose—"would *read* Stanislavski instead of getting him fourth hand, they'd see he always gets his terms of reference clear. If you and I are improvising walking down the street, we still need to know the weather, if it's cobbles or grass, etcetera. . . . They waste so much money this way—all this talking everything out.

"Well, it's just press-on time, and we'll see what we have in Detroit."

A Broadway musical has three directors: the choreographer, who must answer for any kind of designed movement, not just formal numbers; the musical director, responsible for the quality and reading of songs as well as his orchestra; and the titled director, whose work is the acting and informal movement. He is also given over-all command, with veto power over the other directors, as well as general responsibility. . . . Composer, lyricist, and book author are supposed to be around to make or approve changes and, if asked and sometimes if not, offer suggestions, though not directly to performers.

At the Lunt-Fontanne on a typical day during early rehearsal, before the three elements are put permanently together and run through again and again, Greene will be in the basement lounge with pianist Campbell rehearsing chorus, Goldby in the balcony lounge with the Rothschilds as children, and Kidd will have the grown-up brothers on stage. A folding screen is set up in the wings stage right, behind it the stage manager's table with script, stop watch, cooking timer, clipboards, a policeman's whistle, and some temporary props (a

stick to give Prince William authority, umbrellas, ghetto hats).
In the audience a three-by-five sheet of plywood laid over
seat backs at about row M is strewn with attaché cases, scripts,
notebooks, foolscap pads, and coffee cartons. Dust sheets cover
the first ten rows of seats.

Company manager Ted Thompson, in the bunker at 19½,
pores over charts on which the company has indicated its
hotel preferences in Detroit and Philadelphia. Social and professional lines are drawn here, though not enforced; income and
community of function are the guides. Production people stay
at the St. Regis in Detroit, the rest at the Abington or Leland
House. In Philadelphia it will be the Bellevue for production
and creative people, the Sylvania for actors and chorus. . . .
Manny continues to chew over costs: "Ninety thousand for
Pete. Hair's going to be seven thousand. . . ."

Still another audition, for the owners of one more record
company, is in progress on the third floor, and Hilly, with
Osterman and Platt, waits this one out, checking hors d'oeuvres
in the kitchen, pacing in the hall. The producer has a collection of walking sticks, which he keeps in brass and copper stands
here and there in the apartment, and he suddenly plucks one
out and raises it threateningly.

"What's your natural reaction? What is it?"

People cannot react naturally because they are betting
that Hilly won't hit them. Osterman doesn't want to play.
Others grin sheepishly.

"Come on!"

We are supposed to grab and hold the stick; whereupon,
hauling on the handle, he will draw a stiletto from the cane's
shaft.

He looks exhausted and has put on weight.

The audition ends. Hilly asks the prosperous potential

backer, "Richard, you want a prospectus to look at? . . . Manny!"—like a headwaiter—"Prospectus and partnership!"

It is pouring rain, and George and Hilly run around looking for umbrellas to get the man, his wife, and millionaire father-in-law safely to their cars. . . .

In his bedroom later, packing to catch a plane to London for *Oh! Calcutta!* previews and opening, the producer glances over newspaper layouts.

"Can the first names be smaller than the last?" asks Bill Liberman.

"Yep!"

"Shall I line Fred Morton's name under Harnick's?"

"He gets 75 percent of the size."

"Is that the deal you made?"

Hilly gazes sourly at the Elkins-Osterman billing. It is in that order for Detroit but by no means agreed upon for Philadelphia and New York. The capitalization arrangement has been settled. "I had to give up points and take alternate billing. . . . That's show biz. I've been on this seven years. Everyone in the business knows it's my show, and they'll know Hilly Elkins had to give up points and take alternate billing." He adds, however, "Lester could've squeezed me. He didn't."

The magazine *Esquire* had sent a photographer to do an illustration for an edited piece of this book scheduled to appear in its pages in the fall of 1970, and Hilly refused to sit under his portrait of Napoleon and strike the same pose. It is one of the changes being worked.

"They were surprised. It's the first time I ever said no to anything like that."

"I started in this business at fourteen grindin' out movies standin' on a box in Port Jervis," says production propertyman Frank Love. He got into props in 1958, first in summer stock, and soon moved on to Broadway; the work, he says, is not much sought after because it is demanding both of time and energy. He refers often to his age, which is seventy, and is proud of the fact that it does not slow him down. "At eight o'clock the foolin' is over; the curtain has to go up. . . . Nobody has any pride in their work today. It's the unions do it. . . ."

We meet at State Supply Company's main warehouse in the Wall Street district, a company that specializes in properties for entertainment industries. TV is its prime customer.

"We're lookin' for cashboxes and plastic glasses," Love begins. He sits in the ground-floor office, prop list ready, scholarly for the moment in spectacles, pencil aloft. "How about fruit baskets?" A preliminary check will save time upstairs. The office is crowded with odd objects: a Yukon Territory license plate with five zeros, for example.

"What size?"

"Like fruit baskets."

An office boy brings plastic drinking glasses, which Love looks over and rejects. He needs something on the order of cut glass. "If we could get 'em thicker, we could score 'em ourselves. It's a nice glass, though. . . . Sam?" he asks the owner, whose name is Max. "How about red sealin' wax? And, oh— you got a prayer shawl?"

"Parasol?"

"Prayer shawl."

"We got that."

Love explains aside: "I call him Sam."

The warehouse has five floors and an open freight elevator. From the elevator on each floor a pass leads out through ceiling-high properties. I see a monkey-jungle of park benches. "Most of this is used on TV," says Love. "With this guy you can buy. The others generally rent. And he'll get anything he don't have." A great many old juke boxes, all kinds of telephones, outboard motors, ships' binnacles, ladders . . . The office boy follows. Horse harness, carpenter's tools, a two-man saw, parking meters.

"The sabers?"

"With big hilts? . . . Get rid of this." Max hands his Styrocup, empty of coffee, to the boy, and we set off into a dark forest past banks of gutted consoles. "Sixty running feet of the NASA Space Center for a TV commercial. You want a barbershop? Beauty shop?"—barber chairs and hair dryers to the rafters. "Coney Island thirty years ago?" Stacks of angular old canvas finger-pinchers. "I don't wanta sell 'em at any price. You can't *get* the crap." A gondola for an ascension balloon, old luggage. "We did every suitcase for *Hello, Dolly!*" The baskets. Max is on a ladder peering into a loft. "Wine baskets, flower baskets"—searching. "Megaphones. Frank, I'll send you on your merry way for baskets. Try West Fourth Street."

July 22, the Lunt-Fontanne.

A scene has gone particularly well, and Sherman Yellen, gaunt and grinning in his bush shirt, says, "When it goes well, they want me around." And Lester Osterman: "You should have seen it. It raised goose bumps."

A "gypsy run-through" is being planned: the chorus boys and girls (the gypsies) from neighborhood shows will be invited for a Sunday performance to get audience response. Goldby would prefer an audience not directly connected with show business.

Kidd is now getting into the climactic scene, in which the Rothschild brothers force Metternich to come to terms by offering for sale cheaply bonds he is selling dear. There are twenty-four people on stage. The girls, in leotards, hose, and heels, are torn, move back and forth between the brokers' conflicting offers, a hand upraised each time in startled surprise, wanting to buy. The boys, in tight jeans, singlets, or T-shirts, and sneakers, turn indecisively too, not knowing with whom to spend their money—Prince Metternich, to whose class they belong, or the Jewish Rothschilds, who offer a bargain.

Kidd's whistle.

"Sande? Restore the cut."

He has a bullhorn, which he does not appear to like to use, and is dressed in his usual plain style, ineffably suggestive of a tougher, plainer theater world (today he wears the kind of maroon polo shirt boys wore at summer camps in 1938). Bock, who had also risen to set things straight, musically, subsides. The scene is done again and again, broken off midway, discussed. Kidd's whistle keeps ringing out. The brothers are being rehearsed elsewhere by Goldby, and girls, cutely wearing ghetto hats, play their roles. It all begins to come together. The whistle: "Every time you buy a certificate, instead of raising your hand go up and get it. . . . Take a step and a stop, and you have to come back."

"From ze top, Mike?" asks an actor.

Movements grow increasingly precise, controlled, humorous, meaningful.

The whistle.

Bock takes a meerschaum from a sackful of belongings, fills, and lights it. Goldby strolls down the aisle with his brothers, having finished with them; they leap nimbly to the stage. One cups his hands and performs a jazz trumpet while he waits. Bock and Leila Martin go upstairs to rehearse the new Gutele song—"That's How Much I Missed You" (it will be replaced out of town)—and she asks after a time, referring to the key, "Higher?" Linden descends to the lounge with Greene for separate work. Harnick tells Yellen that he has produced some new lyrics incorporating both his and Kidd's ideas.

"None of the girls has any figgers, you see," John Bury is

saying, gazing at the girls on stage. He is discussing the low-cut Regency gowns he designed for the ball. "Then Michael has them raise their arms." He demonstrates. "And they come up over them. Then they lower them and they fall out."

The designer, his wife, who does the drawings of properties that must be built and of details of the set, and builder Pete Feller make a progress tour at Feller's Bronx studios another day.

The raked stage floor is completed. The Rothschilds' ghetto house, built though yet unpainted, has still to have its mechanical doors installed. Bury looks it over critically, ascends its little spiral staircase. The house is tilted back to compensate for the incline of the stage. Elsewhere, a workman applies brick-shaped slabs of Masonite to one of the stage pillars (two sides smoky old brick for the ghetto, two gold and white rococo for the palace; a motor hidden in them will turn them), which is laid out on saw horses. A fly piece of large gilt cherubs playing musical instruments is being carved out of Styrofoam by a sculptor with a saw and kitchen knife. A heavily rusticated piece of wall, its stony texture of glue, paint, and cork chips, lies nearby. Black paint, sand, asbestos, glue, and sawdust give the backdrop of ghetto houses their look of ancient misery.

Bury must be diplomatic with the workmen. "The carpentry can be controlled from the drawing office," he says, "but as you get to completion, as with all interpretive artists, if you push them too far, say too much, give them too many notes, you alienate them and defeat your ultimate purpose. You must be very careful. It's the same with the costume makers." He looks around at the projects going forward in the warehouse studio, some of it better work than others, at the absorbed men. "That's still too bright," he says finally to one busy with a can of khaki-colored paint.

"A lot of John's work is putting himself into other people's minds," Mrs. Bury says. She oversees the work of a man spraying paint on metal flags—"To make them look older, the sort you'd have in Germany in 1780. Old rags." A balcony workshop is crowded with motors and winches to work the scenery, which must also be trucked to Detroit and Philadelphia. . . . Bury has brought along Polaroid shots of Keene Curtis in costume for a royal portrait of William, and he hands them over to the man who will do the job; it is to be painted on Masonite, rough side out to suggest canvas: a prop rather than a painting, it must be recognizable from the balcony.

Later in Feller's offices, which look down on the warehouse work area as on a prison yard, the designer and his wife settle themselves at drafting tables.

"NUDEST SHOW ON EARTH HEADS FOR LONG WEST END RUN."
"*Calcutta*'s just a dirty joke. . . ."
EPIC's receptionist pastes reviews of the London opening into a scrapbook.

"MUCH ADO ABOUT NOTHING ON"—the *Evening Standard*, which includes what it calls a "picture probe" with man-in-the-street interviews like the ones of a year ago in front of the Eden. ("I was hoping to be sexually aroused, but I wasn't at all. It was very feeble.")

The *Daily Telegraph*: "LAUGHABLE INSOLENCE OF OH! CALCUTTA!"

From a letter to the *Times* of London: ". . . The Dowager Lady Birdwood and others—who have written the Director of Public Prosecutions objecting to the work—are therefore merely helping Mr. Tynan and his producers to add another fortune to the one already gathered from gullible, thrill-seeking Americans."

"It is a ghastly show," says the *Times* itself: "ill-written, juvenile, and attention-seeking. But it is not a menace."

Variety in New York breaks the story of the closed-circuit

TV production of *Oh! Calcutta!*, which is set for September 28. It is to be shown in movie theaters across the United States at a $10 top. As of May 31 in New York *Oh! Calcutta!* had earned a profit of $222,660 on its investment of $100,000, according to *Variety*.

Four small Rothschilds play ball with a coffee carton in the basement lounge of the Lunt. They use sofa cushions for bases. The oldest is good-looking and bright, nervously tough. Proudly, he tells of having made stage manager Gray angry because they went up into a loft above the auditorium (there was a ghost, he claims, in the dark projection booth), out over the ceiling of the theater, past where the Phantom of the Opera once hid to cut loose the chandelier on an unsuspecting audience, to a catwalk high in the flies, and then safely to the stage, having knocked some plaster down. He accuses of cowardice in not having accompanied them a stage brother who protests: "I was there! I went up later!" On being asked, each will recite theatrical and TV credits rapid-fire: *Oliver, Mame,* daytime soapers, commercials, etc. . . . Nathan Rothschild, hit in the face with the crumpled cup, takes off after Amshel.

July 30:
The Mayor warns New Yorkers that they must be prepared for the banning of all private vehicles from certain areas of the city and declares the first stage of an emergency alert. An air-pollution panic is in progress, threatening enough for a day or two to move Vietnam off the front pages. Instead, there are tips: slow down, eat less, drink water, go to the movies.

"Our living is causing our dying," cries an NBC radio news commentator, while someone coughs incessantly in the studio behind him. At 11 A.M. the city is like fire, and against its hard dark yellow haze we seem printed flat, as if we had slipped out of the real world at last. Masses of people grow gloomy and take shallow breaths.

Hilly in the heat wave, scarlet-faced ("My heart attack"), natty in the ongoing crises, is maneuvering on his share in the closed-circuit TV deal. "I have taken such nonsense from Floria Lasky," he says on the phone to an agent named Gloria Safier: "I just don't want to go through the chopper with Floria. . . ."

Later, Hilly gone (he is busy arranging for Claire's movie, *Red Sky at Morning*—she is now in Los Angeles to discuss the shooting schedule and costumes—and his leasing of an off-Broadway theater for her Ibsen plays), Malina and Azenberg work out a letter from the producer regarding the division of closed-circuit profits. "We'll say 10 percent for 'other creative elements.' Everyone's going to get hysterical anyway. . . ." Etc. Malina is angry. He pulls a sample orange-yellow *Calcutta* sweatshirt on over his shirt and tie and cries furiously, "George, come here! You want your *kids* to wear this? They should be on toilet bowl covers!" The same people who manufactured the Spiro Agnew T-shirts made them. Manny, outraged as well, agrees. "Sweatshirts with asses on them!" he cries righteously.

"It's all logistics now—getting people hotel rooms, sets moved," says the general manager. "It's departmentalized, and the only thing we can do is hope everyone does his job.

" 'Ultimately money doesn't concern us,' " he quotes Goldby as having said concerning the installation of a new scene in the show. "I said, 'You bet your ass money concerns you. You're in the commercial theater now, baby. You put in a new scene for twenty-five thousand dollars, and do this a few times before New York, and we're out of business! If the show grosses only sixty thousand in Detroit, you won't get a *prop!*'

"It's nonsense-time, panic-time. It's all so transient. It's love-you-today-hate-you-tomorrow-time, and if we have a hit, it'll all be forgotten."

Azenberg gets partner Malina on the phone in a restaurant where he is lunching with Osterman, finds a moment for dialect: "Izzat you, Mista Fettucini? Ah whatsa you sheddule, hah? . . ."

Out-of-town per diem expense allowances—a sampling from the top: Bock, Harnick, and Kidd, $40. Goldby, $50 (more because he is out of his native country). Yellen, $40 . . .

A run-through at the Lunt-Fontanne. It is supposed to be nonstop.

The cast is crowded into the wings at right behind Gray's table in a litter of sandwich papers, knitting, bicycles, and crash helmets. Waiting for cues, they read books, do crosswords, study scripts. A couple of girls in twin leotard-and-tights outfits sit one above the other on a stage ladder. The mood is good; the moment of actually doing the show has drawn close enough to see. Yellen appears with a briefcase. He has been, as always, writing changes and looks ill and stooped. Osterman stands with a proprietary air center stage before the run-through.

"We're going to paint the walls three shades darker to black out easier," he says. "We'll have re-seating, carpeting, new rigging, a new front curtain. Fifty thousand dollars it'll cost. We have a one-year lease, and we can renew. . . ." He looks embarrassed. "Have you heard about the billing? 'Lester Osterman Presents Hillard Elkins' Production of . . .' It's crazy, but it was the only solution." He talks generally about running his theaters; among other innovations he claims to have re-formed his box-office people, a class with an old reputation for rudeness. "They say, 'Thank you,' and, 'I hope you enjoy the show,' " at his 46th Street. . . . "I had to fire two guys to achieve that."

Hilly is on the phone in an office off the stage door. Bock, Harnick, and Goldby confer, the last in blue bells and puffy-sleeved orange shirt. The run-through starts, is stopped, and Kidd leaps to the stage. Again: "Places, *please!*" Gray shouts. The creative element settle in their seats. Greene's hand is upraised; the show will be seen from start to end for nearly the first time. The piano . . .

When it is over, Bock leads the applause.

"Good!"

All stand to applaud the company gathered on the apron. They are asked to appear at ten next morning. Then creators, directors, producers, and principal actors confer. Everyone has taken notes, including the author of this book.

Obvious problems in realizing the musical seem to be in Yellen's department, though some songs are weak or too can-didly reminiscent of *My Fair Lady* and *Threepenny Opera*. There is reliance on Shavian epigrammatic wit, a Yellen weak-ness that is helpful and funny at best but at worst is a strain: a good imitation of an unregretted literary fashion. Small plot flaws beg questions. Why would William's minister confide in Mayer Rothschild? Aren't Mayer and the Prince too quickly friends? Etc. Also, the itch to draw modern parallels has led to heavy work and a didactic tone. The son Nathan grows from imprudent boy to sensible man without conviction, and his love affair seems gratuitous. There are speeches, a tendency to be sloganlike ("Stand straight today so our people can stand straight tomorrow"—a line that will be cut). Everyone is agreed that there is too little music; the staging is often mechanical: the boys' selling in the store; the pogrom; the mother and sons' scene near the end, which is all sit, stand, cross, sit, stand, cross, and so burdened with exposition that our attention fails. . . . All of these problems and others are to be recognized and discussed now and out of town, most will be tackled, some will be solved.

Hilly asks if I have heard of the final decision on billing. Lester Osterman would have preferred to have Hilly present him. He sketches it on an envelope so that it will be clear:

LESTER OSTERMAN PRODUCTIONS

presents

HILLARD ELKINS' PRODUCTION

of

In fact it will turn out to be:

LESTER OSTERMAN

presents

The HILLARD ELKINS Production

of

"You think it's silly, right?"

The producer's humor is improved. There had been recently a suggestion of uncertainty in his business style, and he appeared to be relying on the Azenberg-Malina advising team more heavily than a Hilly-like wish to get his money's worth out of staff would lead an observer to expect. But now, with financing all but settled, even if not to his satisfaction, and Detroit imminent, he appears to be cooler even in the heat wave, to bounce back.

He interviews an Englishman about the chance of producing a show called *AC/DC*. Hilly saw it in London on his recent trip and liked it. The Englishman wears silver bracelets, a fringed belt, high-heeled cowboy boots, a necklace, and shoulder-length hair, out of which a middle-aged face watches carefully. He has brought his scrapbook of reviews: *"AC/DC* begins with a three-way fuck in a photo booth and ends with a trepan operation. If that puts you off, don't go. . . ."

A meeting with the man who is to produce the closed-circuit *Oh! Calcutta!*:
"One of the problems is you're into a lot of long-shot shit," Hilly declares.
They can pick up a third video tape machine for the four shooting days for an additional $2,000. "Get it! Bob, that's cheap! . . ." Etc. He talks to his old friend, agent Robbie Lantz in Los Angeles. ". . . That lawyer's giving me trouble again. . . . 'Eight percent is too low; there are fortunes to be made!' . . ." He gets press agent Sam Friedman on this and other matters: ". . . Lester Osterman presents . . ." etc. "Yep! . . . And we're definitely going ahead in November with *Hedda Gabler* and *A Doll's House*. John Bury's doing the sets. I want a nice tasteful announcement. . . ."
Everyone's eyes smart even in EPIC's airconditioning from the poisoned environment, but Hilly appears unaffected. He quotes Lantz: " 'What'll we get—a point? You're doing the work. For us it's a bonus!' "
Adviser Malina: "It's a matter of *trust*, Hilly."

Polished and cool, having cured Sylvia the maid's headache by manipulating her neck vertebrae ("White man's magic," the producer quotes himself), he meets with a representative of Colormedia Communication Corporation to talk money on the closed-circuit deal. He sits straight, collected, notes the other's figures, looks down his nose at the padful of numbers. He is a veteran of such moments.

"What this does is protect us on the down side," the man says after a pause.

"I think because of that it makes it a little rich in your direction. . . ."

"Why, Hilly? We're gambling $390,000. . . ."

"On 160 situations [i.e., movie houses]?"

"*Hopefully,* yes. Now the down side of that . . . Let's *assume* we get 160,000 seats. There's a piece of it that we should, hopefully, get back. . . ."

"Right! I don't think you're in business, nor *should* you be in business, to break even. Nor am I! . . . No, no. I don't think it's unconscionable. I think it's high." Politely: "I don't think you're being a prick, I think you're being a little heavy."

"I'm trying to protect Harry on the down side and make a few bucks on the up side. . . ."

"Theoretically, I have to go to Paramount and give 'em a check for $250,000. There's a deferment because I'm taking bubkes out of it. . . . I'm prepared to collateralize *Calcutta* and *The Rothschilds*."

"You're a fake."

Azenberg:

"Clark Transfer trucked stuff out today for Detroit—the basic stuff: floor, fly pieces; the electric stuff: boards, cables, lamps; sound gear, tape decks—it all went today. Two forty-foot trucks. Actually one was forty-five feet." He sighs. "Very heavy . . . We're shattering the Hilly mystique of wasting money, though. We'll come in under budget without a lot of garbage. . . ."

Sam Friedman in his office and going full steam:

"You came at a great time. I'm doing my expense accounts."

"A little creative writing," says Louise, his assistant.

(In *The Rothschilds* program's breakdown of staff, Louise Weiner Ment is Company Press Representative, Sam the Publicity Director, his name under Azenberg's, only these two in boldface type.)

A photographer is in the tiny Broadway office with promotion proofs for *Calcutta*. "I like the goddamn photos bled," Sam mourns. "I scream about it. These look like reproductions. They really do. . . . And I like double weight. . . ."

Rothschilds newspaper ads in proof are now on his desk, together with "heralds"—ads to go into other shows' programs —the new Osterman-presents-Hilly billing typed in. *"The Rothschilds, a Musical Legend . . ."*

A very young man comes in seeking *Calcutta* tickets, and Louise appeals to Sam.

"No!"

She is cheerful and kind, a good foil for Sam's angular imperial dourness. "Too young?"

A grim nod. "How old are you?"

"Eighteen."

"Nope." In a gentler tone: "You trying to get us arrested?"

He outlines his immediate job. "There's very little with the columns right now. Most of the publicity is geared for Detroit. I'll be taking Elkins and Osterman to have a go-around there at all the papers. Radio and TV for both . . . You can't call actors away a lot for appearances, since the purpose of out of town is to get a show in shape. With this show it's not too bad. You don't have a Katharine Hepburn everybody wants, who if they don't get it's good-bye Charlie. Fortunately, we have a producer we can utilize . . . and Claire."

Louise will go to Detroit soon to set up publicity, Sam to Philadelphia to prepare the way there.

"Quiet PLEASE," says the sign. "We Are Working Inside."
A run-through from backstage:

Richard Pilbrow appears, having arrived once more from England, is clapped on the shoulder by Charlie Gray and directed into the auditorium through a narrow side passage. Hal Linden and Leila Martin are onstage doing the new song that will be dropped. A dancer crochets a shawl. An elderly actor, who has been dozing, leaps as if stabbed at his cue (*"Money!"*) and dashes onstage, where he examines Rothschild's coins with aristocratic interest. Gutele stands ready with one of her babies—a folded blanket. There is a number of mustaches and sideburns among the male dancers, which will be shaved for Detroit; they wear fishnet singlets and bright sweat bands. The youngest live Rothschild passes himself around among the waiting cast for hugging and patting; and a male dancer, safely hidden, improvises a funny can-can to the inspiring "Sons." . . . Lights out and all onstage for the pogrom, which Goldby allows them to create anew each time: shouting, hooting, beating the stage with sticks, screeching in blood lust—then off.

"Wow! I needed that!"

The ghetto guard calms himself by reading the *Times*.

Gray's kitchen timer pings at the wrong moment, he slaps a hand on it, and hangs his head. In addition to everything else, there are now on his table a cowbell, a liquor flask, an empty champagne bottle, a cigar, a box of Thermodex tablets. The stage manager follows every word spoken onstage.

Someone else's notes: "Hannah-Nathan: she talks soprano. Must cut. . . . Bond scene drags. . . . Be careful, Hal and Leila have a habit of turning upstage. . . . Money O.K. . . . Better *stage* pogrom."

After the run-through Bury and his wife give Pilbrow a drink in a bar near the theater.

"Well, we've lost a lot of the pretties, haven't we?" the lighting designer says, referring cheerfully to trimmed appropriations. "But never mind. What have we got?"

"We've got a floor, the hangings. . . . It's the worst thing you'll ever have worked on. . . ." Bury talks a little later about living in New York. "We like it. Do you remember all those embroidered blouses one used to get in East Berlin? Well, now they're all here in the Village and Liz is buying them. . . ."

Conventionally, Tuesday is press agent day at newspaper offices, but Sam could not make it and comes into Philadelphia on a Wednesday. He talks to Frank Brookhouser and then Bob Williams at the *Bulletin*.

"I'm a little far in advance. . . ."

Williams wants to know who the leading lady is. He seems grumpy: it should be Tuesday. "What happened to Hackett?"

Sam shows glossy photos. "That's Elkins, Osterman, Derek Goldby. . . ."

Williams glances at them. "Well, where's your leading lady?"

"That's the trouble," says Sam candidly. There really is none. He wants to bring Hilly in for an interview.

"Producers do not overwhelm me, frankly. What about Bock?"

"I'll try. Elkins is very colorful."

"I know he's one of the more colorful producers, but David Merrick he ain't, and we just did a piece on Merrick. . . . Personally, I doubt if anyone but Merrick can make news in that way. I don't want to hurt Mr. Elkins' feelings, but with these guys who did *Fiddler on the Roof* immediately you got a million readers. . . ."

Sam Friedman, professional, illusionless, takes it easy. "This is once over lightly far, far in advance," he says outside.

We have coffee with Wayne Robinson, also of the *Bulletin*.

"Sam, are you all here? Is this all the old Sam I knew?" cries Robinson fondly. "Well, you still got that twinkle in your eyes, Sam. You'll live another twenty years."

There is general theater talk.

"You know as well as I," says Sam, "what a lousy town
Baltimore used to be—death. I mean you'd go into Baltimore
for a week and die. . . ."

"You're talking like you want to come into a town with a
show and have a guaranteed audience."

"It better be or there won't be shows on the road any more."

Robinson says later, "Now, you come in September 16 for
three? . . . What about Joan Hackett?"

"Joan was miscast."

"Is it *possible* to make a musical out of this? I keep seeing
George Arliss." And he mentions moneylenders.

"Well, in this they're presented as lending money to the
right causes . . . any minority. . . ." The press agent talks
briefly in his deep sour voice about the dignity of man, and
Robinson nods. Will the closed-circuit *Oh! Calcutta!* be in
Philadelphia? Sam says he will let him know as soon as he
has a theater and returns to the matter of setting up promo-
tional interviews.

"Who are Bock and Harnick?" asks Robinson, at sea for a
moment. And when he is told: "Oh, sure."

The theater manager's office at the Forrest has been redecorated. Sam is astonished. He lifts a brightly designed dust
cover gingerly. "I'll bet that under this psychedelic cover is a
1911 typewriter. . . . No. 1920. They're takin' the hardship
out of travel. Christ! I'll come into Philly more often."

He and the manager set up a budget for ads and other
promotion. "We share the first six thousand dollars." The
house press agent joins them.

"Morrie, what's the average weekly ad budget for a musical
in Philadelphia?" asks Sam.

"Twelve to sixteen hundred dollars . . ."

They go into it all at length: time schedules, proofs, costs;
radio, TV, newspapers, the columnists. "One ad I want to do,"

says Sam, seeing it: *"The Rothschilds, a Musical Legend* by Bock and Harnick Who Did *Fiddler on the Roof."*

"Sure!"

"I can't do it."

"Why not?"

He sighs and slaps the other's waist. "A thing called contracts, son. I can't do it."

The local PA is worried about being able to promote the show.

"Look," Friedman says, meaning it, "don't let this get out. It's serious. It's about Jews who want to be treated with dignity as men. It's good, and it could be very stirring. . . . Also, you *quelle*: it's what Jews call a *heimisch* show. But frankly I'm anxious about how gentile people will react. Hell," he says, "you know me. Comedy and girls. After that, forget it."

Sam, who is permitted to drink little water, asks for and gets an ice cube. His condition irritates him, but he does not allow it more respect than it is worth.

Later, Philadelphia *Inquirer* columnist Barbara Wilson asks, "Who is this girl who's replaced Joan Hackett?"

"Leila Martin. She did *Cabaret*. I mean what's *Hackett* done?"

Friedman has worked for David Merrick. He was agent for Judy Garland for a period ("I adored that girl"). And he worked for Mike Todd, Gypsy Rose Lee, Herman Shumlin, the Shuberts, Billy Rose, and a great many others.

"Rose understood the problems of the trade. 'Hey!' he calls me. 'I see the papers caught you with my fly down. Okay, let's cover up.' I thought he was going to fire me. I loved the guy for that. Rose knew when people disliked him, and why, and could handle it." Hilly knows when and can handle it, but not always why.

The press agent worked for *Believe It or Not* Robert Ripley, who did fire him for leaking a Ripley PR game—the search for The Man Who Was Hanged and Lived—early to the press and for putting the prize money too low (the entrepreneur wanted to announce the contest on his radio show and had decided to increase the amount of his earlier-named prize; Sam had to admit he never listened to the show). He has had expensive offices and staff, small offices and no staff. "My disposition gets bad I move to one room." He worked for Richard Maney, invariably called the dean of American press agents, on *Arsenic and Old Lace*. The list is long. His own favorite client-shows offhand: *Finian's Rainbow, Lend an Ear, Hellzapoppin',* and *The Threepenny Opera*. . . . When asked why his biography, which is at least more colorful than anyone else's connected with the show, shouldn't be in *The Rothschilds* program, he looks incredulous. "Me? I'm the *press* agent, for Christ's sake!"

He worries over the idea, then recalls something written about himself in a magazine article. "Thirty years in this business a press agent," he says, "and the broad writes I'm a public relations counsel. My God!"

Laurence Olivier's elocution woman, not otherwise identified, is present at the final New York run-through. She sits attentively, making brief notes.

"Very good," says Goldby when it is over. He rehearses the cast in curtain calls; Kidd directs the actual bows. "It's so important that you *listen* to each other on the stage," says the director. "It seems a very obvious thing to say. . . . Hannah: *very* good, no reservations, and David was vastly better."

Kidd: "Okay, I'll see you on the airplane, and we can keep rehearsing"—which produces uncertain smiles; he may mean it.

Olivier's woman says to Hannah, "Your 'therefore' was too

soft." And to Hecht: "You staccatoed during 'the cut of my coat.' Otherwise fine. *Very* good."

There are cries of "See you in Michigan!"

Yellen, who will not fly, takes a cab to the train station with a couple of large suitcases. The gypsy run-through (it turned out to be the general invitation run-through Goldby wanted) was a success, he says on the way. He is objective. "A lot of people were affronted by the amount of book in the show, the dialogue. . . ." He says himself, looking both tired and sufficiently durable, of his Mayer-Gutele first scene that it is "gassy." To keep his interest in rewrites alive, he must find a "new line" each time. The playwright is a native New Yorker and perhaps therefore goes to Penn Station by mistake and must cross town again to Grand Central.

The cast meets at nine next morning at the West Side Bus Terminal. Two chartered buses will take its members to Newark Airport. Company manager Ted Thompson, aided by assistant stage managers Actman and Mitch Dana, organizes this matter, which is complex. Some of the cast have families traveling with them; some are saying farewell. Actors drift in and out of the coffee shop. . . .

"There is a point when an actor's medium becomes a director's medium," says Hal Linden over coffee. He is articulate concerning his craft: a gentle, physically powerful, rabbinical-looking man, he wears today an embroidered blouse and fringed suede vest. A large glazed pottery peace symbol hangs from a chain around his neck.

"The kind of stuff that really defines a character—less by what he says than by what he really wants; he may really want self-destruction, for example—these are the things that you look for at first: a large handle by which to get hold of the character. It happened for me about a week ago. It came together. . . . There's a spine for each scene. A series of them makes a road through the play. When all the spines of each scene were put together, Derek and I discovered the character was too hard, too cold. Mayer was messianic. He had total dedication. And this was tiresome at last. Now we've rounded it out, Derek and I.

"Now the director comes in.

"I never subtract. I won't be less dedicated or less firm now" —speaking of the character—"but I will add a factor which enables me to be warmer. . . . I played one run-through, for example, as comedy. It was a relief to me and I'm sure to the audience. I can take some of that and use it. . . . This is what we're going out of town for. Quite frankly, all I have now is the skeleton of the character. *Now* Derek and I can put flesh on it, and in different tones; then Derek may say, for example, 'You've put on *so* much flesh now you can't feel the spine any more.' . . . The first moments of the life of a character are the actor's; then the director's help is intellectual. *Now* he'll create, be an editor. You must trust him. Together you build a role.

"An actor every day uncovers his nerves. You have to be oversensitive to others' feelings to the point where you feel them yourself. Consequently, if a change is made—a line cut that you may have thought was the core of a scene—it hurts. Your function then is to take what's left and make it work.

"Roger, for example"—indicating Roger Hamilton, the ghetto guard, who is having breakfast with his family in a corner of the coffee shop. "It's none of his business what happens to me as Mayer. He lives the life of the ghetto guard. The more detached from me and the more self-involved Roger is, the better that scene will play. . . .

"Acting being a community art form, you must have faith in your director—love him. It's hard for me to give up a life I've built for myself—Mayer—to someone else after I've lived with it personally for a month, and of course you must. It's up to a director to inspire such confidence that you put your life in his hands."

"The dog is in a box or we don't go. That's the way the rules and regulations are, and that's it!"

A crisis. The buses are ready to leave. The plane waits in Newark.

The problem is young Amshel Rothschild's dog, a beagle named Mame who was given Lee Franklin by the cast when he left the national company of that show. The driver of bus two—red with anger at the position he's in, the rules, the dog —wears a safety award patch on one shoulder.

Impasse.

The company gazes from the worried boy to the dog to the driver. Bus one is filled and ready while the greater number of bus two's passengers waits at the rail outside; it is getting late, and we are still only in the silent absorbing first stage of crisis.

Then Ted Thompson appears with a cardboard TWA pet box. Mame won't get in, and it is small anyway. The driver returns from an investigation. There are wooden kennels in a back room, but they belong to the terminal. Money is produced to persuade the man in charge to lend one, and Mame is shoved into it without more ceremony. Keene Curtis, who is Prince William, etc., sits in the rear of bus one, detached, cool on this blazing August day. He is reading the *Times*. On the concrete dock are embraces and farewells. A young actor, with jokes and lingering fondness, embraces another young man whom he must leave behind. Both Linden and Timothy Jerome —grown Amshel—carry guitars slung onto their backs. Linden, who has just said good-bye to his children, holds his stomach to show the pain. Roger says good-bye to his children.

Most of the young Rothschilds' mothers are coming along. "Good-bye. Good-bye . . ." Curtis, as bus one pulls out, the embodiment of the professional on a job, turns a page of the *Times,* not glancing up.

"Just Plain Reality"

XII

Crisis: Detroit, August, 1970

1

"The Rothschilds—A Musical Legend," it says on the marquee of the theater. The theater is on the ground floor of the Fisher Building, which is not in central Detroit but in a gray desert of concrete in an outlying area. On the Saturday before the Tuesday opening, between one and three in the afternoon, the streets are empty of cars and pedestrians. Across a grassless plain are a motion picture house and Howard Johnson motel. A Saks Fifth Avenue chain store shivers in heat beyond another lot, which is gutted and rubble-filled like a bomb site. There is a street as broad as a turnpike yet utterly empty and on the far side of it a few restaurants, a drugstore. Here too is the St. Regis Hotel, a green Alhambra in this place, with fountains, a porte-cochere, a doorman, and Polynesian restaurant attached. It is airconditioned; there is a swimming pool out of doors at back; and it is two minutes' walk to the theater, which is also airconditioned.

The life of *The Rothschilds* company will be lived for a few weeks between the Fisher Theater and, depending on the factors already mentioned, the St. Regis or other, cheaper hotels close by though not in sight.

2

An elevator rises from the basement and substage to the stage, then to dressing rooms above. The basement is for work on props, costumes, wigs, and makeup. Diffen's fitter has come to oversee the end of her job; local seamstresses are at sewing machines. . . . Hal Linden has a balding wig fitted, then moves down the line: "Josephina, I'ma here," he says to the wardrobe mistress. "You aska for me, I'ma here." She sends him to the youthful bearded tailor with the striped apron, who must sew a new pocket to the inside of his presuccess coat. His money pouch is to go into it and has to come out easily. "How's it going to be attached? It has to be somehow so that I can get my hand above it. . . ." He gestures. The boy, working, says to me, "We haven't had any real troubles so far. The problems have all had solutions that are very obvious."

Walls are lined with tables and bulb-framed makeup mirrors. There are cartons filled with soldiers' packs whitened to look travel-dusty, tricorns, shakos, toppers for the brokers in London. There are boxes of scraps for the seamstresses' use in making alterations, wardrobe cases, Love's prop trunks, racks of costumes each marked with its wearer's name and role.

The wig and makeup man stands back from his work on Leila Martin as the young Gutele. "I'm not trying to overmake you up."

"Do you have spies to see about our temper tantrums?" she asks the writer in the mirror.

"There are no tantrums here," says the wig man.

"It isn't a typical production." The grown Rothschild sons call her "mamma" offstage: there is family feeling. "When

David missed a rehearsal, I was upset—as a mother. And I'm not that much older. Even Hal calls me 'mamma.' " She uses a lens of her glasses as a lorgnette to study herself. "How about a white line here? Do you hate that?"

"If you look in the mirror and something don't look right," he says, "it's wrong."

A loudspeaker says, "Onstage for the pogrom, please."

"Good," John Bury in the midst of his installed set declares. "You're writing your book. I've got two more chapters for you." But he continues to squint through the lights at his creation, which now put together in a frame is massively three-dimensional, real, depressing, the dark color of gold.

Pilbrow sits in the center of the Fisher auditorium with Molly Friedel, his American assistant, in telephone communication with the backstage lighting cage. "Forty to full," Pilbrow murmurs pleasantly. Molly, who is trim and pretty with her hair in a long ponytail, transmits through a handset, and the electrician in his sewerful of switches and buttons and endless spaghetti of black cable, which is behind the left wing but in view of Gray and Thoma, pushes a button or throws a switch, so that Bury's set keeps jumping and changing.

"Fifty-three. Fifty-four . . . Fifty-four."

"Dick, how many counts on cue forty-six? We missed it"— the electrician.

"Three. Sixty-five up three. Twenty-four three. Twenty-six three."

Kidd and Goldby sit apart in other audience seats, the latter powerful-sounding on a mike. The company is in the midst of technical run-throughs: the show done in pieces to get sets to work, the lights decided upon—called "focusing"—costumes and fast changes tried out. . . . "A pretty girl is like a melody," an actor sings as Prince William gets the feel of his magnificent coat by strolling across the stage. Bury's golden cherubs, gross buddhas, drop from the flies, then reascend. The ghetto-dwellers gather, foreigners in this elegant theater; they are aloof, contained, righteous, ancient. . . .

"There's no warmth. People just talk to each other." Platt watches the run-through of the early scenes glumly. Yellen is in his room at the St. Regis writing a new first scene. "There's no warmth."

Goldby booms gently into his mike, "There is a flunky missing. Is it Rick?"

Another technical on Saturday evening. Crews and supervisors are in charge: the physical show quells everything: carpenter Artie Finn, electrician Buddy Stern, the flyman, propman Love, stage managers, sound man, wardrobe and wig people, Pilbrow and Bury, Thoma, and discreetly everywhere, expediting, unsnarling, soothing, praising, manipulating, general manager Azenberg.

Builder Pete Feller, who has come to Detroit with his work, says, "Okay, Alan. He's probably gonna give you an even shorter count next time. . . .

"Your bank flat and your stock exchange sign . . . Hold it, hold it, *hold* it! Take it up again. It's the first time. You'll develop it easier as you go. . . . Kill all your trims, please. We'll give you a low trim on that silver flat. Mark that, Dick. Take those two downstage carriers on sight-line. . . . That's good. Are you hung or swinging?" Pilbrow and Molly have stopped only for a sandwich. His voice drones cheerfully: "Eight . . . 281, 282, 283, 284—full."

An actor-dancer goes over costume changes with one of the dressers, an elderly lady draped in male coats and vests, two hats on her head, a stick in one hand, a rolled paper in the other. She must wait in a specified changing area, help him into the new costume, send him back. "I should be wearing the green waistcoat buttoned. . . . I come off, take off this coat, come back, take this off, put this on. . . ." He shoves the scroll into his Empire shirt bosom: "This *has* to go in here. No! You'll keep this. I'll need the cane. Getting back into this red coat is just a matter of five counts. . . ." She must deal with changes for several of the cast. Dressers have detailed notes of their own:

Right after Mr. Linden's change #3, Mr. Hecht will be coming off on stage right for a moderately fast change into his Rothschild and Sons Outfit. As Mr. Hecht comes off stage he will slip off his apron and shoes. Have boots on the floor ready for him to slip on and the black vest in your hands ready for him to put on. The vest will be put on first so that while he is slipping on the boots you can grab the coat and have it ready for him to put on. Have the black wide-brimmed ghetto hat on your head ready for him to take from you. Be sure that the black arm band is on the left sleeve. Also be sure to have the scroll untied and the briefcase ready to hand Mr. Hecht when he is ready to go on.

"On the act curtain—may we lower it, please?" asks Mike Thoma. "May I have the house lights up, please?"

"You have 'em." The electrician peers out of his cage. "Oh. I thought we had 'em. . . ."

"All quiet, please. Dick, Dick, can you set the bank flat down? Beautiful! That's beautiful. . . . Stand by, please. May I have the house lights to half? . . . You're not ready? Okay, relax. . . . House lights to half, please."

"You got it."

They will perform Act II, a piano dress rehearsal.

"House out, please," says Thoma. He stands at the stage manager's desk, a headset on.

"Out!" echoes the electrician.

Actors and dancers in costume wait.

Music.

"You got sixty-eight."

"Got it."

"Go!"

Stern punches a button. The stage blazes. Pilbrow continues to address the electrician from the audience as the act begins, and Thoma must go on giving him script cues: "Stand by seventy-one. Go!" Etc.

They pause midway through the act to work out a snarl.

Goldby waits in the audience with his shoulders draped against the airconditioning in a white woolen shawl. Actor Hal Linden waits in the cramped second-floor study of his house as lights flash and change color. He is old. "I am the ghost of Hanukkah past."

"Marvelous!"

Bury gives a bark.

"How are you up there, Hal?" Goldby asks. "All right?"

"Dying"—a white smile deep in the beard.

Sherman Yellen appears, grinning around his pipe. He has done the new scene and seems not to be displeased. And he has rethought Mayer in reference to a song, "I Will Bow," that will be dropped anyway later. "His motive is *not* obsequiousness. He's a good banker and knows it. . . ."

Hilly sits nearby, quiet, dressed in brown.

Michael Kidd directs the ball scene, occasionally whistles. A powdered wig flies off during the waltz, and its giggling owner retrieves it. A large jewel clatters to the stage. A podium, supposed to glide smoothly onstage, jerks on like a warped dresser drawer. Over everything onstage under Pilbrow's light is Bury's brass-coin color.

At 11:40 P.M. Bock and Harnick slump silent. Platt stands in dark glasses, watching the emptying stage in a somber way. Bury chews at a knuckle. Pat Cummings goes to sit beside Kidd, who is still alert and deep in whispered conversation with Hilly. Yellen studies the sets. They "ride the play," he says, rather than the other way around: "They must be scaled down . . . brilliant but overpowering." Azenberg explains why the stage hands and actors do not go on longer with this evening's rehearsal (he would like them to in spite of the hour): unions. "If we go to two in the morning, we can't call them till two tomorrow afternoon." There must be twelve hours off, except between dress rehearsal and first performance. "Then we're allowed eight hours."

3

The St. Regis pool is Hilly's and Osterman's office and everyone's meeting place. There are comfortable chaises, metal tables and chairs under umbrellas, waiters in white jackets bringing meals and drinks, phones. . . . The hotel has other guests, but the theater folk outnumber them and are catered to for the long-term trade they bring.

Claire Bloom lies reading *Under the Volcano*. Sam Friedman and his wife are side by side in bathing suits and sunglasses. Kidd descends from his room in dotted bathing trunks, other belongings in a plain man's Woolworth shopping bag. It is the Sunday before Tuesday opening. There is to be a clean-up rehearsal at one, dinner at six, half-hour call at seven-thirty, and dress rehearsal with orchestra at eight.

"CALM CLAIRE KEEPS HER COOL: BLOOM IN BEDLAM"

Sam and Louise have done their work, and there are feature stories with photos in both major local newspapers: that these appear the Sunday before opening is an indispensable condition of press agentry.

"HILLARD ELKINS—GAMBLING BIG ON 'THE ROTHSCHILDS' "

He is "that long-haired flamboyant showman." There are telephone and motor scooter stories, phone interruptions. "I am unusually sanguine about 'The Rothschilds,' " he says to the interviewer. There he is in Claire's *News* interview: phone calls again and talk of the difficulties of financing shows, as well as of Claire's movie, for which she must soon go on location, and the projected Ibsen repertory. "I provide the crass and she provides the class," says Hilly.

Kidd does a couple of lengths. Linden has appeared in trunks and, the beard suggesting the first Baptist, dives in. Pilbrow takes breakfast under an umbrella but must soon return to his lights. Goldby and Bury come down; the *Times* Sunday theater section is passed around. Mrs. Harnick is here, and other wives. There is talk of a sale of bathing suits at the Saks chain store. . . .

"It's far enough away from New York to prevent casual unsolicited helpers from dropping in," says the producer under his umbrella. It is why he likes Detroit for out of town. Also, it has one of the best plants for musicals—the size, the acoustics, sound setup. Most important, the Nederlanders, Detroit-based Shubert-like owners of many theaters, have a well-organized subscription campaign. "Except for L.A., it's the only place where your base income is set for shows that haven't yet established their credentials. . . ." Hilly was here with *Golden Boy*.

He gives Claire a kiss.

"You're looking ten years old and acting nine."

Platt, asked if there is an osteopath in Detroit, says there is a whole school of osteopathy. He remembered other preopening sciatic attacks and checked at once.

"Call tomorrow and tell 'em to send their best student."

Osterman, in an interview-giving mood, is plain and toughminded.

"We'll get roughly sixty thousand a week. Philly, you'll do thirty thousand on Theater Guild, but they're big on musicals and mail orders. I never played Detroit. . . . The Fisher is capable of making ninety thousand-plus in a week, but you can make money here and lose it again trucking to Philadelphia. . . . You rig it, hang it, fly it. . . ." It makes him thoughtful. "If we can get into New York without having lost money on the road . . . Well, it's tougher and tougher to make it on the road, and this is an expensive show. It's a big crap-shoot. Reviews here will affect us in Philly, and maybe word will trickle back to New York." ("Reviews" unqualified by any adjective means good reviews to the theaterman.) "Here in Detroit," he goes on in his direct way, concerning how they must handle a setback, "only Bock and Harnick are sacrosanct"—presumably because of their craft, which resists substitution by its nature, as well as their reputations. If they don't get reviews, they will have to do something: "Derek and Sherman are expendable." Unlike Bock and Harnick, they are not stars. Goldby and Sherman "have never been here before"— done a musical—"and are unfamiliar with the context. We all know where the problems are." He outlines them readily.

"Hilly," the co-producer winds up in a remote tone, "has everything riding on this. They say if he fails here he'll never produce another show."

Mrs. Kidd has brought the new Kidd baby to the pool, and the choreographer indicates the husky cheerful boy's high instep and short toes. A dancer's foot? He is reluctant. *"Any* athlete," he says didactically at last.

4

Dress rehearsal.

An orchestra makes all the difference. It bears, with sets and costumes, the same relationship to theatrical faith that a chapel does to religious faith. We see the entire show now as a deep complexly faceted thing, filled with surprises and as professionally set, as hard, as a jewel in a ring. It is finished. It will be finished over and over again starting from this point until New York is reached; but it is already fixed, the sight and sound of it remorselessly in the domain of perfection. If later it will be more perfect and now it is less perfect, perfection remains its aim and character—technically, rather theatrically speaking, its racial character. And it is seen in dress rehearsal that the orchestra effects this character as the sea effects the passage of ships: it is the components' medium. Finally, such is the magic of concert well rehearsed, of wit and skill, that one innocently agrees to the presence of greatness, though greatness is not present. It is why we feel good at a good musical and so let down when we leave it.

The Rothschilds works, and it is on its way to working better.

Kidd grins as the brothers return from Denmark and the smoke of Napoleon's armies rises thickly to the flies.

In the entr'acte Claire says that the orchestra had sounded more imposing in the compressed environment of the lower lounge where it rehearsed. Osterman says in his candid way, "I thought it was too dark for a musical." And, when someone asks where Hilly is: "He went out and shot himself." Kidd's baby is handed around. Hilly appears and assumes his consulting stance with Goldby—arm across the other's slim shoulders, head pulled close. A Styrocup of coffee is spilled; Osterman shakes his head. "It won't come out. If this was my theater . . ."

Act II. Hilly and Claire sit close, Barbara behind them with her notebook. Bock is one seat from Harnick, cigarette aloft; Harnick is with his wife Patti, a former actress. Azenberg and Yellen are side by side. Derek is with assistant Janet O'Morrison, Pilbrow with assistant Molly, both still at work, Platt alone; Sam is with Mrs. Friedman, Osterman with his wife. . . .

Mayer's death leaves us unmoved. Prince Metternich appears without his wig, on advice: it is Keene Curtis, bald as an egg, much more ominous. All in all, the second act is not a success, and applause is wrung from the watching professionals. The cast indicates conductor Greene, and it applauds him. It is a chilly moment, the hardest work still ahead. Kidd will go straight into further rehearsal. Actors get out of costume and regroup; they practice difficult bits on their own. Bury fusses with the gate to the ghetto, and hammers echo in the wings. There is to be a midnight meeting to discuss the second act; the writer of this book is barred. "John," asks Hilly, referring to some mechanical difficulty, "is that going to be solved?" Bury doubts it unless money is spent.

"Let's start thinking of approaches, then."

A male dancer gropes for a contact lens on the stage; another looks strictly at a pretty, pleased female dancer: "I thought I told you to keep clear of those winches"—protectively, regarding her long, winch-tempting hair. Numbers are rehearsed. Bury at midnight stands alone ruminating among his settings. Pilbrow is finishing his lights for the night. The two Englishmen will stay away from the meeting and instead order a bottle of Scotch sent up to Bury's room at the St. Regis "to celebrate"—perhaps an end to a chapter in their work, though the notion may be intended humorously. For a moment the designer, towering and bearded, is illuminated in the midst of Frankfort, then the lights go out.

5

There are room and poolside meetings, almost mystically private, at night and all of Monday morning. There is to be another dress rehearsal, a preview with an audience Monday night, and then the opening. An early sense of crisis prevails, the certainty, not new, of "something wrong" (though everyone says he knows exactly what is wrong), coupled with a certain expectation of high praise. Whatever the reviews, they are going to change the show.

Bock and Harnick, devising new songs, almost never leave their rooms; their faces are seen now and then, imprisoned, gazing down at the swimming pool. Yellen rarely stops work. Staff and crew, actors, directors—all edge fractionally closer to exhaustion. Bob Malina flies to New York and while he is there gets a pair of shoes for an actor because there is an air-freight strike; or he brings swords; it is uncertain. Reports find their way out of the war tents, but in fact it is tame stuff. Bury has been attacked for not "breaking down" the costumes enough; they are too new, too "Technicolor . . . a little German cobbler look to them." Certain scenes are wrong, as known. The small boys' shop scene, which at this point paints them as kids kids love to hate, is always a target. Also, *why* don't Mayer and Gutele embrace after their long separation? (No warmth?) The urchins aren't ragged enough. And, of course, Act II . . . Hilly is "into" soul food and sends a "gofor" out into Detroit at night in a cab for it: fried chicken, spare ribs, collard greens. . . . The principal purpose of these meetings, Platt points out, since they have only now seen the show with full orchestra, is to decide what can be done to improve the show for its opening without upsetting the actors.

I pick my way across a wasteland of heat and spend too much on a pair of bathing trunks at Saks. Only the women's suits are on sale. "Schmuck," says Hilly from the pool. "Why didn't you buy a woman's suit? That's typical of your chauvinistic attitudes. . . ."

Mrs. Sherman Yellen has arrived. Poolside word games and old-movie games are embarked upon to ease the tension. Bock releases himself at last and appears in a bathing suit. Osterman also appears, having been to the pre-preview dress: "It went more smoothly today." And to Yellen: "Your hat joke is out," breaking the news. "That's fine with me," the writer replies. Mrs. Bock and Mrs. Harnick are in bathing suits. "Jerry says he'll feel *he's* made it," declares Mrs. Bock apropos of Cornel Wilde seeing Gene Tierney reading his novel on the train in *Leave Her to Heaven,* "when he hears someone on a subway platform whistling one of his tunes." Hilly does his Anacin commercial. Osterman wonders whether or not they ought to dress for the preview.

The word "legend" has been dropped from the subtitle on the marquee. Harnick smokes a cigar seated on a banquette in the inner lobby.

An audience.

Yellen looking skeptical, somehow shrewd, is probably nervous. Osterman's broad face is expressionless, though he has confessed to a feeling of nervousness: "Believe it or not," he says. Malina and Azenberg look solemn, authoritative, yet there is a suggestion as always that they are watching themselves; they gaze around at the crowd they have helped command. Hilly wishes Harnick, Bock, and Yellen luck. "Here's to your income"—to Malina. Goldby wears a sweater and no tie. Pilbrow and Molly are spruce, but nevertheless carry notebooks under their arms. Bury wears a tie. "This is chapter twelve," he says, pleased: " 'When the Shit Hits the Fan.' " He heard the expression recently for the first time and it impressed him. "Don't quote me." But it is asking a lot. The jokes are generally weak. "That's a *good* author"—of Yellen in his flag-red trousers and shirt—"he's wearing the show card."

The ghetto-dwellers' costumes are seen to have been shredded in response to the criticism of too much affluence. The audience is lively, appreciative, and critical in a genial way. Yellen's lines get laughs, which makes him grin, but there is coughing during expository work. ("They'll cut that out," says a theatergoer concerning a scene.) In the interval Claire signs programs, and says later, after trying to, that she can never overhear comments except awful ones. Yellen, however, hears someone say, "This knocks *Fiddler* off the roof."

There was a problem with a cable used to move a stage truck with half of the ghetto shop on it, and intermission is extended. Osterman appears before the curtain: "Due to technical difficulties . . ." The delay seems endless. Backstage Linden is shouting, "Get chairs and play it on the deck!" while Goldby paces, chewing his lip. "Don't you pull!" cries a crew member from deep in stage left. "Let us pull!" "A whole chapter this is!" propertyman Love cries. Hilly, Osterman, and Kidd—all cool—confer in Prince William's palace. Then Artie Finn, the bearded production carpenter, plucks wire-cutters from a toolbox. . . .

Act II is played without part of the set.

It goes well enough, and there is enthusiastic applause at the end of the show and a flattering number of curtain calls. People tell each other they enjoyed themselves. They go out of the cold lobby into the hot night. The theater's front doors are locked, the stage work-light lit. Then a depressed pause before a crew attacks the guilty winch and cable and pulls them apart.

Cast, creative, and production people cross the turnpike street for a drink, though at separate tables. Claire remembers the audience: "There wasn't a black face in it," she points out, which is true: not in front of, on, behind, or under the stage. The mood (not because of this) skids lower, grows gloomy and silent. There are to be more late-night St. Regis meetings concerning changes. . . . "It was a good audience," Ted Thompson says. "Alert. They *listened* to the long explanations." But it doesn't seem a great deal to say.

Opening night in the morning.
Manny has praise for the crew, which worked on the winch

until four and finally got it fixed. "I give them aces. They're terrific. They worked their asses off. You don't see them by the pool. This is a *very heavy show. . . .*"

Pilbrow and Molly are already in the theater.

"Hard focus, Johnny. Get it upstage here"—to a boy pointing a spot. "It may just work." He goes up the ladder himself. The failed half of the ghetto shop is all right again. Frank Love cuts pieces from a long snake of rubber to nail to the butts of the rifles. "So they don't make so damn much noise." Bury, harassed-looking at last, is touching up on command the shield for the top of the ghetto house. "Chapter ten: 'The Day the Designer Hit Me over the Head.' If anyone asks me how I'm getting on, I will." He waves a brush charged with red paint.

Detroit sports columnist Pete Waldmeir is to interview Lester Osterman at a restaurant in the Fisher Building arcade. He is late, and Sam Friedman apologizes.

"Don't worry," Osterman says. "So we'll have lunch. If I'm not near a telephone for an hour, I save a fortune." He means he won't buy stocks during that time. Osterman is courteous, patient, a good listener, yet speaks willingly. The columnist, when he arrives, gets at once to harness horses. Osterman picked up his first in a claiming race. "It took off, won purses. . . . I was hooked. It's a sort of hobby that got to be a little fun."

Sam prompts him: "What about your baseball team: how'd you get started in that?"

"Oh, it was B League—minors. We sold Ruben Gomez to the Giants. . . . It was a lotta fun—a neighborhood thing."

"So, what makes horse racing like the theater?" Sam asks. "To give Pete a legitimate angle . . ."

"The risk, the gambling . . ." He explains that his theater real estate offsets production risk, then he gets into that: "You get your nut back on one show in seven." Horses and the theater: Osterman says, "You gotta be dedicated. It's mostly for love. . . . It's not like MGM doing a picture. It's a personal thing if you own a horse, or a ball club, or a football team, or if you do a show."

"We've got a million advance on *The Rothschilds*," Sam declares. "*Figure* a million. Danny Kaye can sell three million up front—on Broadway, not TV, not movies. . . ."

Reminiscence in the millions.

"We had the Jets offered to us for *around* a million," says Osterman. "That was before they got big," which leads to football stars, and gets them back to show business: "Zsa Zsa sits in Sardi's till 9:40 finishing her dessert"—a cue waiting for her in a theater across the street: "They go crazy. . . ." He is glad there are no stars in his show. . . .

Sheldon Harnick is at poolside with his notebooks. As always, he is generous with information. "We're going to try to restructure the opening. There'll be a new scene between Mayer and Gutele. More after the boys come up out of the cellar. One or two new songs at the end of Act I . . ." Etc. Hilly dictates memos—producer and Barbara both in bathing suits: "Dear Jerry and Shel"—though Harnick is a few feet away. Osterman, finished with his interview, takes a poolside call, looks hopelessly up through Detroit's filthy sky as if at God: another winch has gone wrong—burnt out.

Opening night in the afternoon.

Goldby is at the pool in golden trunks, Bock in ragged denim shorts laced up the back. There is a pale air of holiday on the part of the creative people—of having handed in this exam, though others are to follow. Platt emerges from the water, red-bearded and fiercely grinning. Actors—Linden, Hecht, Martin, Clayburgh—gather. Pilbrow and Molly order Bloody Marys and sit down to their sheets of cues. Manny hands out the tickets. I ask Goldby for a quote: "Nope!" At

5:30 the sun remains muffled, hot, ominous. More Bloody Marys, disconnected talk about which hotel in Philadelphia is best . . .

No one wants to have supper: "With the party afterward, and considering last night, and my nervous stomach," says Platt, "I'll wait." The Ostermans dine in their suite. The Bocks, the Harnicks go off in separate directions. Hilly and Claire will eat later.

Harnick paces inside the stage door at 8 P.M. "I thought I used up my nervousness last night. I find I have a lot left over."

"Fifteen minutes, please . . ."

Hilly, in the lobby, is in black, a foaming white stock at his throat, eighteenth-century Beau Brummell cuffs. Claire, in boots, a long Civil War–looking gown, and fringed shawl, describes herself as Beth in *Little Women*. . . . Act I . . . Intermission. People smoke and look generally well pleased. "They're fluffing the lines," someone says, but indulgently; out-of-town seems to know it's out of town, though it pays heavy prices for tickets, that it's for the work and worry. "Great," someone else says, then at once qualifies it: "It will be, it will be. . . ."

"The hell of it is, the Rothschilds are still at it. Look what they did to Bernie Cornfeld."

"It's *good*. How could they compare it to *Applause*?"

Backstage during Act II.

The quick changes are performed with violent speed: "Shit!" "God!" "Still writing your book?" They hurl themselves off into the dark wings, then back again into the blazing light. Hannah Cohen waits to tax Nathan Rothschild in the London Stock Exchange, hitches her shoulder bag, strides out into the brilliantly colored refulgence of a musical stage. Thoma paces with a headset on. Gray limbers up, touching his toes. Lights go down on the count of six. Kings, queens, the upper crust of early-nineteenth-century European aristocracy gather backstage; they kid around a little, waiting. The crew works in its best, ready for the party. Electrician Stern, dressed to the teeth, says, "I've been up seventy-two hours straight and felt better than I do now. . . . I'm emotionally drained. If someone asked me a question, I'd stutter. When that wire shorted out today, I thought I was finished. . . ." The final curtain falls, and Hecht runs offstage grinning. "Ten outta ten for da crew!" and slaps his hands together. Mike Thoma applauds as the cast comes off. Everyone looks happy. There are three curtain calls, a reminder by Gray on the public address that there is to be a matinee next day; upstairs to the dressing rooms; a king gets on the stage-door pay phone. . . .

"Nice, but it needs work," says Hilly's father in the lobby. "The first act. It's talky."

Audience gone, work-light on, the company stands here and there—in the aisles, onstage. It is the same as other nights and completely different from them. "It's crystal-clear what it needs," Hilly declares. "It's major, but it has to be done."

The party is at Topinka's—Hilly and Lester have hired the whole place—across the boulevard. ("Old Friends and Old Wine Are Best," says a sign inside.) Keene Curtis is presented by the company with a large squash, which has comic meaning most here appear to understand. John Bury coming from the buffet with a filled plate complains that he cannot find a real apple in the United States. Conductor Greene, at ease, matter-of-fact after the battle: "I just kept cool and went after what I wanted." Hilly is the courtly co-host, his secretive smile on, as if he knows what the morning will bring. He does not drink at all. Derek sits with the children Rothschilds, their mothers looking as if they are not quite invited to the opening-night party. "Hilly's *father?*" says Greene, astonished, meeting him. Osterman makes his rounds. "You're all too sober!" Yellen, with his exhausted unbending gaze, declares that Janet O'Morrison counted seventy-six laughs. There is little prognosticating. The tentative line is that since the show needs a lot of fixing good reviews might be a disadvantage, even a barrier to it. Bury is saying of his designs, "I'm monochromatic. That's my work." And: "If I'd known Michael was going to have hands on thighs and up skirts, I'd have given them tutus and red bows on them, but I didn't know, you see. . . ." Things break up relatively early.

Room service delivers the early edition with a red rooster stuck on it. "Good morning!" the bird says bravely; but in the news are wars, and air disasters, murders, and bad reviews.

6

Yellen smiles powerfully. "If we'd opened in New York with last night's show, we'd have had a success!" (The reviews of Yellen's share of the work were good.)

"The worst thing we can do is overreact," Manny says soberly but not too weightily. "You gotta do exactly what you were gonna do yesterday."

Bock appears at his window high over the pool.

"Don't jump!"

"I'm afraid they'll want to rip it open all the way and change it." Reading the *Free Press:* "For example, he dislikes the court scene. I think the court scene is extremely effective. . . . They're in character, and they're effective!"

Breakfasts are brought, eaten distractedly under the umbrellas.

"I always expect disaster because I'm Jewish. . . . I *resent* that the love scene's trite!"

Bock comes down in a bathing suit.

"They like Mayer because he's the underdog," someone is saying. "Nathan's a success, so they don't like him."

"We'll get them to like Nathan," Bock replies grimly.

Hilly on the phone in his suite: "First we have to agree on the problems—I've written about five pages of my views—then we have to determine the theoretical part and how to handle it. Then we have to do it. We'll put the new Nathan song in. . . ." Etc.

He is asked about his director.

"One: he can make a major contribution. Two: he can make no contribution. Three: he can interfere with us."

Claire is sneezing and red-nosed.

"She's allergic to failure."

"I'm allergic to *any* kind of emotion."

Hilly seems cheerful and ready to fight: shaved, alert. Sam Friedman looks in with an advance of the *Variety* review, which is a good one. (The New York theatrical weekly paper uses stringers out of town to do pre-Broadway reviews, rather predictions of what New York reviews may be like; when they can be, they tend to be generous to the trade.) As always, a bar has been set up in a corner of the suite's living room. Osterman's Lola calls. (There is competition among secretaries—a subtheme; their being here at all is a questioned factor in the budget. Hilly's Barbara, not asked for at this all-day meeting, will feel "superfluous . . . guilty.") Why not have the meeting in the co-producer's suite, which has just been cleaned?

"No!"

Claire relays the "no" diplomatically on the phone, I am banished, and the crisis meeting, high-level with only the three creators plus Kidd, Goldby, Osterman, and Hilly present, begins.

"Hello, treasure," says Doreen, Diffen's associate, in her pleasant Liverpool. She is one of Bury's "people" whom the designer has invited to be his swimming guests. "Bathing suit?" She looks over the pool. "You don't think I'd disport meself, do you?"

Platt has what amounts to a visa to the meeting of the seven and looks in on it now and then. Wives appear one by one, sit at metal tables with bags of knitting or books, and cast glances up at the hotel windows. Platt reports when he learns something. "This is the big one." It turns out that Hilly, on his own, asked William Gibson to come out. "Hilly will probably say he just wants the opinion of a bright outside playwright. . . ." (Yellen feels, anyway, that he has been put upon, his royalties "pecked away at," as if to say one more thing won't matter.) Platt says, "Derek should give up points."

Bury has clipped the part of a review that alludes to the costliness of the sets and sent it to Peter Hall in England: " 'The truth will out,' I wrote."

At the matinee stage manager Actman is heavy-lidded and Janet O'Morrison, who counted the laughs, depressed. "They act like we opened on Broadway." Charlie Gray, having thoroughly enjoyed himself at the cast party, is today clean, clear-eyed, and ready at his nerve-center podium. Yesterday's telegrams on the bulletin board: "Break a leg. Go get them." . . . "Sorry we ran out of money. Good-bye and good luck. Hilly and Lester."

There is a brassbound peep hole in the house curtain, and it is pleasant to look out at paying customers coming in. Backstage is a cool cavern carved out of a hot afternoon: dark, smoothly busy, even consoling. . . . "The *Press* was worst," says a knowing Frankfort street child.

A duchess retails the review to a stage hand: "Kidd should have done more. . . Keene was good. Hal was good. Paul, no . . . The book was—"

"Fair"—the urchin.

"Fair. All in all," the duchess says, "it wasn't a real good review. . . . *Variety* was good?" She claps her hands. "I didn't know that. I'll have to buy *Variety!*"

The counter girl in a snack bar in the Fisher arcade: "Did you hear the show got bad reviews?"

The meeting continues at three in the afternoon. Claire has been driven by the cigarette smoke out of her room to the poolside, which she swore she would not visit again. A wife says to the writer, "Put down the way they took it this morning —optimistic, unwilling to be panicked. . . ." Mrs. Osterman comes in from the theater during intermission with reports of overheard remarks. "They *like* it. . . ." Mrs. Yellen and Mrs. Harnick will not go to the theater tonight but instead will go to a movie or to bed with a book.

Five o'clock.

John Bury, having been to the theater and returned, is in his room changing once more into a pair of trunks.

"No, I wasn't invited to the meeting. It's all upper echelon. They're talking about us. I have a notion that Hilly will ask us all to take royalty cuts next week. I'll go along with Bock, and Harnick, and Kidd. . . . I pray they sack me," says the designer, who wants to go home.

He descends for a swim, and, looking down from the fourth-floor room, I see him dive into the pool. The wives are under an umbrella, waiting out the endless meeting; it is almost six. It starts to rain, and when Bury returns, he says in astonishment, "I was talking to them, and Mrs. Yellen groaned at a certain point and said, 'Oh, my God, what a long day!' I thought it was a very nice day, no longer than usual. Then I realized she was suffering spiritually with her husband." The wives, even in the rain, remain by the pool under the umbrella.

XIII

Crisis Continued: New York, August–September, 1970

1

At Sixtieth and Fifth Avenue at 5:30 in the evening traffic is at a standstill. Cabbies are out of their cars, staring ahead. A squad of police moves off from in front of the Pierre, an American flag decal on the summons book in the hip pocket of one. The snowy CBS news truck makes an island in the crowd that fills Sherman Plaza and flows into Fifty-ninth, up the Plaza steps, and across the police barriers. On top of the truck a newsman in a game-fishing chair revolves his shoulder camera slowly, an aide with a walkie-talkie next to him. "MEN, STOP KILLING VIETNAMESE WOMEN"—on a sign. The march leaders, ready an hour late, carry among them a twenty-foot black-on-green banner: "WOMEN OF THE WORLD UNITE."

Auto horns blare, which may be part of the demonstration.

"FREE ABORTION ON DEMAND."

A boy in cutoff jeans, hair in a ponytail, paces the sidewalk behind the barriers talking excitedly into a tape machine. "I

269

had to stop," he tells his machine, which hangs around his neck: "I had to stop! It was really amazing! All of a sudden, this transformation!"

"BITCH, SISTER, BITCH."

The signs alternately kid and are deadly serious.

"PRAY TO GOD, SHE WILL HELP."

"Q: AND BABIES?

"A: AND BABIES—THE MASCULINE MYSTIQUE"—with a photo blowup in color of dead southeast Asian women and children in a row on a road.

Slowly the demonstration forms up and rolls into heavy motion, men as well as women marching. "STOP TOILET FA-CILITY DISCRIMINATION NOW." A youth climbs to the rim of a concrete tree tub, looks over Fifth Avenue filled with people. "Wow! What a mob!" In a crawling lead car, smiling, sit three generations of suffragettes.

"Freedom NOW!" all chant in rhythm, marching along well at last. Men gaze down from the balcony of the University Club at Fifty-fourth. In front of Saint Patrick's a great deal of booing from some professionally hard men is heard: "Hey, fellas! Hey, fellas!"—mincingly.

"DRAFT WOMEN" . . . "EQUAL JOB OPPORTUNITIES. LET'S SEE YOU DIG A DITCH."

Politician Paul O'Dwyer is with the women.

"Hey, O'Dwyuh! What the hell ah you doin' theah, O'Dwyuh!" shouts an opposition woman.

"Up yours, faggot!"—showing a finger: "Hey, *fag*-got!"

"Butch-dyke!"

The marchers smile at first, not quite understanding. A man leaps enraged from his car at Forty-eighth: "I gotta god-damned train to make! Let's go!"

"Hey!"—a man strangled with anger: "I wanna get preg-nant!"

"HOORAY FOR WOMEN'S LIB! DOWN WITH ALIMONY"—an onlooker's sign.

A few reply, most keep their eyes ahead. "Some people just hate," a girl says to her marching companion. The police talk shop: "This will affect the men in Eightieth station"—because the march got off late. The parade of demonstrators rallies behind the public library. Two men and a woman, taking advantage of the crowd, pass out antiabortion literature: "Don't be a homicidal maniac. Stick with God. He hasn't changed His mind. Stop the degenerates who arc killing our babies. . . ." The news agent in his box at Forty-second: "You see everything. I bccn here thirty-one years. You see it all. . . ." A black with a challenging boll of hair and a white with a bricfcasc, inspired, argue in the midst of an attentive crowd, using the multisyllables of intellectuals infuriated. "Is it in the history books?" the black man shouts at last, beside himself. "Is it? *Is it in the history books?"*

2

Hilly makes flights almost daily between New York and Detroit.

"The Pontiac *Press* and Windsor, Ontario, *Star* loved it. Raves."

Gibson was there as Hilly's guest and made suggestions. Now the producer has invited the Boston critic, Elliot Norton, who was so helpful in a friendly way about *Golden Boy*, to come to Detroit. It is a secret. Sherman Yellen is "defining a new plot outline from start to finish." There are already two new songs and more are being written. "I'm very enthusiastic," says Hilly in New York.

Concerning Gibson and Yellen's response to him, he declares in a restrained way, "There's always discomfort if someone from your own field appears." The accomplished playwright said he wants to have the brothers humiliated once more as, rich now, they return to the ghetto for a Passover feast, perhaps be searched by a guard; no one is sure about this: perhaps a real rock through a window. There is to be no more auctioning off of the eighteenth century (an early stylized opening), the song in praise of money is out, and much more. . . .

Hilly is wound tight. The subject of the director is avoided. He sits with his eyes closed in a chauffeur-driven limousine on the way to the airport. That ghetto gate, he is persuaded, eyes shut, must be used again in Act II: it is the play's antagonist. And: "I *hoped* for bad reviews." He had made all his notes, he says, the night before. Certainly he should have seen solutions as well as problems much earlier: "I was distracted by other elements of the production. Also, sometimes you have to see it on the stage." He apologizes for being uncommunicative. Claire, in Hollywood for costumes for her movie, telephoned the previous night, and he could not get back to sleep; there were "problems" today.

In a Kennedy coffee shop the producer looks over fellow passengers with awakening interest. Faces. "Those are sad faces," he says of a family sitting on stools at the counter. A few questions turn up the fact that the comment is descriptive only: "I don't feel sorry for them. I hate sadness. . . ."

George Platt reports by telephone another day. Kidd has been made over-all superior, Goldby under him on straight scenes too. "They haven't worked out billing yet." The actors are upset because they were not consulted and because they don't know now who is in charge. Also, Goldby is generally much liked by the cast. A sample problem is offered: the director asked the actors if they approved the freshly written material and wanted to do it; if not, according to report, he rejected it; whereas there can no longer be the elections and options of democracy in this crisis: "Hilly is going for a straight commercial hit." But no one believes that the producer will fire the director. Detroit is described as "chaos."

Another day.

The Lunt-Fontanne street doors are opened to the hot morning. Burlap-wrapped bales of Lees carpeting fill the lobby and packages from the Globe Ticket Company marked, "Rush, Rush, Rush." Orchestra seats have been torn down to their frames, and men are at work on them; the walls are being painted; the red *Rothschilds* sign is up. Dinty Moore's across the street is ready to open after its summer holiday. The Helen Hayes is dark, but down toward Eighth Avenue the Imperial is ready to receive the new Danny Kaye show. . . .

"Major, *major*," cries Platt at 19½.

"He said to tell no one. . . ." He goes on, making heavy pauses:

"It is major! Mr. Azenberg also asked me to say nothing to anyone."

They are waiting for Hilly to arrive. Platt makes a throat-cutting gesture with his hand. "He's coming in, going back tonight, back here tomorrow morning, back to Detroit tomorrow night. . . ."

"Poor Eddie Fisher," says Barbara reading *Variety*. "It says he owes over nine hundred thousand dollars."

"Hilly owes that much."

"Oh, come on. That's just being one-up."

What about the Alice restaurants?—trying to pull loose threads back into the tapestry. The group that had been doing them is bankrupt. No one seems much concerned. The mood is high.

Hilly arrives. He wears a black-leather and knitted-cotton combination. He hurls a list at Barbara: names to get on the phone. He grins ferociously, scarlet-faced.

"Goldby's out."

"Did it hurt, Hilly?"

"What?"—hands spread out on his chest: "Hurt *me*?" Understanding it: "Don't be an asshole. I don't like to hurt *any*one. . . . It only took me a year and a half. . . ."

"Does the cast know?"

"Paul and Hal do. I met with them last night. I'll go back tonight."

"Was there an argument?"

"There was a meeting. You know I never argue."

"When did you do it?"

"At two this morning I finally got it done."

"How did Jerry take it?"

"That's what the meeting was about." He shouts into the intercom: "Goering! Goebbels! Eva! . . . Page? Would you ask my two friends to join me here in the Reichsministry?"

It is like old times.

The hi-fi is tuned loud, the director's contract fetched, Azenberg and Hilly embrace. Claire has returned from Hollywood; she wishes Hilly did not have to go straight back to Detroit. "A couple of nice things have happened to me in the past year," the producer says historically: "With *Alice* and *Calcutta* . . . Now *The Rothschilds* is going to be a smash." He wants to talk to Kurt Vonnegut about the final option payment for *Cat's Cradle,* the balance due this day.

Claire declares that she enjoyed being on her own in Los Angeles: she rented a car, drove to the beach. . . .

Azenberg asks if she will play a Southern belle in her film.

"I'm no longer a belle."

General contractor Jerry Simek reports. "I did a lot. . . ."

"The window?"

Not that.

"Sam called," says Platt. "He wants three hundred posters for New York. Okay?"

"Yep!"—reading mail.

He says on the phone later, "Listen, you want to lend me forty-five thousand for two weeks? I'll give you 2 percent a day."

He talks to Lantz, Goldby's agent. Afterward he announces, "They're behaving honorably."

Barbara spells out Vonnegut's name to a phone operator. Calls come in faster. There is discussion concerning the *Calcutta* taping, scheduled to start in a few days, and backing for the Ibsen plays. The producer grows increasingly scholarly in tone about Detroit: "We discussed our problems, examined our options, and decided that this option made the most sense for the show. . . . I told Derek. He took it very well, said I was making a mistake. It did not come as a tot'l surprise. . . . *Hel*-lo, Yvette"—to a phone: "I'm fine." Low, solemn: "That's right. Michael Kidd . . . I'm having dinner with Paul tonight after the show to relax him. Being an actor and therefore insecure . . . I'll talk to him honestly and he'll feel relaxed *and* enthused." To Claire: "What did you call me? Bullshit artist? Do you mean I'm a liar or the way I express myself?"

The latter. She is repairing a blouse with needle and thread.

"He's going to write it down, and you'll be hysterical."

"Mr. Vonnegut's showing a friend around Cape Cod," Barbara announces. "That's why we can't get hold of him."

"If we plaster the city with those three-sheets, Con-Tact can make a fuckin' fortune, and so will we," the producer says on the phone again. "Cool it. Wait. We'll make *money*." And again: "I'm gonna have a bite with Paul and relax him. . . . He could have held out for a full royalty"—Goldby—"but agreed to a one-half cut. . . ."

Azenberg snaps scissors at Hilly's head. "We could save a fortune if I cut your hair. . . . Will you tell me how you got the cast of *A Doll's House* down to seven people? Did you eliminate the children?" he asks Claire. And to Hilly, when she says she did: "*Why* are you going back to Detroit tonight?"

"To see Paul, who's uptight . . . for him to know I'm coming out to see him. And for Mike, who needs someone there to say, 'Hello, how are you?' . . . I called Hal and Paul last night to tell 'em before the company heard and before Derek told 'em, and no one felt raped—not Derek or anyone else." He gets Osterman in Detroit: "Les, it's better than we hoped." He outlines the agreement with Goldby. ". . . and nothing on anything else . . . underlying rights . . . billing's out.

"There are guys around now who'll pay a hundred"—another call—"a hundred and fifty thousand for *Cat's Cradle,* so if I wait till Monday I'll be in the toilet. . . ."

The press release concerning the change: "Artistic disagreement."

"I understand the market was jumping all day," Hilly declares.

"It's of no concern to me," Malina says.

Hilly chokes with laughter. "I didn't tell you. I'm going public! . . . Got you there!"

"Dear Kurt"—a telegram: "I appreciate your position and hate to put this on a personal basis. . . . The project represents considerable investment, emotional and otherwise on my part as well," etc.—requesting permission to delay payment. "I don't think it'll work," he declares after it is sent.

The limousine.

The producer stuffs his attaché case with cigarettes, notes, *Variety*. . . . If the writer accompanies him again, he promises not to sleep. "I had all this other stuff on my mind. . . ." No? He is off, jaunty, swift-moving, a fresh cigarette going, tinted glasses in place: the crisis appears to be resolved. Everyone in the office is on a separate phone, and there are no good-byes.

(Derek Goldby will return almost at once to England and

begin work on a play. He will not fail to phone and send cables to each *Rothschilds* opening.)

3

Hilly plans to lease the theater part of the ground floor of the Henry Hudson Hotel on the West Side for Claire's Ibsen repertory. On a morning early in September he and Claire meet theatrical builder Pete Feller, the English director Patrick Garland, and Bury, released from Detroit and armed with preliminary plans for redesigning the theater and for the sets. The building agent escorts them; they also look into a rathskeller kind of restaurant next door, which the producer may develop. He says aside of Detroit: "I think we've broken the second act. . . ."

Later, in a cab with Bury going uptown to look in on one of the TV taping sessions of *Calcutta,* a sketchy amplification: the family reunion scene in the second act—not Passover now, after all—was a stumbling block, as stated elsewhere: wordily expository, static, overpopulated, didactic. Hilly himself, he says, solved it in outline form (he does not quite say wrote it), "and then Sherman appears independently with the same scene written. . . ."

He hustles designer and writer into a delicatessen at Eighty-first and Broadway, buys what is needful for the Hilly Sandwich: a half pound of cream cheese, a half pound of lox, plus leeks on a bagel; it is eaten dripping, standing in the store.

Across the street at Tele-Tape Productions' Second Stage the "Taking Off the Robe" opening sequence of *Oh! Calcutta!* is being blocked, and the producer moves here and there for whispered consultations. A girl directing the sequence is on her stomach at one side, watching narrowly: "Move your *feet!*" Robes are whipped off, then on, then slowly off, showing the naked bodies a year older. "I'm having a terrible time with my robe!" cries the girl on the end whose job is regularly in time to the music to turn, kneel, and flip her robe right over her head to reveal her bare behind, then slowly straighten. The camera crews seem occupied with technical things. One man, for example, is feeding his juggernaut of a camera's dolly from a tank of air. But the grips lean goggle-eyed over the rail of a catwalk. "We'll spend two houhs on this fuckin' numbuh because nobody's gonna get it right!" cries a robed actor.

"Hey, Mike, they book you next?" yells a grip to his friend.

A break, and the middle-aged-looking (though fit) *Calcutta* man shouts in what could be a reformer's rage, "I'll entuhtain yuh!" throws open his robe, takes his penis in hand, and makes gestures of what one had once supposed were actionable obscenity at the girl director.

From somewhere a workman says, "My God."

Bury, eyes closed, appears to doze.

More rehearsal.

When the blocking is completed, a boy and girl, naked, embrace in a comradely way. It is notable that none of the cast, on September 2, has a sun tan.

19½ East Sixty-second now says 9½. The writer wonders why anybody would steal a "1."

"I guess somebody wanted a '1.' "

Does the producer still have his collection of "H's" and "E's" on the walls outside his bedroom?

"Why not? Have I changed my name? Am I any more secure?"

Once upstairs, he gets Friedman: "Sam? *I* want that full-page ad. Call it my ego. . . . Right now we've got to go strong suit—for the morale of the cast. . . ."

"You take a full-page ad in the *New York Times* you know

what the word's gonna be?" asks Platt, overhearing. "You're broke. You're in trouble."

There is talk of casting the Ibsen plays. "We might *just*," Hilly muses, "wind up with a brilliant company." And Claire, who is present: "Wouldn't it be marvelous to make it possible for really good actors to come to New York?"

George writes to the people who manufactured the sweat-shirts, enclosing a list of U.S. movie houses—with seating capacity—in which the closed-circuit *Calcutta* will play: ". . . could break the sweatshirts out into a big selling item. I don't believe any article of clothing has ever had a send-off like this . . . a conversation piece about a conversation piece"— urging a coordinated promotion in Varsity House outlets with the telecast and with EPIC's bookstore and record shop promotion.

The box-office gross for The Rothschilds Company for the week ending 8/29/70: $62,366.50.

Detroit word-of-mouth has been good, people are buying tickets in spite of the reviews, and the weekly gross will increase.

XIV

Pulling the Show Together: Philadelphia, September–October, 1970

1

Not long before the company's arrival Sam Friedman takes a suite for the day at the Warwick Hotel in Philadelphia. Here Hilly will meet the press. "He'll be wild with only one phone—*and* in the bedroom," Sam says gloomily.

Ernie Schier, a Philadelphia theater critic, arrives with local press agent Morrie Yuter. Hilly is in a tomato-red shirt and matching tie; he is a little restrained.

"I think I'm losing my mind," he begins.

"Why?"

Schier is insistent.

"Well, there's a show in Detroit called *The Rothschilds*. . . ." The closed-circuit deal, the Ibsen. . . .

"That doesn't sound like much of a schedule for a man of your ability." He wants to know about the filmed *Calcutta*. Will it be toned down? Will there be close-ups? . . .

There is an art to being interviewed. The producer measures the other and mends his pace. An elocutionary tone: ". . .

what a discriminating viewer would see from the fourth row . . . It is not a skin flick. We're neither trying to pander nor hold back."

How much will he make?

"Ah, it's difficult to assay. . . ."

"One million? Two million?"

"Not the first night." Hilly laughs, but Schier does not and after a pause repeats the producer's reply encouragingly.

"It'll probably gross between one and a quarter and one and a half million. . . . I'll get my share."

"Ultimately, will it go into the Samuel French catalogue?"

Sam laughs, and Hilly says, "I hope not."

"Why? What's the source of your anxiety?"

And so on. (*"Why* are you doing Ibsen?" "I believe in good works.") At length, the semicombatant part done, they settle into a fairly friendly talk. Hilly is impressive about the Ibsen plays in the context of contemporary politics and in themselves; he has been reading to good effect. They go from there into the complications of franchising ("Being a lawyer as well as an accountant helps"), movie-making ("Everybody gets screwed in movies. The basic formulas are formulas for screwing"), cable TV and his ambitions in the field of cassette tape libraries ("If I'm doing Ibsen, I plug into college towns . . . *$100,* I plug into black neighborhoods"), the desuetude of the theater, the anility of audiences, more *Calcutta* ("The daily reviews were a Rorschach test of every guy's sexual hang-ups. We got three hundred reviews—more coverage than the moon shot. Everyone who had a pencil and a mimeograph machine reviewed it. Auckland, New Zealand, passed a *law* forbidding this show, and if all those people get upset, it was well worth doing, right?" Schier replies firmly, "Right"), and at length, with Sam steering, to *The Rothschilds.*

"You did it to be taken back into the church?"

"The *schul*"—but seriously: "I have a hang-up on ghetto stories. It's one of the reasons I did *Golden Boy*."

Ralph Collier radio-interviews the producer in a room at the top of a center-city club. "A-N-A," Hilly murmurs as the second hand makes its last sweep, "C-I-N . . . not just one but a combination of medically proved and tested ingredients . . ."

A challenging question from Collier, Hilly invokes Aeschylus, goes to the closed-circuit show (it is due in town in ten days), then to his musical, which Collier plugs generously. Concerning both the diversity of Hilly's projects and nudity: "Are there *any* limitations today for a producer?"

"Yes, his talent."

(Later he tells Sam, who was not present, about this reply and chuckles.)

There is a third interview over lunch, and the producer, tired now, grows first irritable, then laconic. As the young man writes, he grimaces over his head at Sam and finally ignores him to talk shop with the press agent. He wants to run *The Rothschilds* newspaper ad framed in a Star of David.

"You want to chase *all* the gentiles away?"

"It's a natural logo."

"You'll get Arab bombs exploding in the goddamn theater."

"Also, I want to invite Golda Meier and Abba Eban to the New York opening. I don't know whether to do it officially or just chatty: 'As long as you're in New York drop in.' . . . No? More formally."

"I'll get Lindsay to ask 'em," says Sam in his illusionless voice.

Hilly goes to the suite to rest, and the interviewer departs. "This always happens," says Sam, worried. "He was persnickety. He's great the first couple of interviews, then—it's usually with some woman—he gets persnickety. I gotta talk to him about So-and-so"—an expected newsman. He follows the producer up, looks into the bedroom. "I saw your face and got a little worried," Sam says. "He was only doin' his job."

"I know, but he had absolutely no knowledge. . . ."

"You don't answer in two syllables," says Sam gently. Himself not well, he says, "Okay, get your rest."

There are three more interviews—one with a major daily, one with a syndicated campus journal, the third with the representative of a chain of neighborhood weeklies. Hilly is forthcoming, intimate, and friendly, voluminous and minute. His Lord John of Carnaby Street jacket is off, tie pulled down. Drinks are ordered: nothing is too much trouble. In short, admonished by Sam, he is once more a professional at work, and the newsmen like it.

". . . You can learn from negative comment. No, not in New York. That's the end of the line. . . ." Ibsen: "Nora wheedles and fucks her way into things. . . ." *The Rothschilds*: "I'll take a C in history and an A in drama. . . ." Good reviews and bad reviews: "It's part of the human condition that we tend to think people are bright who agree with us. . . . It's one thing to shoot a horse who's broken a leg; it's another to break the other three legs. . . . I'd love raves, but I want honest reviews to make me think and everyone involved think—to fix the show. If I were coming in with a road show, I'd want good reviews to make money. . . . I happened to be doing a paper when I was taking a degree in, ah, economics . . ."

"Well, you don't measure success by the length of a run?" asks the campus interviewer.

"I gauge success," the producer declares, "by how much I like a show." And abruptly to local PA Morrie Yuter, "Listen, I want twenty-five-cent tickets for kids to *The Rothschilds* starting right away!"

"Fifty cents," says Sam.

"I want *kids. Poor* kids: black, white, pink—I don't care! And I don't want publicity on it. . . . You do it through the schools, Sam, you do it through the schools! We'll supply money for a bus. That's what the twenty-five cents is for. . . . Bullshit: it'll *work.* . . . We'll get 'em if we have to have 'em under guard and handcuffed. We did it with Sammy Davis. . . . Of course, I admit that was more relevant. . . ."

The interviewers, dazzled, leave, and Hilly says, "I'd like to do something about that. I'd really like to. . . ."

Presently, they go over the local ad. Sam has prevailed, and the frame will be a courtly-looking shield.

"Say '*Variety*, the Bible of Show Business,' " says Hilly. "What the hell."

He wants a radio campaign: "Saturation, starting Thursday night."

"It did nothing in Detroit."

"Eighty thousand dollars?"—referring to the latest weekly gross. "Sam, get the wrap! Get the wrap! I want a radio campaign; and prepare a disaster set: 'Shirley Eder says . . .' " Shirley Eder is a syndicated Detroit-based columnist who has been friendly to Elkins and his show. The campaign is mapped. Hilly will clear it with Lester. It must be arranged to paper (distribute free tickets for) the house for preview performances, since the producer wants the theater at no time less than 60 percent full.

Personal promotion: "I haven't been on Carson or Cavett. I've been on Merv Griffin. I'll go on the *Today Show*. . . ."

"Will you get up that early?"

"I'll get up that early. . . . Sam, did you hear? I'm trying to get the floor of the New York Stock Exchange for the opening-night party."

He gives the hotel operator half a dozen numbers to reach

in various parts of the country, returns from the bedroom doing a fast step: " 'I can't dance, don't ask me . . .' I must lose nine pounds. . . ."

Later, he talks to playwright William Gibson.

"We introduce a gate into the second act. . . . There's one other adjustment: I want to postpone Mayer's death, so that all the stories will converge after Aix. . . ." Etc. ". . . give us ten days or two weeks of your time. . . . Five days? . . . We're talking about perhaps ten minutes of material. Yes, well . . . I fucked up your life once for a long time. I can't do that every time I get in trouble out of town, say, 'Daddy, do a show for me.' . . . Yes . . . I will. I will. And if you get any brilliant thoughts, you might holler. Right? . . . I'll buzz you. Peace."

2

The company appears to like Philadelphia. When there is a little time off from the take-in of scenery and equipment at the Forrest and from rehearsals in a Sylvania Hotel ballroom, members make excursions—out to the river, down to the Independence Square area, or in the neighborhood of the theater itself, which is, at least in part, a picturesque tangle of cobbled streets and cul-de-sacs with shops and old houses like gift boxes piled three high and covered, in September, with morning glories. Morale appears to be good in spite of the personnel problems and constant text changes. In any case, New York, which is home, is getting nearer.

The Forrest is a contrast to Detroit's Fisher: red velvet, gold leaf, cut glass, and it is relatively intimate; also, it has just had a new stage built for it. It is a theater notorious in show business for its architect's error: dressing rooms, unplanned for originally, are in a building across an alley behind the stage's back wall (there is a subterranean connection too).

Bits of Bury's set litter colonial Quince Street alongside, among machinery, costume and prop trunks, trailer trucks (Clark Transfer: "Let's Get the Show on the Road"), musical instruments ("Don't Drop: Harp"). A bulletin board notice invites the cast to use the Variety Club ("The Heart of Show Business") in the Bellevue Hotel. Brother James Rothschild shows up hot and tired, having toured old Philadelphia; he must go at once to the Sylvania, where a new number, under Kidd's direction, is being rehearsed.

Europe's rich and titled aristocracy, outwitted by the Rothschilds, now sings in a frenzy of frustration, "Oh, there's no way *out!*" Brothers Amshel and James, reunited in Philadelphia, greet each other with pleasure. The cast, during breaks, is forthcoming in a way it had not been in Detroit, seeming to feel a security and forward motion that had been wanting. Keene Curtis talks in a general, not excessively cautious way about directors, saying prefatorily, "I don't know *any* Broadway director who can teach you anything if you don't know your craft. . . . You find the limits of all of them after a time. One will block poorly but be brilliant with bits of character; another will block brilliantly, and so on. . . ." He liked Goldby's work. "Michael is wonderful at things like pace and action and rhythm, and he also makes good suggestions for character. . . . Some actors don't like a director to give them too much. They want them to mold a bit"—he uses sculptor's gestures—"after they've gotten the feel of the part."

"It's a better show," Kidd himself reports. "Of course, we'll be working right up to the end changing in Philly. Word-of-mouth got around in Detroit, and we were doing sellout business when we left and could've stayed another week." When asked how he likes Philadelphia, he stares. "Well." It is not relevant. "It's three blocks to me: here, the theater. All places are X to me with a show. I work."

He returns to it.

Howard Honig (ghetto-dweller Blum and Mayer's understudy): "Even when Derek was fired, the company generally rolled with it pretty freely. There was no feeling that the show was going to fall apart. The good atmosphere we had going in Detroit didn't flag."

Someone else: ". . . It was just that when there were problems nothing was happening. I guess they felt a need for uni-leadership. The changes in the show have helped. We *know* as actors. It's hard to get a response during the show—there are no applause-stops—but it's visible to us at curtain calls. . . . If we opened in New York now, we'd get by. Changes now are frosting."

Propertyman Frank Love sits calmly on a chest of props in the stage-door alley. "It's a big show, no question," he says comfortably, "but not mammoth. It's movin' too, tightening up. It's a *good* show. Nice. None of that filth in it."

Mike Thoma observes the bearded and indefatigable Artie Finn at his work. "He figures on going until the curtain drops Wednesday"—the preview before opening. "It's a big fuckin' show: a four-hour take-out. You know it's a big show then."

Back and forth: the Sylvania's Wedgwood Room to the Bellevue Hotel, to the theater—Kidd's three blocks in a humid Philadelphia heat wave—and back to the Sylvania.

"It's going in the right direction," Hal Linden declares, finishing a scene. He likes the Sylvania as a place to live but misses the old John Bartram, where he had once stayed and which has been torn down.

"Peggy, did you get a note about speaking louder as you go off?" Kidd asks.

"I've been inventing. . . ."

"Just a little louder"—firmly.

The pogrom is no longer an improvisation but is highly

stylized and rhythmical—dancelike; it ends with a single scream: very scary now.

" 'What more do you want? . . .' " Kidd objects to Gutele touching her ambitious son.

"I'm responding to what I see in his face," she argues.

"It looks more sincere if you leave it out."

It is hot.

Prince William comes in from the Sylvania's Ritz Lounge with a bottle of Schlitz and watches.

The offstage watchman, legs up on a chair, William Goldman's book about the theater, *The Season,* open on his lap, sings, "Jews and aliens of Frankfort: the ghetto is clo-osed," in a big voice.

Grown son Nathan declares, "It'll take a fortune to stop that song."

Linden briefs the writer on his own character's progress: "He's undergone changes. Their changes and mine . . . I have to know what I am, what they're saying about me, or else I begin to lie onstage. He used to be a man who knew what he wanted and what he was willing to do to get it—a militant man. I had that song, 'I Will Bow.' It's gone. Now he's an I'll-do-what-I-can man." He taps his chest. "It's all more inside now."

A check of the neighborhood has been made by actors not rehearsing. Well-remembered delicatessens are gone. Favorite theater and sports place, Lew Tendler's, is gone. Saddest of all, the Russian Inn is gone, now a go-go joint. Where are the decent restaurants? Out-of-town has changed and keeps changing.

A heavy ghetto roof is being carried into the theater through the side doors at ten o'clock at night. "Okay, boys, easy, easy . . . just the way we did before . . . goin' down, like the girl said at the picnic . . ."

The radio in a coffee shop: "*A-o! Calcutta!*" in a mincing

Philadelphia accent. The announcer seems to hear his own announcement and is astonished by its meaning: *"A-o! Cal-CUTTA!???"* And assuring us, like it or not: "Yes. *A-o! Calcutta!* You can see it now. . . ."

The orchestra pit is too shallow or too close to the apron of the stage, which makes a problem, since Bury's floor hangs far out over it in a precipitous lip. Charlie Gray, with Mitch Dana behind him making notes, goes from one rehearsing musician to the next in the theater's basement lounge measuring each from floor to top of head; their chairs must be sawed off. Both stage managers are smiling. . . .

"No celli, no bass: violins and violas . . . once more," Greene is saying, Bock present. *"And!"* Greene pats the air energetically. They play. He taps his stand, and they stop. He makes air-clearing gestures. "I asked for fourteen." They are rehearsing the new second act overture—the entr'acte—and, this being a new city, it is a new orchestra. Bock attends quietly to his score, makes a change. Greene announces it: "Listen carefully. . . ."

Upstairs Artie Finn, tough, sweating, patriarchal, continues to oversee the take-in; chain hoists wait with heavy set units aloft: "Slack it off, keep slackin' the chain off. *Wait* a minute, Tommy. . . ."

Thoma has not moved from his orchestra seat at the theater for two days, it appears. Will the set get hung by tonight in time for the preview? "Maybe," the production supervisor replies. The orchestra crashes from downstairs. Pilbrow and Molly, at work in Philadelphia, wear matching costumes: jeans, denim shirts, embroidered suspenders with Mickey Mouse clips. Bock, all in blue, with his clogs, curved pipe, and electric bush of hair, is a Dutch sailor now rather than a burgher, which may be due to increased confidence. John Bury is also in Mickey Mouse suspenders. He has been given his mail. "The nanny smashed up the car," he announces, reading. Was she hurt? "No, unfortunately . . . I've several more chapter headings for you. Later . . ."

Sherman Yellen, with most of the higher company ranks, is at the Bellevue. "Hilly had visiting nobility in Detroit to see the show," he says bitterly. He is eating a sandwich in the hotel bar. "They suggested everything from a Passover dinner to a prolonged deathbed scene." The suggestions were not to his taste. When he talks about Goldby now, though he was one who wanted the personnel change, it is in part to praise him. "He contributed style, to the English sequences especially. He was good with Paul and Jill and got performances they wouldn't have given another director. He was an excellent editor, had an appreciation for language. . . . He gave the show its consistency, made it all of a piece, gave it a special look. . . ." Etc. Kidd is "rational . . . has a good sense of timing, of audience. . . ."

Sam is at the preview, the night before opening; stable-seeming Osterman is here, Yellen, Hilly ("Hello, there, young fella . . ."), Platt, Bock—all seated in a rear row. Kidd, Pat Cummings with his notebook, pace. . . .

Scenery sticks, then works. The new songs are clearly a help. It is hard to see what differences Kidd's direction has made, but there is a difference, and the show is improved commercially speaking, which is the point now, its tone generally lighter and more amusing: this appears to come from songs, scenes, and direction together. Mayer, as reported, has changed: a bit sly, readier for the opportunity, less regally proud. The boys in the shop are more like boys and instead of cheating their customers give things away; and the pogrom goes well.

Pilbrow and Molly sit on dim-lit balcony steps doing cues. Harnick crouches out of sight below the orchestra half wall chewing on a thumbnail, rises to peek, crouches. Bock remains calmly seated. An order of scenes has been reversed to good effect. "I'm in Love" makes sense of the courting, though it is one more *Fair Lady* song. Another new one (Sammy Davis and others are to record it some months later) for Act II—"In My Own Lifetime"—has the contemporary political and social relevance Goldby was always seeking. ("I want to see the fighting cease," the song goes on.) Except for a banker's practical wish for the financial stability peace brings, it is nonsense in this story: out of context, message-carrying, purposeful for an ethical good. Yet it makes dramatic sense of the will-reading that follows. . . . Here is the much-talked-about second act ghetto gate scene, but it is staged without a further humiliation, is ironic instead, which is Yellen at his best and first-class writing: the guard is now seen to be respectful, loving even, and old ghetto friends, unrecognized and thought to be beggars, are tipped by a rich, Anglicized Nathan. (The irony will be bowdlerized for New York.)

The Mortons are in town. "I still think they should pass out money afterward," says Fred Morton when the preview is over.

Yellen: "Don't let Hilly hear you. It'll be your money."

"I think we're 75 percent home"—Osterman: "But I've yet to hear anyone stand up and scream. Did you hear 'bravo' tonight?"

The co-producer asks Yellen if he can't give Hannah more to do in the vexed family reunion scene near the end.

Jill Clayburgh had spoken to him too. "I told her all Tolstoyan heroines dwindle into domesticity."

"Maybe you could take a line from the mother," suggests Mrs. Osterman.

"You want to see bloodshed in Philadelphia?"

There will be a matinee preview next day, then the critics' opening.

Calcutta posters bloom all over town—on lamp posts and building sites, in shop windows:
"DIRECT FROM NEW YORK BY THE MAGIC OF ELECTRONICS." Six local movie houses are named. Tickets cost $10 each, though one theater also offers $8 seats. "SUGGESTED FOR ADULT AUDIENCES ONLY."
It will be shown about ten days after the musical opens.

Storms of applause follow the matinee preview next day, and bravos this time. The audience loved it. It stands in the aisles to applaud and cheer. It won't go home. Kidd is elated, the cast delighted; it can be seen in their faces during curtain calls. Production people grin. It has been a good solid Philadelphia matinee audience, for which affection is felt everywhere in the world of the theater. The performance flows into 7:30 opening-night curtain. Greene sends off his orchestra from substage into their now cavelike pit and sawed-off chairs. "Have a good time. Enjoy yourselves." . . . "Five minutes, please"—Gray's voice. Manny is here. ("Everything all right?" his tone suggesting that anything else is not possible.) Winches work, sets move, cues are not missed. (The writer, however, doing research, is mowed down by Napoleon's soldiers, who come roaring off and must turn into English stockbrokers. "Clear out!" they cry.) "The rise of Jewish makeup," critic Schier declares premonitorily to a friend during intermission; there will not be as much wit in his review. "I feel guilty," says local radio personality Frank Ford. "I don't know whether I like it because it's Jewish or because I like it." (He will treat it well.) Sam and Hilly, nose to nose in the lobby: "It's gonna be the best fuckin' show there ever was!" cries the latter. "I'm scared of good reviews! I don't want good reviews!" He is red-faced, excited. "I'm *not sanguine!*" The bell. The lobby empties. The producers remain. "Let's get the reviews," says Osterman, counting up: "Let's get the show fixed; then we're home. We're coming into the stretch."

Hilly flings an arm around him.

"The producers disagree. I want bad reviews, he wants good."

"Good means money business in New York."

Hilly and Sam wait out Act II in the lobby and discuss the producer's imminent trip to some U.S. cities where he will do promotion and whatever he can to oppose censorship of his *Oh! Calcutta!* telecast: Chicago, Columbus. . . . Sam proposes bringing Tynan over, getting some of the writers—Lennon, Beckett, Feiffer—to go to the towns and plead for the show. ". . . in a group! Beckett would come—a Nobel prize-winner! It'd mean a million and a half at the box office!"

The second act.

Bravos for Hal Linden and Paul Hecht.

A relatively genteel party at the Variety Club.

Bad reviews.

3

The remainder of the time in Philadelphia is difficult but not despairing. The reviews—the important ones, in any case—are damaging without being, in the producers' view, helpful. Hilly makes his promotion tour and returns. He invites more of what Yellen called visiting nobility—writer-director Mel Brooks and playwright Christopher Hampton foremost among them—to see the show and offer suggestions, which are, in the nature of things, always forthcoming. There are constant strategy meetings from floor to floor in the Bellevue. The weather is tempered. Ticket sales continue to be good, though not sellout. Hilly is in New York and Philadelphia on alternate days, Claire still out west shooting her movie. Bock and Harnick, tired, work at new material: a market day song for Linden, a new end for Act I, and a number of other, lesser changes. Yellen, close to exhaustion, works on in his room looking over Broad Street as summer ends. The playwright objecting, Joseph Stein, who wrote the book for *Fiddler on the Roof*, is hired to write additional material for this show.

Stein had not understood, he says, that the incumbent objected; it is distressing. He works fast and well on any handy typewriter, or even on scratch paper standing up in the street. Changes are made at once; by the time the company gets to New York more will be made, some of them effective. It is difficult to ascertain which writing belongs to whom, so closed are the sessions, but it is not major work. Yellen is annoyed because the rest of the creative element accepted help; Kidd got his directing job, he feels, in part because of the writer's opposition to that incumbent, and he senses that the new director would not hesitate to expend him in turn if circumstances required.

There appears to be no possibility now of delaying the New York opening, though Hilly would like to, as he says, to improve the show further and to let the new Danny Kaye show get in first. He is unable to carry the wish.

Kidd works on calmly. The cast is cheerful enough. No one thinks that the Philadelphia reviews are necessarily fatal. The new material—rehearsed all day, bits put in at night—renders the show, as it should, clearer, lighter in weight, tauter: somehow more important, in spite of the constant edging toward commerciality; alternatively, perhaps due to the salutary effect of chipping away at the didactic to get at the popular. In any event, it is more believable. By the end of its Philadelphia run the musical will be improved. Mayer's new fair song, an unembarrassed attempt to seduce the audience, works well because he is trying to win affection and customers in his native market place: not, in this context, an un-Rothschild-like thing to do; also, by placing him among non-Jews as a man instead of a Jew, it gets away from the remorseless us-and-them war tone of the original play. The characters' fictional world expanded is by that much more credible. The second act remains irreversibly bookish, since the drama never ceases to be the means to a message, but it too is both a bit lighter in weight at length and steadier on its legs, due to internal changes, by the time New York previews begin.

Al Hirschfeld, the cartoonist for the Sunday *Times* theater section, comes to do his caricature. The cast does not stop enjoying Philadelphia and begins to be recognized on its streets, which is pleasant. It gives post-opening interviews to the papers. Pat Cummings takes notes at each performance: dropped cues and lost lines ("fumpfs," of which, with new material, there are many), attempts at out-of-context individualization ("So-and-so is wearing his Kabuki makeup again"), etc. The customers still like the show, and matinee audiences adore it, to the delight of Kidd, who grins at elderly ladies and gentlemen who stand to cheer his work. John Bury makes minor changes in the set ("They're going through one of their murky bits again now," he observes of the new crisis and the final pulling together) and Pilbrow's Molly (Pilbrow is in England for a few weeks) in lights.

The telecast's time comes around, and it is not a success. Done as if it were live at the Eden, though it was filmed earlier in a studio, the taped audience laughs and applauds, while we, unwilling voyeurs (a purpose of the show with its cheerful athletic sexuality was to remove that burden), are silent, gazing with misery at the purple fuzzily naked figures on the tiny screen, listening to jokes that were never good and are here reduced to obscene tickles, some so brutally raw in this unsuitable environment that one is now shocked by what had been amusing. The Justice Department is "thinking" of bringing charges against its promoters. Six or so cities halted or canceled it, and Hilly, on his side, is thinking of suing Keating, a U.S. pornography commissioner; though he could not get an injunction to stop the telecast nationally, the commissioner's publicized desire to was probably influential in the cancellations. Hilly and the authors made money on it, but its actual producers, Colormedia Corporation, will be, he says, "in the hole."

The Rothschilds alters, rehearses, alters. Yellen moves from fury to fury and finally to a sort of working calm like a ship at last in the lee of land: the show, in fact, looks as if it might make port. Bock works in his J. S. Bach sweatshirt, Harnick in turtlenecks. Actor Hecht cannot put in certain new material at once ("I need a night to pull myself together"). Kidd loses his temper occasionally in a quiet way: "It's very aggravating. I haven't slept in three nights working on the scene, and then I come in and there's no technical . . ."—but regains it at once when he does. It is a friendly company, as often stated. ("I *like* your boots!"—a brother to an actor-dancer during a break.) Hilly appears regularly: "Mike, you gonna put the new stuff in tonight?" As far as changes are concerned, as exemplified by Mayer Rothschild's extended life, he has had his way. He says that he intends to go through with his lawsuit on behalf of *Calcutta*. "For twenty-five million. I'll settle for a little less." He delivers a talk at Philadelphia's Poor Richard Club for member theater buffs, first being introduced as having been by education an attorney (the degree from any one of a number of law schools; he will explain, if asked, that he and Barbra Streisand have different backgrounds for different occasions). . . .

The show's last night in Philadelphia.

Three of the boys' voices, on the road too long, are cracking with puberty, but it goes well in spite of that. Mayer, with his faults, is at last an attractive, almost wholly real invention. There is still no eleven o'clock number—no show-stopper at the climax; Hilly would like one, but it is evident that he will not get it. The cast boards a bus to go to New York after final curtain. Harnick, who saves what he can, intended to go along but in the event does not. Ted Thompson has checked in the last actor, the last piece of luggage, and they are off. Manny Azenberg oversees take-out (first trucks leave by four in the morning, and the Lunt-Fontanne take-in is to begin six hours later). Sandwiches and urns of coffee wait for the stage hands. Dressing rooms are emptied—pieces of script left behind, crosswords, paperbacks. . . . Charlie Gray and Manny place bets on when the last equipment will go. The long night drags, and Manny sits comfortably watching. The fact of his being here— management seeing this hard stretch through to the aching end —is good for workers' morale: the ghetto dismantled, palace taken down, the beautiful floor taken up, all the treasures packed, costumes and props crated: work not to be done again for years, it is hoped. . . .

"I really think that of all the shows coming in," the general manager says in a comfortable way, "this is the best shot."

XV

"I just paid a little attention": New York, October 19–20, 1970

1

". . . the strongest memories of my childhood are of spending Saturday afternoons in Macy's toy department, and Mother said I could buy . . . bargains, and, ah, I got to know the toy department very well . . . and vice versa."

"Ah, whaddya mean?"

"The toy department got to know *me* rather well."

"Ja ever lift anything?"

"I used to hang out there. . . . Not at Macy's. That was home. I mean, you go to Woolworth's. . . ."

"When I was a kid, I stole things from Woolworth's."

"Macy's . . . that was home."

"No. In Philadelphia there was no Macy's."

"Gimbel's . . . Now, be smart. . . . There was a period when Mother was . . . quite ill . . . and I spent a period of time in what was a partial boarding school and partial orphanage, and I came away with a tremendous dislike of . . . graham crackers and tin cups . . . didn't like to drink my milk in tin cups. I also remember taking coeducational baths, not sexual but interesting, and, ah, having a tremendous crush on a girl who I said good-bye to by jumping on a swing she was swinging on—doing a romantic number. First day I was entered into kindergarten I found it a very uninteresting way to spend a day, so I took off on a streetcar and went to Coney Island. Then I came back. The other thing I remember very, very clearly was a teacher I liked who liked me. And a . . . pocket watch had been taken from a kid in the class, and . . . I had taken the watch. I didn't need a watch, but I had taken the watch. And she didn't consider that I would have taken the watch, and we all lined up against the blackboard, and I threw the watch across the room. I felt very guilty about that, and she felt very badly. . . . Miller . . . Ah, I went to school at P.S. 130. It was on Ocean Parkway, and I remember associating with that school a kind of municipal pier feeling, like I did later with a radio station called WNYC . . . hospitals: kind of large, impersonal, and uninteresting."

"What was the first movie you ever saw?"

"The first response . . . the first thing that came into my head was Sonja Henie and Jack Oakie. I hope that isn't true. Nope. No, not *City Lights*. Ah, and I almost . . . It's funny, we used to go to movies on Saturday . . . *Sunday* afternoons, and we listened to concert programs; and it was a ritualistic kind of . . .

". . . I dived under the water and kissed her. I had never kissed anybody in my life. I was eleven and a half years old. . . . And she invited me to a party at her house, and they was all *rich* kids, and all I had was this pair—and I'll never forget it—of faded blue pants and a blue jacket, and I had never learned how to dance. . . .

"And I went to this party, and they were all jazzed up, and I watched them dance for about half an hour, and I determined that I was going to get up and dance better than anyone in that room, and I did. . . .

"By fourteen I was a snappy dresser because I had money: duck's ass, peg pants, the whole *schtick*.

". . . first job I got paid for: *first* job was selling newspapers door to door. Nonexistent newspapers. Well, they turned out to be nonexistent: *Veterans Weekly,* things like that. I was a very good salesman. I used to make two, three hundred dollars a week while my father was making eighty. I learned then that they don't reward you for being wise and kindly and artistic. But I said we'll change all that. Fuck 'em. But then if that's what they want, that's what they get; so I kept selling more papers. Then I discovered I could make more money on radio. . . .

". . . I had no sense of values. I feel—wow!—I feel my fifth to tenth years were wasted. . . . Oh, the teachers dug me, but it was all bullshit. I could ad lib on any subject; I always could. And that's why turning it around from getting fifties to getting ninety-eights was nothing. I just . . . you know: paid a little attention. That was easy. . . ."

2

The vest-suit formal Hilly had ordered wholesale ("Make Outs—for the Party Circuit by After Six") lies on the couch in his office, its cuffs unfinished due to a factory mix-up. He will have to wear something else.

Abba Eban will come with Lindsay. Aurelio . . . Maybe one bona fide Rothschild; George Platt is not sure which. Len Garment of the President's kitchen cabinet will not be there, though he had meant to be. It is reported that he pulled his Achilles' tendon.

It is opening night at noon.

"I love you," says Hilly to his father on the phone, having discussed with him turning Claire's mini red fox coat into a midi by adding to it. "Keep your fingers crossed. Your life is at stake." He throws a letter opener at his cork wall. "I want you all to know that whatever happens tonight I won't change. I'll be just as obnoxious. . . . I was once a knife-thrower."

Claire has been in stores trying on other fur coats: "The craziest thing I could think of to do on this day when the empire may be crumbling."

Yellen appears with a parody of II-7—the second act family reunion scene that has been so vexed—to be Xeroxed for distribution. Except for brief periods he and the producer have skirmished ceaselessly, Hilly, operating from his greater strength and particular ethics ("Tell the truth!" he will admonish a secretary. "It's your best protection!"), taking the points: but this is a different sort of day. The producer hurls his gift at the writer—a Jewish coin from the period of the second revolt against the Romans—and the small box knocks the pipe out of Yellen's mouth.

"Hilly, we've come a long road together, but Jesus! . . . What is it—Seconal?"

"Cyanide."

A gift for broader distribution is the *Rothschilds* show card in red Con-Tact, framed in gold, with an inscription ("With grateful appreciation and warmest memories of our association") and Hilly's and Lester's signatures in gold imprinted across the bottom.

New York City no longer delivers local telegrams; Yellen has brought along his greeting, neatly typed, which he will tack to the stage-door bulletin board: "Be as great as you are! Remember"—using a line from Mayer Rothschild's will: "I am the stuff from which the good God makes an angry playwright. I love you all."

"It's been a long time," says the producer in his office to no one, abruptly crepuscular and still.

In the afternoon there is a line at the Lunt-Fontanne box office. Malina and Azenberg, in front of the theater, read Yellen's parody and roar with laughter ("Momma, what do you want?" . . . "Me? Another line, a song of my own, a flower pot, and you out of my house. I want everything. . . . In my own lifetime/I want to see my sons get theirs. . . ."); he will not show it to the cast until after the opening. Gifts are being passed around backstage. Pilbrow and Bock appear, the latter in a maroon jacket with velvet collar and velvet trousers; he kisses Charlie Gray. From the stage the redecorated theater looks handsome: new seats and walls are a pleasant, not too bright shade of blue; chandeliers sparkle. Harnick and Bock present enameled Rothschild shields for lapel pins, or crown brooches to the ladies, notes accompanying. The cast is doing a read-through in the balcony lounge, coats and crash helmets piled on the floor. Next to Yellen's note on the bulletin board are others: "May you run as long as us poor Jews in *Fiddler*." . . . "There goes the neighborhood. . . ." A memo tries to enlist the cast in a theatrical bowling league, another is about the Actors' Fund, still another urges theater musicians to vote to have their own attorney: ". . . PAY AS YOU PLAY—FOR THE BETTER DAY." Rothschild children now wear gold and red Rothschild sweatshirts, gifts from Bock and Harnick, and "Jewish Power" buttons (Hecht's gift). Linden as well as others ask the writer if this is his last chapter. Yes.

Cast members are generally optimistic: "The matinee ladies love it, and they're powerful at the box office. . . . Even if the reviews are bad, it'll probably go"—and are vaguely out of control. "Are they gonna sing it?" Greene demands of Kidd. "Because they're just foolin' around."

"They have the option not to sing it. We're doing it mostly

to think over the values of the show," Kidd says. "We decided ahead of time. I'm sorry."

"General insanity setting in," says an actor. "It's just nervous energy."

On the corner at Forty-sixth and Broadway the ghost of what New York once was in reality rises from the theaters and restaurants up into the old dinosaurs of billboards, blazing with electric light at midday, the art in them as simple as a child's. People and cars flicker like fish in and out of the October sunshine. Two small Rothschilds chase each other from the theater to the corner and back. . . .

Young Jacob on the stage-door pay phone: "Room 1108, please . . . Mom? It's me! My gift: you'll never guess! It's a *Rothschilds* poster with the entire *Rothschilds* cast—signed! . . . Yeah. Just come over. Okay?"

Harnick and Bock seem to be everywhere in the difficult day, loyally and quietly solicitous.

"How iss you?" a male hairdresser asks a girl dancer in the basement.

"I'se fine. That was a fine haircut you gave me."

"Angling for another?"

Mrs. Kidd settles into a chat with the wardrobe supervisor. "How's the baby?" Josephine asks.

"Unfazed by the whole thing."

Boxes of flowers are now beginning to arrive.

Dinty Moore's, where the party is to be (the Stock Exchange turned them down): two cakes are carried in—giants inscribed one to Hilly, the other to Osterman: the restaurant owner's gifts. ". . . Ask if we can get a photographer, because they're not gonna give us the right time. We gotta get what we can. . . ."

Barry Gray has agreed to originate his radio celebrity show from Dinty Moore's to give his audience the excitement of a

Broadway opening night, the party, the reviews as they come in. . . . Hilly and Lester have bought six bottles of very expensive Rothschild wine—Château-Lafite 1874—in addition to five cases of less imposing but still expensive wine.

The cast descends from the lounge, the read-through over. "It won't be long." A worldly veteran, years from enchantment, quotes Kidd's pep talk: " 'Play the scene. Don't let the opening-night audience throw you. It's an added performance. . . .' "

"Well, tonight the tale will be told," a dancer says, bouncing down the steps. Kidd himself offers a little grin. "I have no quote, Kit," he says simply. "I've been too busy with the show to be phrasing quotes."

Hal Linden needs a pair of shoes for the party and when he leaves the theater strolls over to McCreedy & Schreiber nearby.

"I feel confident," he says. "I know my job and feel I can do it. I'm not nervous. I'm excited. This is the big shot after years of stand-by where people say you can take over but not originate a role. . . . So many friends are hoping for me on this shot. I'm grateful to Jerry and Sheldon for giving me a chance. Sheldon thought of me while they were still writing it. . . .

"That San Remo model in the window"—to the shoe store man. This is a theater place (many of the shoes for *The Rothschilds* were made here), and Linden is known.

"Get Mr. Linden the San Remo line with removable buckle, Number 2429, size 10." He buys them. $35. "This guy struggled for years," the manager declares angrily to the writer, to the world, and he punches the actor's shoulder hard. "You *better* get a success."

A 50-percent-off clothing sale in a store around the corner: "Generally pretty faggy but worth a look." No. "Junk, waste of time . . ."

The actor's opening-night supper will be in White's on Forty-fourth Street. He buys the writer a bowl of clam chowder. Until now he has made the luxury part of his living as voice-over in TV commercials: Pan Am, Ivory Snow, Alpo, Noxzema, etc. Actors are paid by the commercial—scale, which is $102 basic, and residuals. The residuals do it: "An account could easily pay, where you're the only voice, twenty-five to thirty-five thousand a year. . . ."

More flowers at stage door: a Star of David in yellow chrysanthemums from Janet O'Morrison; more wires. The opening-night audience begins to arrive on foot, in limousines and cabs for a 7 P.M. curtain; there are policemen with blue helmets (only a few years ago they would have been mounted on horses). The inner lobby is the place for production people and their families. They will remain standing, or sitting on lounge steps, or pacing throughout. The Yellens are here with their son Nicholas. Osterman stands weightily apart. Claire comes with playwright Terrence McNally and her daughter Anna. Pilbrow and Molly in evening clothes retreat constantly to the cloakroom to pick up a headset and speak softly into it. Fred and Marcia Morton are here; Barbara and the EPIC switchboard girl. Souvenir programs with Con-Tact red covers and gold tassels did not arrive until late. "I had to go up and down the aisles handin' out plain ones to the critics," Sam says.

The show . . .

Yellen folds up onto the lounge steps like a clasp knife.

Hilly, pink-faced, smokes, pauses to look, paces. (Black velvet jacket, black and gray trousers.)

Kidd, carefully dressed as for a union election, stands with professional strictness at the back of the center aisle, feet planted apart; perhaps he is seen from the stage; his apparent ordinariness and calm would be a comfort.

Pilbrow is perched on the cloakroom counter; he applauds obediently, leans back to whisper instructions.

As the new market place number begins, Harnick, agonized, ducks into the well of steps to the lower lounge, cautiously returns. Mike Thoma paces in evident misery.

Kidd sneezes, and Hilly shows him a warning finger. They smile.

There is much applause from production people where called for. Harnick laughs at the script's jokes.

At intermission I accompany Sam Friedman to the Howard Johnson on the corner, where the press agent orders an ice cream cone. Abba Eban had to go to Rome and therefore is not here. Ed Sullivan is here, Earl Wilson. Lindsay came with a party, perhaps including a Rothschild but perhaps not. When we return we find ABC-TV cameras shooting the intermission crowd, the lights like fire in the glassy Rolls-Royces parked before the theater. Newsman John Schubeck asks Sam to point out celebrities. There are not a great many. Someone says Edward Kennedy came tonight, but he is not to be seen.

Act II.

The audience has been warm, as New York opening audiences tend to be; now that warmth increases, and Hilly looks cheered. Yellen asks me, "How do you think it's going? I thought that goddamned scene sort of dragged. . . . No? Good . . ."

It is soon over, and there is a great number of bravos and curtain calls, which I forget to count, yet one of *The Rothschilds'* creative people whispers, "One fuckin' flop," grinning with tortured ferocity.

"The Jewish *Porgy and Bess,*" says a member of the audience and even more mysteriously: "Some nice gowns . . . tits . . ." The house empties, a chauffeur comes in, looks around anxiously.

Evelyn and Guy de Rothschild were supposed to show up, Barbara says.

3

The war room this time is in the general office upstairs at Dinty Moore's.

Barry Gray, who is a tall lank man with farmer's hands, a deep voice, and eyes both merry and guarded, has been set up at a table at the far end of the farther of two rooms. The cast, guests, and staff are downstairs paying no attention to the place cards Manny and George arranged; they come to the war room at first by invitation, later pretty much at will, and the upper floor is soon jammed and smoky. The buffet is below, but there is coffee here and a small bar, and it is here that the Château-Lafite is being decanted. It was picked up at Christie's in London by a New York wine merchant from whom EPIC made its purchase; for a fee the company has sent an expert to pour it—six squat, serious-looking black bottles filled for the Earl of Rosebery, an English Rothschild connection, nearly a hundred years before. "I once opened one," says the wine man, "and it made the front page of the *New York Times*."

Barry Gray is telling his listening audience about the "private, invitational-only party of *The Rothschilds*. . . . Opposite me is Hillard Elkins and his lovely wife Claire Bloom, and her daughter Anna. . . . How could they make a musical out of *Golden Boy*?" he asks joking. The crowd is dense but, in the presence of an actual broadcast, disciplined. Three photographers dart agilely about, flash guns going.

"Having wrapped twelve-five today . . ." begins Hilly.

" 'Wrapped?' " The broadcaster glances around alertly as the producer explains: box-office and mail-order receipts.

Claire sits straight, holding her daughter against a knee (Anna is soon to be taken home). A girl photographer squats on a windowsill for angle shots. There is a glimpse of Mayor

Lindsay, larger than life like a figure in a post office mural (also like Joy, his hand ever at his lips bidding adieu), just leaving, casting his superb smile. (He has today endorsed Arthur Goldberg's doomed candidacy for Governor.) Gray flew in from Paris for this show and, while Hilly looks impatient, tells of his affection for that city. The pourer of wine has opened several of the bottles and, smiling, lids lowered, decants some into a dozen glasses, which he puts before the broadcasters and selected others. The bottles are worth $240, I am told, though it is uncertain if that is altogether or not. Sherman Yellen edges through the crowd toward Barry Gray; various people connected with the show are being interviewed at the four table mikes. "Why doesn't Sherman just knock him" —Hilly—"off his chair?" says one of the playwright's relatives *sotto*. Keene Curtis, almost Far Eastern in his affability, describes with pleasure Yellen's parody of II-7 during his interview: then Yellen himself, who does not deny his identity as author of the skit "Delicious Indignities" in *Oh! Calcutta!* The girl photographer, in a purple pants suit, hangs aloft, camera drooping but ready. A Nassau County politician, who seems to have been a backer of the show and who liked it very much, speaks briefly. His picture is not taken. The Château-Lafite is ignored, and I sneak a taste from someone's glass. It's good. . . . The noise grows, that first respectful quiet forgotten, and the two rooms are so crowded at last that when a place is found it must be kept. His father at his elbow, Hilly sends a wink: "Look at me," the wink declares. "Look where I am." Fred Morton is introduced and takes a vacated seat. "You look marvelous!" cries Gray.

"I've seen the show four times, and today I came nearest to crying."

"How come you only came *near* crying?" Later Gray returns the conversation to Paris and his 747 flight, which impressed him.

"I saw you sip the wine," the expert says, working his way over to me. He is upset because the vintage has been snubbed. "It's beautiful, isn't it? Unmistakably 1874 . . . Just slightly over its peak now. If you served it to me blindfolded, I'd say, 'This is an old claret, just a little over the hill. . . .' "

Suddenly Lester Osterman brings a small silence into the room.

"Edwin Newman hated it."

"He had some good things to stay, but he basically hated it." The co-producer, having done a stint with Gray, had been in the restaurant owner's private office for TV reviews. "Leonard Harris liked it, Newman hated it." (Harris liked it, "warts and all." Newman asked if there might be a connection between costliness and dullness.)

But then, nearly on the heels of this report, comes the first intimation of success. Barnes seems to have liked the show. Osterman's son has appeared from somewhere, stepped into the war room waving scraps of paper: "Clive Barnes gave it a good review!" The *New York Times* daily review is, of course, life or death; off-Broadway, as demonstrated by *Oh! Calcutta!,* can survive Barnes, but Broadway cannot.

" 'Moral force . . . show-stopping . . .' "—the young man reading aloud from his notes to the people nearest the doorway. " '. . . box office . . .' " Morton claps his hands. It is not possible. It must be a mistake! Whistles and applause. Someone kisses Mrs. Osterman. "You're in!"

"You're *sure*?" And she says to me with justice and joy, "It's easy to hate you. You can't care."

Hilly leaves the room and returns shortly, making long-distance nods, eyes popping, crimson-faced. "ABC said, 'Not a good play, a *great* play!' "

Osterman at Gray's table once more—the show is off for commercials—had emptied an inner pocket of cards and letters and, exultant, slaps this packet hard onto the table. Gray, back on, interviews Linden. The good review is only hinted at for the moment: more pictures are snapped. Osterman: "I'm sorry you didn't see Hal tonight, because he was really good. . . ." The wine expert, moving from glass to glass in the room, is finishing them off. "I was in Paris," Gray says. . . .

"Now this is Lew Funke of the *Times*"—Osterman referring to their source of news about Barnes. "And he's very reliable. We're playing it by ear, but it looks good. . . ."

Hilly grabs a mike.

"We don't have Sammy Davis! We don't have Danny Kaye! But we have a brilliant show, and I think we'll be here a long time! The box office opens in the morning, and the line forms on the right!" . . . Hal: ". . . no jealousy in the company . . . no feeling about who's got the big number . . ."

"The net result of all those fights and disagreements," Hilly cries to his radio audience, "is, *I* think, a great show!"

Mrs. Don Walker is on a sofa in the front one of the two rooms. "I'm the wife of the world's greatest arranger," she declares. . . . It is 12:25 A.M. Mayer Rothschild kisses his son Solomon. The owner of Dinty Moore's embraces Osterman and says to Mayer: "I loved you . . . adored you. You are the father of the world!" Lewis Funke himself, silver-haired, pipe-smoking, is calming someone. "Did I ever lie to you?"

"I just want it to run long enough for me to play Mayer," says Howard Honig.

Actual copies of the *Times* for October 20 are brought in at last.

In the body of the restaurant downstairs the company stands in groups listening as the review is read aloud. One reading is finished to loud applause while another still goes on. The restaurant is a dark Victorian-looking place with etched-glass doors, and mirrors, and a heavily carved old bar, burgundy carpets and tablecloths: seen from the head of the stairs, the actors are absorbed into the decor like figures in a carpet. One group blooms with cheers, another, then they disappear. Bill Liberman has finished reading to a group that includes Platt, Bury, and others. "Will your book have a happy ending?" asks Barbara.

"A last line for you," says Bury: "A hit by mistake. No. By accident." He stares a little fuzzily. "It means they were aiming at it and made it by accident."

Another reading of the review on the other side of the restaurant; then, gradually, the place grows quiet.

There is less to say. The burden is lifted, the need for clamor dissipated. It is not necessary for the moment to go on selling the show, but the impetus to do so remains, and there is a letdown, as well as the old human difficulty in knowing how to handle victory when prepared for defeat; simply remembering victory's unfamiliar phrases is irritating work for accustomed losers. Yellen wants ice cream, and he leaves. Claire is quiet, red-eyed. "I've had hits. I've had flops," Hilly says. "Hits are better." But he speaks in an absent-minded tone.

It is too late for Sardi's. A group goes to Reuben's on Fifty-eighth Street.

Of a reviewer who will be heard from next day, Claire says, "He couldn't have liked it in a million years. He's a half-wit."

"If Watts gives it a good review, can you use it?" Morton asks.

"Sure."

"Shall we order? Captain . . ."

It is late. The too large place is empty except for this party.

"What'll the line be tomorrow, Hilly?" asks Osterman, referring to the review-quoting ad they must decide upon.

"Big." The producer is brooding.

Silence.

There may be a rush at the box office, not an overwhelming one necessarily. It will be the factor to watch. There is some talk anyway of passing out hot dogs and coffee to waiting ticket buyers.

"You know, Barnes said 'solid,' " someone declares. "It was. He was right."

2:10 A.M.

"I call my sugar candy"—the middle-aged piped music.

They eat mostly in silence, no particular mood coming, then bit by bit Hilly picks up; his eyes are congested.

"We're in good shape! . . .

"We have three or four years on Broadway.

"An international success: England. It'll be a smash in Israel! Whatever they say about it, it'll be a movie!"

Then he shouts—the unexpected apparent point—angrily: "This show, *don't kid yourself,* is 40 percent of what it could have been! . . . But! We have a show! And that's"—the real point: *"pretty fuckin' good! . . .*

"The trick, Lester, is not to kid yourself in this fucking business. From now on when I do shows I'm not gonna do dinosaurs! *Candide* was gold on the road. . . . No more of that! . . .

"Considering what we had to work with and where we came from, we did a pretty damned good show! . . ."

The producer shouts: *"We did the best show possible considering the circumstances!"*

Silence.

Osterman: "Well, thank God we got the *Times.* This was a good audience. . . ."

"It was not."

"It was."

"It was *not,* Lester!"

"Well . . . we're gonna know ten-fifteen tomorrow morning at the box office what we got."

"We would've paid off anyhow, Lester."

"Between ten and twelve if there's a hundred on line would be good. If we can wrap fifteen to twenty thousand tomorrow, that's goin' good."

Silence again. Good nights on the sidewalk in front of Reuben's.

" 'The Rothschilds' is a good and solid start to the musical season," Barnes wrote.

4

It is a perfectly clear, bright blue New York day; it is cool, the sun is shatteringly bright; there are mornings like it on the high plateau of Mexico. A girl reading on a Fifty-seventh Street crosstown bus laughs aloud in delight at something written in her book. Two schoolgirls get on and settle themselves.

"Where was the dance where you got ripped off?"

"Temple Israel."

"Is that where the bathroom's downstairs?"

"Yeah. And that's where Chad broke up with Holly."

"Were you at the Riverdale dance?"

"Yeah, I got ripped off there too."

"They just ripped *me* off for some *umbrella* I had with me. . . ."

The city is covered with election campaign posters. Boys and girls hand out Buckley literature from behind sturdily suburban bridge tables on street corners. The temperature is 60 degrees more or less. There is little wind.

The producer, composed and clear-eyed, is this morning wearing a Bill Blass tweed with blue squares.

"George, get a cost from Nathan's on how fast I can set up hot dogs and grape drink," he says quietly.

"Hilly, may I ask why you feel you have to feed people who stand in line and who've never been fed before?"

"Press purposes"—quietly.

I ask how it feels to have a hit.

The producer looks at me. He constructs an expression. It is heavy, bug-eyed, entire: a joker's ultimate look: he is both the eggs and the fox. He says nothing.

He is behind his desk in the throne of a chair. He places a leather letter folder carefully on it. The Barnes review is alone inside the folder. He lights a cigarette and reads the review, tapping his neat serpent-twined fingers. It is quiet. He is like porcelain in this odd almost Mexican light: scrubbed white and pink, gems winking, gold gleaming, whiskers (they are trimmed to perfection) white as frost; smoke curls up in a smoothly unwinding blue-white sheath that twists and ripples at the ceiling. It is an Oriental moment, still as jade or painted porcelain.

"Get me Sam Friedman at the agency," he says gently.

Sam is at Blaine Thompson, the theatrical ad agency in the Sardi Building. Hilly is past due there.

"Sam, what do you want to use as your lead out of Barnes? . . ."

Manny reports by phone on the box office: a steady line twenty to thirty people long since 10 A.M.

"How's Lester holding up?"

"Nervous as a cat."

He says quietly to someone else, "The Barnes review, I think, won't hurt us. I was prepared to go without critics, and I'm delighted to have them."

In a little while the producer takes a cab to the Lunt-Fontanne.

Osterman is there standing on the sidewalk, and the co-producers shake hands. Thirty-two people are at the box office at 11:25 A.M. Osterman's associate, Horner, is here, Hilly's associate, George Platt. They stand in the crystal October light looking up at their theater or across at Lester's Helen Hayes, which is being painted. ("What a coat of paint does for something!" Osterman murmurs, watching.) Manny emerges from the Lunt-Fontanne stage door, Malina with him. They stand on the sidewalk. The line maintains itself at about thirty, and from time to time one or another of the group strolls in to look at it. No one is in a rush to get to the ad agency, though they are late. Mrs. Azenberg stops her car before the theater, and her husband leans casually in for a talk; Forty-sixth Street is like a country road: the car, these people, Broadway nearby all in brilliantly etched focus. There is a vivid whiff of charcoal and scorching chestnuts from a vendor's cart. A couple of girls with glossy, volcanic, black-wool naturals, combs in their hip pockets, stagger past whooping, hanging onto each other for dear life in the alcoholic air. Hilly works out approaches yet remains quiet, as if lightly hypnotized. As men are rarely permitted to be, he is, here before the Lunt-Fontanne near noon on October 20, 1970, in the right place at the right time. When someone asks of a review, "How was Chapman—really bad?" the producer answers, "Really bad," gently. Soon they will walk to Broadway—Hilly in the lead with his fast mobster's swagger—down to Forty-fifth, down Shubert Alley to the Sardi Building. They will work on layouts, exploit the meager praise Barnes has given them. By one in the afternoon the box office will have wrapped $6,500, and Sam will say, "It'll run, it'll run," which means it will. They have only the Barnes review, really. Other reviews—the most important ones—are either indifferent, or negative, or faintly praising, or angry at this way of using money to make money in a difficult time.

(*The New Yorker* will be all but clinically enraged, as if its critic had really been driven mad by Hilly.) The election will hurt box office, and the pre-Christmas (and pre-Lent) weeks. Like most of Broadway, it will go on only one good leg, its future insecure, but the show is a hit: not a *Fiddler* or *Oklahoma!* kind of hit that runs forever and earns for everyone connected with it undreamed-of sums of money, but a hit that runs, that has a chance of paying back its investment, and earning money. Israeli Foreign Minister Abba Eban will finally see and like it, and a photograph of him with Claire and Hilly is soon to appear on the brown cork wall next to the framed show cards. Ed Sullivan will present a scene from the *Rothschilds* on his program, singers will record its songs, a rabbi will use it as a sermon text, and other things still hidden will come of it. Hilly will buy *Cat's Cradle* outright at last to try to make it into a film. *Alice's Restaurant* is to be recut (a nude scene eliminated) for GP distribution in company with *The Night They Raided Minsky's*. Hilly's present intention is to cut *Revolution for the Hell of It* himself as a documentary and distribute it—it is uncertain; produce a satiric revue with the current Vice President of the United States as its central figure; begin his own cassette library with Claire Bloom and other front-ranking actors reading children's stories and poetry; produce the Ibsen plays in their new translations (Claire Bloom is to have a great success in them). *The $100 Misunderstanding* script will be rewritten. *The World's Greatest Play* (humbly presented by Hillard Elkins) is to be scrapped as an EPIC project. Manny Azenberg and Bob Malina, with their secretary, are to leave during a general budget cutback before Christmas, the bunker surrendered, the static-filled intercom removed. Elaine May will file suit against EPIC and others to prevent use of her name in the credits of *A New Leaf;* the film is not now hers, she will say; it had been edited to four hours when taken from her: "a catastrophe," the producer is to say. (It will head the Easter bill at Radio City Music Hall, get good reviews, and make money.) The Alice chain of restaurants has failed. Mitty the Weimaraner has died of old age ("Passed away," says Hilly, "quietly in his sleep"). *Oh! Calcutta!* continues to run in several parts of the world; in New York it will move from the East Village to the Belasco on Broadway. Projects will be abandoned, new projects put in hand, foremost among them a musical to be written by the Englishmen Newley and Bricusse. ("Then I'll take six months off, if I'm alive," Hilly says. "If not, I'll take seven months off.") This is in the future. Now the producer stands in front of the Lunt-Fontanne on a bright October day that is not too cool or too warm but is just right.

Epilogue   June 2, 1971

It's a rather gray afternoon, Hilly writes some months later, *the last Sunday we are going to spend in Westport—an overcast but happy day. I have carefully reread the book and I like the cuts very much. I also, on thinking and reflecting, feel that unless one wants to make a totally different book than you intended and have written (which I don't want to do), there's very little or at least much less thought that I want to add or comment on. . . .*

I think a lot of the motivation I was concerned about is either clear or as clear as it can be without your sitting inside my head. Certainly clear enough . . .

There are some lines of connective tissue that don't come through, that you had no way of knowing. For example, when I was first in the army and making plans for getting out, through a mutual friend I met and got to know and like Mike Stewart. Out of that relationship really grew my management business, because Mike led me to Adams and Strouse. I used Mike for Candide, *which gave him his first shot. Through Mike I met Neile Adams, who then married Steve McQueen and led*

318

me to Steve, and through Mike and Strouse and Adams Bye Bye Birdie *came to be, and from that relationship Adams and Strouse went into* Golden Boy. *Through the* Golden Boy *experience, I met and got to know and love Bill Gibson, and know and like Arthur Penn. Our working relationship was good, and through that experience Arthur asked me to do* Alice's Restaurant. *Also through Gibson and Penn, I met and was asked to help Elaine. I took her over for a while and that led to* A New Leaf. *As side note, because Arthur had asked me to do my first picture (he could have had his choice of the field), I was very concerned about the film business, which at the time had a mystique for me based on lack of experience. . . . I subsequently learned that there is no mystique. It was a business like the theater business or any other. . . . Hopefully, when the book comes out, I will be involved with Arthur in a new project, and Elaine as well. These relationships keep going and grow and are, perhaps, the single most important element of our business.*

Calcutta *had a particularly strong meaning for me. Getting into an area that I thought was very important to expose. Some of the material was taken out, as you kind of indicate, because it was just too strong and tended to confuse the audience when their minds were being blown on another level. Hopefully, if we get* Calcutta II *off the ground, we will use this kind of material, which, I think, will add up to the kind of show that will be enormously interesting and as different from* Oh! Calcutta! *as* Oh! Calcutta! *was from anything else.*

I guess The Rothschilds *is one of the three projects that I got hung up with and I really liked. The others are* One Hundred Dollar Misunderstanding *and* Cat's Cradle. *They have all taken seven to eight years. Only* The Rothschilds *has been done. I think* Cat's Cradle *will be done shortly, and I think* One Hundred Dollar Misunderstanding, *which will have a new writer, may get before the cameras this year. (With or without me directing.)*

Golden Boy *and* The Rothschilds *are, I guess, my "getting out of the ghetto" period. Strangely enough,* Golden Boy *was a bit too early and* The Rothschilds *a bit too late, but they were both, I think, worth doing. It took me a long time to solve* Golden Boy. The Rothschilds, *under the circumstances, working with the talents involved, kind of talents rather than degree, didn't enable us to solve that one, but we may turn it into a "hit," which is the only thing left.*

The most important thing that has happened to me, of course, has been Claire. I have discovered what it means to really care for someone totally. She's a remarkable lady: neurotic, beautiful, superstitious, brilliant, naïve. You don't know her as well as you might have had you not been writing the book, because, as you may have caught on, she kind of stopped talking. She has a tremendous concern for her privacy. She has turned my head around. She has made me evaluate what I am doing, what my talents are and aren't, how much of an investment one makes in what one does, how little time really remains, and how careful one has to be of committing, and how complete that commitment must be. Things that really failed are the things that I haven't delivered on. I delivered on Golden Boy. *I delivered on* Oh! Calcutta! *I didn't on* The Rothschilds. *Some of the problems go into financing; I am trying to solve those. But, basically, it's one's attitude toward one's work.*

Broadway is becoming a very, very difficult arena, more so than ever. But at least it gives one the privilege of doing what one believes in if one takes the time and effort. You're not, as in the film business, subject to a limited number of buyers. . . . But that may change also. In addition, I find it necessary in every situation to believe totally in what I am doing; you caught that.

That's all I have to say or add that I think may be of some value. If there is anything you want to discuss, please do. . . . As I say, on studying the material, I don't think it's really necessary to do any more. Also, it's not possible, without hurting other people, to go into the motivation, mechanics, techniques, etc., any more deeply.

Best,
Hilly

72 73 10 9 8 7 6 5 4 3 2 1